TRANSFORMING
EAST ASIA

TRANSFORMING EAST ASIA

The Evolution of Regional Economic Integration

NAOKO MUNAKATA

RESEARCH INSTITUTE OF ECONOMY,
TRADE AND INDUSTRY
Tokyo

BROOKINGS INSTITUTION PRESS
Washington, D.C.

Library of Congress Cataloging-in-Publication data
Munakata, Naoko, 1962–
   Transforming East Asia : the evolution of regional economic
integration / Naoko Munakata.
      p.   cm.
   Includes bibliographical references and index.
   ISBN-13: 978-0-8157-5887-7 (pbk. : alk. paper)
   ISBN-10: 0-8157-5887-1 (pbk. : alk. paper)
   1. East Asia—Economic integration. 2. Regionalism—East Asia.
   3. East Asia—Commerce. 4. East Asia—Economic conditions—
   20th century. I. Title.
   HC460.5.M86 2006
   337.1'5—dc22   2006018349

                    9 8 7 6 5 4 3 2 1

Typeset in Minion

Composition by OSP, Inc.
Arlington, Virginia

Printed by R. R. Donnelley
Harrisonburg, Virginia

For my parents

and for

Toshinori and Aiko

Contents

Preface   ix

Acknowledgments   xiii

Abbreviations   xvii

1 East Asia in Transition   1

2 The New East Asian Regionalism   8

3 The State of Regionalization   37

4 Competing Proposals for Regionalism   62

5 The Primacy of Asia Pacific   81
   Economic Cooperation

6 New Assumptions about Regionalism   102

7 The Race for a Free Trade Agreement   115

8 Major Powers and East Asian Economic Integration   133

9 How Economic Integration Changed East Asia   169

Notes   187

Index   245

Preface

I did most of the research and writing for this book between September 2001 and June 2004, while living and working in Washington, D.C. Many Asian friends asked me why I had chosen Washington instead of some Asian capital to study economic regionalism in East Asia. It was a particularly valid question at the time, as the September 11 terrorist attacks, which took place days after I arrived in Washington, fundamentally refocused U.S. attention on the immediate crisis and subsequently the war in Iraq, leaving little attention for Asia.

The answer was straightforward: I chose Washington because U.S. policy toward East Asia significantly shaped Japan's policy options on East Asian regionalism in the past and, in my view, will continue to do so. I first encountered U.S. reactions to East Asian regionalism in the early 1990s when I was deputy director of the Southeast Asia and Pacific Division at the Ministry of International Trade and Industry (MITI, later renamed METI). At the time, Washington's strong objection to Kuala Lumpur's proposal for an East Asian Economic Caucus (EAEC) confronted Tokyo with a dilemma: if it supported the Malaysian proposal, it would risk antagonizing the United States. The mainstream argument was that this was a risk Japan could not afford. Those who disagreed were considered anti-American and leftist or simple-minded.

The episode left me with a few questions. First, would the United States, which had once supported European integration, be against Asian integration forever? Second, why did Tokyo not try to persuade Washington that an East Asia–only framework would have its own merits and could also serve U.S. interests? Could Japan not have good relations with the United States and an identity as an East Asian country? Third, could Japan earn the trust of the United States and its Asian neighbors as a regional leader? These questions lingered as I participated in preparations for meetings of regional forums

ix

such as the Asia Pacific Economic Cooperation (APEC), the meeting between ASEAN economic ministers and the minister of Japan's Ministry of International Trade and Industry (AEM-MITI), and the Asia-Europe meeting (ASEM); developed aid packages for Asian countries in the aftermath of the Asian financial crisis; and explored the feasibility of free trade agreements for Japan.

These questions all point to a common conclusion: Japan cannot confidently promote regional cooperation in Asia without a solid understanding of U.S. global strategy and Asia's position within it. Consequently, these were the issues I sought to explore as a guest scholar in 2001–04, first at the Brookings Institution and then at the George Washington University.

I started to examine these issues with a simple argument: East Asian economic integration will stimulate change within countries across the region. Why? Because unless they become open, promote competition, and trust other countries' commitments to abide by agreed rules, economic integration on an institutional basis will not be achieved. What is more, enhanced interdependence and institutional ties will focus regional economies on mutual interest and thus help overcome residual mistrust. These developments will make Asia more peaceful and prosperous, which will serve economic interests of the United States, while reducing its security burden in the region.

Upon arriving at Brookings, I realized that this argument was never obvious or appealing to Americans. One American scholar told me, "Your argument is interesting because it is counterintuitive!" As a result, it took me a while to actually sit down to write the manuscript. I kept wondering how I should structure my argument so that it would find willing ears.

I concluded that the best I could do was to describe in detail why and how institutional frameworks in East Asia have evolved, how the role and behavior of the United States have been perceived, how countries in East Asia have changed, and how moves toward economic integration have accelerated domestic reforms, stabilized regional relations, and thus complemented U.S. strategy in East Asia. Such evidence of the positive impact of East Asian economic regionalism would provide an alternative perspective on its merits.

Since I completed the original manuscript and went back to my government job in Tokyo in June 2004, there have been major changes in the circumstances surrounding East Asian regional cooperation. The tension between a rising China and a relatively declining but more internationally active Japan increased in the spring of 2005 with violent anti-Japanese demonstrations on the streets of major Chinese cities. These manifestations of deep-seated distrust between Japan and China, the single most important obstacle to East Asian regionalism, prompted questions about its viability. I did not have time to update the entire manuscript in response to these developments, but an additional observation is in order.

One of the historical lessons identified in the book is that when the momentum of regional cooperation is weak, the prospective participants tend to focus on who should be invited to cooperate, rather than what they will cooperate about. We saw this symptom in the preparation for the East Asia summit held in December 2005. This is an undesirable trend.

Instead of getting bogged down in questions of membership, the countries in the region should focus on defining the goal of an East Asian community, developing a roadmap to achieve it, and defining specific milestones and the conditions necessary to reach them. If they are not ready to move in this direction, then they should focus on functional cooperation under the ASEAN + 3 framework, while pursuing agreements for trade and investment liberalization and facilitation on a bilateral or subregional basis. Functional cooperation will help develop needed institutional capabilities within the region. It will also give prospective participants opportunities to redefine, if appropriate, the most effective geographical scope for cooperation.

Little will be gained by prematurely trying to develop East Asian institutions with meager substance. Building a regional community will take a major transformation or metamorphosis of East Asian countries. Until this happens, the dream of East Asian integration will not come true.

Acknowledgments

This book is based solely on my personal opinion and does not represent any organization with which I am or was associated. However, in the course of preparing the manuscript, I received generous support from many organizations and individuals.

I wrote the first draft of this book while I was in Washington, D.C., as a visiting fellow at the Brookings Institution's Center for Northeast Asian Policy Studies (CNAPS) (September 2001 through June 2002) and as a visiting scholar at the Sigur Center for Asian Studies at the George Washington University (July 2002 through June 2004). During this period, the Research Institute of Economy, Trade and Industry (RIETI) sponsored my research on East Asian economic integration and U.S. policy toward the region. My employer, the Ministry of Economy, Trade and Industry (METI), made this project possible by seconding me to RIETI for those three years.

My current and former colleagues at MITI/METI gave me valuable insights into various policy issues and opportunities to witness the historical events in the region. While it is impossible to mention everyone that I benefited from, those who gave me specific advice and assistance with my research for this book include the following, listed here with family name first, in the Asian fashion: Kuroda Makoto, Hatakeyama Noboru, Konno Hidehiro, Sano Tadakatsu, Okumura Hirokazu, Tanaka Nobuo, Kuwahara Satoshi, Umehara Katsuhiko, the late Takatori Akinori, Tsugami Toshiya, Kuroda Atsuo, Terazawa Tatsuya, Yanase Tadao, Hatano Atsuhiko, Ishikawa Masaki, Sumita Takayuki, Nakazawa Norio, Tojo Yoshiaki, Ohta Takehiko, Iida Hirobumi, Kobayashi Izuru, Nishiwaki Osamu, Nakanishi Tomoaki, Aizawa Takahiko, Saito Junko, and Shinohara Miyuki.

Okamatsu Sozaburo, former chairman of RIETI, and Aoki Masahiko of Stanford University, former RIETI president, helped me go to Washington, D.C., and encouraged my research there. Aoki, in particular, urged me to undertake this project, introduced me to American scholars knowledgeable about U.S. policy toward Asia, and gave me valuable advice on academic publication. Yoshitomi Masaru, current RIETI president, and Tanabe Yasuo, vice president, offered generous help to enable me to complete the project after returning to METI. While at RIETI, I benefited greatly from discussions with and input from former RIETI colleague C. H. Kwan, senior fellow, Nomura Institute of Capital Markets Research; Shiraishi Takashi, then of Kyoto University (currently vice president of the National Graduate Institute for Policy Studies); Soeya Yoshihide and Kokubun Ryosei of Keio University; Tanaka Akihiko, Fukagawa Yukiko, and Takahara Akio of Tokyo University; Fukao Kyoji of Hitotsubashi University; and Yamashita Kazuhito, senior fellow, RIETI. Current and former RIETI staff people gave me crucial support for my research away from Tokyo. I thank Matsuda Hiromi and Katsuno Masahiro for their kind support for the publication of this book after my return to METI.

At the Brookings Institution, Bates Gill, former CNAPS director, gave me enormous help, providing a precious learning experience, introducing important contacts, offering valuable suggestions about my papers and commentaries, and, with his wife, Sarah E. Palmer, making my life at Brookings a lot easier and happier. I thank Michael H. Armacost, then president of the Brookings Institution, and James B. Steinberg, then vice president and director, Foreign Policy Studies, for their support of my research. Brookings also provided an opportunity to meet and learn from current and former resident scholars, including Lael Brainard, Catharin E. Dalpino, Nicholas R. Lardy, and Edward J. Lincoln. Virginia Q. Rosell, center administrator at CNAPS, who remembered everybody's birthday, spared no efforts to have the six visiting fellows in our group spend time together and form memories to cherish. Among the visiting fellows that year, I particularly thank Lho Kyongsoo of Seoul National University and Jia Qingguo of Peking University for their valuable input into my research. Current CNAPS director Richard C. Bush III facilitated my research in Washington and the publication of this book.

Mike M. Mochizuki, director of the Sigur Center for Asian Studies at the George Washington University, kindly invited me to spend my remaining two years in Washington at his center. He patiently encouraged me to work on the book, introduced me to many academic contacts, provided various opportunities to present my research, and helped organize study meetings to get feedback on my manuscript. I particularly thank Hugh T. Patrick of Columbia University, Muthiah Alagappa of the East-West Center, Ellen Frost of the Institute for International Economics, and Amy Searight of the George Washington University for reading through some or all of the chapters in the manuscript and providing valuable comments and criticism. I am grateful to Harry Harding, dean of the Elliott School of International Affairs, for his encouragement and support. The Sigur Center provided me a great opportunity to meet professors and visiting scholars focused on Asia, from whom I learned a great deal, including David L. Shambaugh, Michael Yahuda, Young-Key Kim-Renaud, Robert Sutter, and Daqing Yang of the George Washington University; Katharine H. S. Moon of Wellesley College; Min Wan of George Mason University; and Junhua Wu, chief economist, the Japan Research Institute, Limited. Young-Key Kim-Renaud provided me generous help in arranging a research trip to Seoul, introducing valuable contacts there. I thank Ikuko S. Turner and Debbie Toy for their kind assistance, which facilitated my stay at the center.

While based in Washington, I benefited greatly from discussions with scholars, policymakers, and journalists, in addition to those noted above. Those who provided valuable comments on my manuscript and related papers include Richard Cronin, Gerald L. Curtis, Brad Glosserman, Edward M. Graham Jr., Miles Kahler, Peter J. Katzenstein, Adam S. Posen, John Ravenhill, and Etel Solingen. I also thank Claude Barfield, William T. Breer (and Peggy, his wife and my teacher), Steven C. Clemons, Robert C. Fauver, Geza Feketekuty, Yoichi Funabashi, C. Laurence Greenwood, Kongdan Oh Hassig, Walter B. Lohman, T. J. Pempel, James J. Przystup, Christopher J. Sigur, Tang Shiping, Yoshibumi Wakamiya, Tsuneo Watanabe, and Zhang Yunling for their insight and kind help.

Thanks also go to those at Brookings Institution Press who helped to shepherd the book through production, including Mary Kwak, acquisitions editor; Janet Walker, managing editor; Vicky Macintyre, editor; Larry Converse, production manager; and Susan Woollen, art coordinator.

I thank my husband, Doi Toshinori, and my daughter, Aiko, for their understanding and for supporting my passion for this book project and my job, more generally. I also thank my parents, who have always encouraged me to work hard and achieve my goals.

List of Abbreviations

AEM	ASEAN economic ministers meeting
AFTA	ASEAN Free Trade Area
AIC	ASEAN Industrial Complementation
AICO	ASEAN Industrial Cooperation
AIJV	ASEAN Industrial Joint Venture
AMF	Asian Monetary Fund
ANZCERTA	Australia-New Zealand Closer Economic Relations Trade Agreement
APEC	Asia Pacific Economic Cooperation
ARF	ASEAN Regional Forum
ASEAN	Association of Southeast Asian Nations (Brunei, Cambodia, Indonesia, Laos, Malaysia, Myanmar, the Philippines, Singapore, Thailand, and Vietnam)
ASEAN + 3	ASEAN plus three (ASEAN countries and China, Japan, and South Korea)
ASEM	Asia-Europe meeting
AUI	ASEAN-U.S. Initiative
BBC	brand-to-brand complementation
CEP	comprehensive economic partnership
CEPT	Common Effective Preferential Tariff
CER	closer economic relations (between Australia and New Zealand)
EAEC	East Asian Economic Caucus
EAEG	East Asian Economic Group
EAFTA	East Asia Free Trade Area
EAI	Enterprise for ASEAN Initiative

EASG	East Asia Study Group
EAVG	East Asia Vision Group
EMS	electronics manufacturing service
EPA	Economic Partnership Agreement
EPG	Eminent Persons Group
EU	European Union
EVSL	Early Voluntary Sectoral Liberalization
FDI	foreign direct investment
FTA	free trade agreement
FTAA	Free Trade Area of the Americas
GATT	General Agreement on Tariffs and Trade
GDP	gross domestic product
GNI	gross national income
GNP	gross national product
GSP	Generalized System of Preferences
IDE	Institute of Developing Economies (Japan)
IIT	intra-industry trade
IMF	International Monetary Fund
IPR	intellectual property rights
IT	information technology
ITA	Information Technology Agreement
ITC	International Trade Commission (U.S.)
JETRO	Japan External Trade Organization
JSEPA	Japan-Singapore Economic Partnership Agreement
KIEP	Korea Institute for International Economic Policy
MAFF	Ministry of Agriculture, Forestry and Fisheries (Japan)
MAS	Monetary Authority of Singapore
MFN	most favored nation
METI	Ministry of Economy, Trade and Industry (Japan)
MITI	Ministry of International Trade and Industry (Japan)
MNC	multinational corporation
MOF	Ministry of Finance (Japan)
MOFA	Ministry of Foreign Affairs (Japan)
MOFAT	Ministry of Foreign Affairs and Trade (South Korea)
MRA	mutual recognition agreement
NAFTA	North American Free Trade Agreement
NICs	newly industrializing countries
NIEs	newly industrializing economies
OAA	Osaka Action Agenda
ODA	official development assistance

OECD	Organization for Economic Cooperation and Development
PAFTAD	Pacific Trade and Development
PBEC	Pacific Basin Economic Council
PECC	Pacific Economic Cooperation Committee
PMC	post-ministerial conference
PTA	preferential trade agreement
RIETI	Research Institute of Economy, Trade and Industry (Japan)
RTA	regional trade agreement
SARS	Severe Acute Respiratory Syndrome
SMEs	small and medium-sized enterprises
SOEs	state-owned enterprises
SOM	senior officials' meeting
SRF	Supplementary Reserve Facility
SRTA	subregional trade agreement
TIFA	trade and investment framework agreement
TRIMs	trade-related investment measures
UN	United Nations
UR	Uruguay Round
WTO	World Trade Organization

1

East Asia in Transition

The most dynamic region in the world today is East Asia, with one-third of the planet's population and one-fifth of its gross domestic product (GDP).[1] The regional economy sprang back to life in the 1980s, when deepening interdependence began spreading economic benefits throughout the region after a century of wars and ideological struggles between various powers, which eventually saw greater sense in development and cooperation. Even the socialist countries among them were introducing some market reforms before the end of the cold war. This focus on economic development, together with the security presence of the United States, has defused potential sources of conflict and maintained regional peace and prosperity.

East Asia now faces a historic geopolitical transition, however, owing to the rise of China and relative decline of Japan. The continued stability and prosperity of the region, not to mention the world, will depend on the course of this transition. If the violent anti-Japanese demonstrations on the streets of major Chinese cities in the spring of 2005 are any indication, managing it will be no easy task.

In response to the challenge, there has been a surge of political interest in the vision of an East Asian community. Such an entity could help accommodate China's growing power and influence, stabilize Sino-Japanese relations, and maintain regional peace and prosperity. But enormous difficulties stand in the way of its realization. East Asia is not a monolith. Regional economies differ widely in their stages of development. And deep-rooted distrust and historical antagonism bedevil relations between Japan and China.

1

As a result of these and other factors, including the reactions of extraregional powers, political support for East Asian cooperation has wavered greatly. A growing concern, especially now that Japan is slipping from its earlier position, is that China could dominate the region, using East Asian institutions as a vehicle of influence, which would make it difficult to maintain a stable balance of power within the region. In reality, there appears to be no immediate prospect of Chinese domination, for it is commonly understood that any East Asian community should be based not on hierarchy but on equality and mutual respect. Nonetheless, concern about the potential for Chinese hegemony continues to curb the political momentum behind East Asian cooperation.

As this book argues, these difficulties should not deter the countries of East Asia from promoting regional cooperation as part of a multilayered approach to international cooperation. Initially, their efforts should focus on economic issues. The development of dense production networks across the region has already deepened economic interdependence and given local governments a clear common interest in reducing transaction costs for businesses operating in East Asia. By acting on this common interest, they can make the region more disposed to competition and innovation. It will not be easy to negotiate the necessary reforms, owing to domestic political resistance to economic liberalization. Nonetheless, such an effort can have a large payoff by helping to focus the region's attention on economic development, rather than on political power plays.

In the early stages of reform, regional governments should be flexible and choose the most appropriate forums for dealing with particular problems. At present, this may mean working within the framework of ASEAN + 3 (the Association of Southeast Asian Nations, China, Japan, and South Korea), as well as through other bilateral, regional, plurilateral, and global institutions.[2] (Note that plurilateral agreements involve more than some but not all members of a larger multilateral agreement and differ from subregional or regional agreements in that the membership is not tied to a particular region.) Eventually, when regional leaders are ready to articulate common goals and agree on the membership, they can take further steps toward building an East Asian community.

Although the vision of such a community is still somewhat vague, its realization is an important goal. East Asian countries need institutions that will allow them to deal with the region's unique problems on their own. Though they still lack the mutual trust necessary for such institutions to work, the alternative—having outside powers act as a counterbalance in the region—

would only intensify tension and rivalry. By contrast, greater regional cooperation can help overcome lingering distrust and antagonisms and turn East Asia into a more comfortable place to live.

Institutional Economic Integration

Over the past fifteen years, enthusiasm for an East Asian community has increased dramatically. At the beginning of this period, the region was already benefiting from de facto economic integration induced by market forces—a process I call "regionalization." Up to 1998, however, East Asian governments shunned formal free trade agreements (FTAs) in the region, instead pursuing liberalization in the global arena on a most favored nation (MFN) basis. They also hesitated to create East Asia–only intergovernmental forums to promote regional economic integration.

By the fall of 2000, however, all the powers in the area had embarked on bilateral FTAs. In addition, at the ASEAN + 3 summit that year, East Asian leaders started to explore such ideas as an East Asian free-trade area and an East Asia summit. Since then, the rise of China has accelerated the process of regionalization and strengthened its neighbors' incentives to promote "regionalism"—meaning the pursuit of regional economic integration through intergovernmental institutions—and to integrate this huge country into rule-based systems at both the global and the regional level. Also, China's decision to conclude a free trade agreement with ASEAN accelerated the race for bilateral FTAs and compelled interest in adopting a more coordinated approach to liberalization.

What direction are these developments likely to take? I see East Asian regionalism as a dynamic process of transformation. Over time, the region will evolve from a group of countries separated by residual protectionism and bureaucratic inefficiency into an open and integrated market. As domestic demand increases, the region will become less dependent on U.S. markets, and trade with the United States will become more balanced. Now handicapped by weak market institutions and vulnerable to economic shocks, the region's economies will develop solid institutions conducive to competition and innovation. Instead of being divided by political rivalries and historical animosities, East Asia will become a regional community bound by common interests and aspirations.

Despite frequent comparison with the European Union (EU), an East Asian community is unlikely to achieve the EU's level of institutionalization. Instead, its institutions and arrangements will be suitable to East Asian reality and thus be more akin to the North American Free Trade Agreement (NAFTA). Countries will conclude bilateral agreements that are later combined to form a regionally seamless agreement. Regional governments will therefore be able to participate in various international arrangements and explore institutions that differ by membership and scope, depending on the particular problems they face.

Ultimately, if the vision of an East Asian community is to become reality, each member country must reform its domestic economic and political institutions in ways that make its economy and society more free and open. In addition, governments must become more sensitive to their neighbors' concerns and priorities. Given the scope of these tasks, East Asia may not fully achieve the vision described here. Even so, any effort in that direction is a force for positive change.

The Feasibility and Efficacy of a Regional Community

Unfortunately, the current trend toward institutional economic integration in East Asia is not necessarily welcome in other parts of the world. According to some critics, the obstacles to East Asian regionalism are so great that hardly anything significant can be achieved. Others see the momentum toward integration building but fear this might turn East Asia into a closed, inward-looking bloc. This book questions these negative views and provides an alternative perspective.

Despite formidable challenges, East Asia has made significant progress in promoting trade and investment liberalization at the regional level, which would have been considered impossible in the past. Both Japan and South Korea have concluded and started to enforce bilateral free trade agreements with third countries that involve the liberalization of agricultural products— a highly sensitive issue—and negotiations for a Japan-Korea free trade agreement have begun. As already mentioned, China and ASEAN have also concluded, and now started to implement, an FTA. Japan, Korea, and China are contemplating a trilateral investment agreement. And ASEAN + 3 has expanded its scope, adding ministerial meetings in a variety of sectors. These rapid developments of the past few years suggest that these countries may eventually overcome the remaining obstacles to further integration.

One of the largest obstacles is the political rivalry and deep-rooted mistrust between Japan and China, as illustrated by the great tension between the two in the spring of 2005. Regional frameworks were vital in keeping channels of dialogue open when bilateral relations became thorny. Fortunately, in the future, the region's deep economic interdependence, regular summit meetings in regional and international forums, and the involvement of extraregional powers, notably the United States, should continue to help diffuse tensions and keep regional efforts on track.

In the following chapters, I highlight East Asia's progress toward regional integration, arguing that it is not likely to become a closed economic bloc. The economic frameworks being pursued are not fundamentally different from the regional frameworks proliferating around the world. If anything, they are likely to be more open and outward looking than similar arrangements in other regions because East Asia's dependence on extraregional markets gives it a strong interest in increased trade liberalization on a global level. Significant changes in the behavior of Japanese firms, which some regard as closed and inward looking, also strengthen the prospects for openness. Note, too, that East Asian regionalism does not rest on exclusivism rooted in anti-Western or anti-American sentiment among some individuals in the region, but rather on pragmatic calculations of economic interest, as well as a desire for mutual trust and a sense of community. Far from turning inward, as skeptics fear, East Asian regionalism will no doubt serve as a valuable pillar in the framework of institutions that govern the international economy.

Plan of the Book

Since this book is about the evolution of institutional economic integration in East Asia, the central concern is cooperation in trade and investment rather than in finance or political security. However, the forces at play cannot be fully assessed without examining the political aspects of East Asian regionalism, such as the debate over the East Asian summit and East Asian community.

The discussion opens in chapter 2 with the breakthrough events presaging regionalism and the ensuing controversy as to whether free trade agreements are "building blocks" or "stumbling blocks" en route to global liberalization. The focus here is on the significance of East Asian regionalism and the major factors that have promoted it (defensive regionalism, intraregional economic interdependence, and intraregional competitive dynamics), as well as hindered it (the lack of cohesiveness, extraregional dependence, and hesitancy about institutionalization).

Chapter 3 concentrates on the process of regionalization since the latter half of the 1980s and its role in promoting both cooperation and competition in East Asia. Regionalization has not only created a common interest in reducing transaction costs in the region, remaining open to the outside, establishing a common front toward protectionism in other regions, and promoting the growth of regional domestic demand. It has also stimulated a desire to become a regional center for business activities, spurring competition particularly among countries with similar economic structures. Some influential factors in the evolution of regionalization are the international environment, the activities of businesses, government policies, and above all ASEAN, a major player in shaping East Asian regionalism, particularly in its early stages. Production networks—with their fragmentation, modularization, and agglomeration—have also contributed to the regional economy and help explain its uneven integration by product type, prevalence of extraregional linkages in terms of markets and sources of investment, and growing domination by China. Recognizing the need to adapt to the regional environment, Japanese business networks have begun delegating more decisionmaking authority to local subsidiaries instead of extending their "closed" domestic system into the region.

In chapters 4–7, the discussion turns to the four distinct stages of East Asian regionalism since the mid-1980s. The first stage, between 1985 and 1992 (see chapter 4), is marked by four competing proposals for greater regional emphasis: bilateral FTAs with the United States, Asia Pacific Economic Cooperation (APEC), the East Asia Economic Caucus (EAEC), and the ASEAN Free Trade Area (AFTA). Between 1993 and 1998, as outlined in chapter 5, APEC established its primacy and, over time, nurtured cooperative relations among the countries in the region. However, APEC's limitations became evident after the failure of the Early Voluntary Sectoral Liberalization (EVSL) initiative, which awakened the region to the need for a multilayered approach to international economic institutions. Chapter 6 deals with the third period, which began in the wake of the 1997–98 Asian financial crisis and ran until late 2000. During this period, the region's governments experimented with arrangements that were formerly taboo, such as FTAs as opposed to liberalization on an MFN basis and East Asia–only forums. The fourth period (covered in chapter 7), from late 2000 to the present, is marked by China's growth and impact on East Asian regionalism, as well as acceleration of an FTA race. In addition, East Asian governments have developed a greater interest in pursuing pragmatic regional cooperation through various channels, notably ASEAN + 3.

Several findings emerge from the analysis. First, East Asian regionalism sprang from defensive motivations but then was largely shaped by the intraregional desire to deal with common concerns. Second, on balance, intraregional competition has promoted cooperation rather than conflict by encouraging countries to pursue bilateral FTAs. Third, although historical obstacles to regionalism persist, countries are overcoming them. Fourth, as chapter 8 explains, the course and pace of East Asian regionalism depends in large part on the policies of three countries: Japan, China, and the United States. Chapter 9 summarizes the de facto and institutional impact of economic integration on the region. It also provides some policy suggestions for Japan, China, and the United States, especially in view of the political uncertainties surrounding East Asian regionalism.

2

The New East Asian Regionalism

On October 22, 2000, Japan's prime minister Yoshiro Mori and Singapore's prime minister Goh Chok Tong arrived at an agreement of vast economic implications for East Asia.[1] In January 2001 they would launch formal negotiations for the region's first preferential trade agreement (PTA) under Article 24 of the General Agreement on Tariffs and Trade (GATT), for a new-age economic partnership to be known as the Japan-Singapore Economic Partnership Agreement (JSEPA).[2] The term "new age," coined by Prime Minister Goh, reflected the entrepreneurial spirit of the talks and the hope for new solutions to a wide range of problems facing the business community.[3] These discussions were expected to create a model for future moves toward economic integration. Little did policymakers in Tokyo or Singapore suspect that developments would begin in less than a month.

Ending a midnight round of golf on November 16, 2000, at the meeting of Asia Pacific Economic Cooperation (APEC) leaders in Brunei, U.S. president Bill Clinton and Prime Minister Goh announced that their governments would soon start negotiations on a bilateral free trade agreement (FTA).[4] In the past, the Clinton administration had been cautious about pursuing FTAs with a limited number of countries in Asia, such as the agreement among the Pacific five: Australia, Chile, New Zealand, Singapore, and the United States. Instead, it had preferred to rely on APEC and on multilateral negotiations at the global level.[5] Signaling their desire to move quickly in a new direction, the two leaders instructed their trade ministers "to endeavor to conclude negotiations before the end of the year."[6] These negotiations were to take as their model the U.S.-Jordan FTA, the first such agreement involving the United States that incorporated environmental and labor standards. U.S. Trade Representative Charlene Barshefsky also urged that the talks "focus on 'new economy' issues such as electronic commerce and information technology."[7]

The next day, it was reported that China would propose a free trade area with the Association of Southeast Asian Nations (ASEAN).[8] On November 25, 2000, at the Fourth ASEAN + China Summit, China's premier Zhu Rongji called on the ASEAN members "to explore the establishment of a free trade relationship" with his country, and to convene a group of experts to discuss possible efforts to deepen economic cooperation.[9] Although Zhu avoided the term "free trade agreement," his statement apparently implied that China was open to establishing FTAs.[10] This was a marked departure from its previously cautious attitude, expressed earlier that month by a Foreign Ministry official: "Free-trade cooperation is beneficial to promoting economic development in APEC, but we also do not wish such cooperation to become an exclusive trading system."[11] Within a month, each of the three major powers active in Asia—Japan, the United States, and China—was taking an important step toward the conclusion of bilateral or broader free trade agreements in the region.

On November 24, 2000, the ASEAN + 3 summit convened by ASEAN, China, Japan, and South Korea yielded two other proposals related to the idea of East Asian identity: for an East Asian summit, and for an East Asian free trade area or free investment area. Although the early intention was merely to have a study group explore these ideas, even this modest step met with some uneasiness.[12] Still fresh in some minds was Malaysia's proposal of the early 1990s for an East Asian Economic Caucus (EAEC), which had conveyed at least to Westerners a decidedly anti-Western flavor.[13]

In response to questions about how the proposed summit would develop and whether Washington should be concerned, Prime Minister Goh asserted that the new era dawning in East Asia posed no outside threat:

EAEC has always been a good idea; having the East Asians meeting as a caucus. But at that time, some countries, which included Singapore, were not in favor of EAEC because we wanted to get APEC going. . . . [N]ow that APEC is firmly established, with regular Summits, Singapore's position would be quite one of confidence. If Asians want to meet as a group, I do not see why we should not, because North Americans do meet as a group. . . . So I see no problem in ASEAN + 3 evolving, if that is the desire of the leaders, into some kind of an East Asian Summit.

I do feel that [as] East Asians, we do have common problems and we do want to talk about cooperation within East Asia, not about keeping others out. . . . East Asia should be open to other countries in terms of trade relations so Washington would have nothing to worry about.[14]

In short, Goh's message was that the countries of East Asia would be guided by their own interests, not the preferences of outside powers, in choosing appropriate forms of deeper regional cooperation, yet would remain open to the outside world.

Changed Attitude, New Vision

As recently as 1998, the countries of East Asia still showed little or no interest in promoting regional economic integration through the formation of intergovernmental institutions, such as free trade agreements or customs unions—a process henceforth referred to here as "regionalism."[15] Instead, since the mid-1980s, the region had relied on "regionalization," or de facto economic integration through market processes, to generate dynamic growth.[16] This was not a particularly surprising choice. Many observers considered Asia to be too diverse for institutionalized integration to succeed.[17] As John Ravenhill has pointed out, it was laden with "the bitter legacy of wartime hostilities between Japan and other states in the region."[18] Furthermore, the colonial legacy shared by ASEAN's members made them wary of dominance by big powers. Above all, U.S. foreign policy in the post–World War II era had established bilateralism as the dominant pattern in East Asia.[19]

Despite some interest in the new trend, apprehension lingered.[20] In the late 1980s and early 1990s, many outsiders worried that East Asia might turn into a closed, inward-looking bloc. With Japan seemingly poised to dominate the regional economy, many thought the spread of Japanese business practices, which were believed to bias Japanese markets against foreign firms, might have a similar effect throughout East Asia. This fear was fueled by the region's high growth rate, Japan's rapid economic rise (at a time when many foreign companies experienced difficulties in entering the Japanese market), and the central role of Japanese production networks in East Asia's regionalization.

An added concern, particularly of the United States, was that the creation of regional economic institutions might solidify the perceived anti-Western attitudes in the region. The confrontational way in which Malaysia's prime minister Mahathir bin Mohamad presented his 1990 proposal for the establishment of an East Asian Economic Group (EAEG)—the precursor to the less ambitious proposal for a consultative East Asian Economic Caucus—made Washington even more opposed to East Asia forums. As a result, the region's governments spent most of the 1990s trying to recover the freedom to meet without offending the United States. This preoccupation delayed a pragmatic, substantive policy debate on how to make the best use of various institutional options, which issues and problems various institutional frameworks could address, and how regionalism would work.

Instead, local governments became euphoric about the robust pace of regionalization, giving little thought to the lack of a solid form of regionalism such as preferential trade agreements. Their strong economic performance, tied largely to extraregional markets, made them confident that their single-minded reliance on multilateral frameworks for liberalization, such as GATT and later the World Trade Organization (WTO), was the way to proceed. Whereas the United States warned against giving Europe a free ride and suggested turning APEC into a free trade agreement, East Asian members believed that the forum should remain open to the outside by keeping liberalization on a most favored nation (MFN) basis.[21] Ryutaro Hashimoto, then Japanese minister of international trade and industry, argued:

> The primary force [of Asian dynamism] is direct foreign investment. Most notably, the liberalization of trade and investment in the region has not been brought about as a result of regional negotiations for free-trade agreements, based on reciprocity. Rather, it has been the result of individual countries' strategic judgment that it was best to create new growth opportunities by competing with their neighbors to attract foreign capital. In other words, individual countries have pursued liberalization on their own, in the end creating a high level of economic interdependence among themselves. That I would call the Asian experience. . . .
>
> Further liberalization within APEC should continue on a nondiscriminatory basis. . . . There is no need for East Asia to take steps that would suffocate its own economic dynamism.[22]

This resistance to an APEC free trade agreement was based on the firm belief that East Asia would jeopardize its prosperity by turning into a self-sufficient bloc and therefore needed to avoid any discriminatory forms of regionalism that might stimulate a backlash in important markets. Consequently, its commitment to the GATT principle of nondiscrimination seemed destined to remain in place for the foreseeable future.

Impact of the Asian Financial Crisis

The Asian financial crisis of 1997–98 shattered confidence in the "Asian miracle." Old habits changed drastically as regional governments realized they could not rely on global institutions to protect and promote their interests. Now they were eager to use all available tools—including those that were formerly taboo, such as East Asia–only forums and preferential trade agreements—to revitalize their economies. However, the crisis cannot by itself explain the turn toward regionalism. The major force underlying regionalism, already at work before the crisis, was the growing sense of common interests.

Rise of China

Another large contributing factor following the Asian financial crisis was the rise of China. As China became a leading market and an important node of regional production networks, intraregional trade and investment grew. At the same time, specialization increased and production networks became more tightly integrated, making it increasingly urgent to reduce transaction costs and strengthen the investment climate across the region. Attention thus turned to stable, institutionalized solutions to these problems. With the development of Chinese markets and complementary relations among East Asian economies, regionalism seemed more likely to yield significant gains. Furthermore, China's active pursuit of an FTA with ASEAN elicited a strong competitive response among countries in the region and accelerated various negotiations for other FTAs. In the wake of China'a economic, political, and military rise, they also felt the need to build a strong East Asian community that could firmly integrate China into a rules-based system at both the regional and global levels.

The Vision: Metamorphosis of East Asia

The vision for an East Asian community actually goes beyond economic cooperation. As the 2001 report of the East Asia Vision Group (EAVG) explains, it extends into the "political, security, environmental, social, cultural, and educational arenas," with economic cooperation serving "as the catalyst in the comprehensive community-building process."[23] Although the institutional structure of such a community has not yet been clearly defined, it is likely to aim for integrated national markets; the free flow of goods, services, capital, information, and people; the avoidance of future wars; and a regional identity. In pursuing such goals, East Asian nations will gradually build institutions, including legally binding agreements, to integrate their economies, making the management of their relations more stable and predictable.

Although these are not unlike the goals of the European Union (EU), the level of institutionalization in East Asia will no doubt be less complex and its components more appropriate for the region. As U.S. ambassador Howard Baker has pointed out, East Asian nations "must integrate a more diverse cultural landscape with an even longer history than Europe has."[24] A hierarchical structure clearly seems out of place, with equality and mutual respect the preferred foundation.

To this end, the region must undergo a vast transformation—from a group of countries separated by residual protection and bureaucratic inefficiency to an open and integrated market; from a group of exporters overdependent on U.S. markets to an economy driven by domestic demand with more balanced trade with the United States; from economies with weak market institutions, vulnerable to economic shocks, to ones with solid institutions conducive to competition and innovation; and, eventually, from nations divided by political rivalries and historical animosities to a regional community bound by common interests and aspirations. These changes can only take place if each country reforms its domestic economic and political institutions, making its economy and society more free and open and more sensitive toward each other's concerns and priorities. East Asian regionalism will thus be the instrument of a dynamic metamorphosis.

Ambition and Pragmatism

By the autumn of 2000, the East Asian vision was slowly passing into uncharted waters. First, countries removed taboos regarding "East Asia–only" forums and preferential trade agreements. As a result, they obtained autonomy in designing their regional cooperation, but they could keep this autonomy only by gaining the confidence of the private sector in the effectiveness of their regional institutions, as well as earning the trust of extraregional governments in the positive contributions the region could make. At the same time, these efforts have complicated the task of reform by unleashing a competitive dynamic among the major powers. Today, the region has overlapping bilateral and subregional FTAs at various stages of development without a shared vision of how to attain regionwide economic integration.[25]

This stands to reason because East Asia is not a single power. Naturally, its member countries have separate interests. Japan, feeling uncertain in the wake of China's rise, wants to revitalize its economy and to keep the region peaceful and stable, hoping that regional and global institutions will integrate China into rules-based systems that will make its policies and actions more predictable. For its part, China would like to secure a stable international environment so that it can focus on domestic development, avoid international obligations to implement domestic reforms, and eventually build up its own strength, at the same time forging a coalition with other states for counterbalancing the superpower ("multipolarization"). Neither Japan nor China would like to see the other dominate the region. The ASEAN countries are particularly bent on preventing external powers from dictating to them. They want to present a united front when dealing with external powers so they can influence and offset those powers. However, internal competition and jockeying for position within the organization is a recurring problem affecting the cohesion and effectiveness of ASEAN, prompting some more developed members to collaborate with external powers without waiting for the ASEAN consensus to form. Within ASEAN, country relations with external powers may also be affected by ethnic composition, geographical proximity, and historical experiences. South Korea, like the ASEAN countries, is bent on offsetting the influence of major powers, such as China, the United States, and Japan. It is also keen to participate in the growth opportunities of the region and eventually become a regional hub of economic activities. As different as their priorities are, the countries of East Asia all want to maintain peace and prosperity in the region and to have the mechanisms needed to do so.

Well aware of the difficulties of their enterprise, East Asian leaders now have more realistic expectations about what they can achieve in the short run, and focus on facilitating changes that would serve their long-term goals. Spurred by the new dynamics in the region, attitudes toward competitive reality, economic opportunities, and government roles are changing and thus paving the way for further reform and eventual fulfillment of the region's great potential. With its modest but steady progress to date, East Asian cooperation seems on the right path to overcoming mutual mistrust lingering in the region and promoting peace and stability. The question is, can the momentum of regionalism be maintained if interrupted by further hostile demonstrations like those of spring 2005? Will countries really be able to cooperate on substantive issues when they had difficulty reaching a consensus on the purpose and membership of the First East Asia Summit in Kuala Lumpur in 2005?[26]

To ensure that the long-term vision survives the political ups and downs, which, more fundamentally, stem from the current difference in value systems and threat recognition among major powers in the region, countries need to agree on and define precisely their concept of an East Asian community, as well as the specific steps required to reach this end. Until they can cooperate on such matters, they will have to work within the ASEAN + 3 frameworks and bilateral or plurilateral arrangements.[27] This would at least help them develop some of the institutional capabilities needed to build a rudimentary community framework and to establish (possibly redefine) the appropriate geographical scope for solving their problems and promoting their common interests. Beyond that it would be premature to establish formal institutions until individual countries completed their reforms.

In this connection, the newly created East Asia summit will not fundamentally change the prospect of East Asian regionalism. It just means that East Asian countries have obtained another forum to devise solutions to particular problems, and the division of work between the ASEAN + 3 and the East Asia summit will essentially be determined by the nature of the issues to be dealt with. In the meantime, however, the East Asia summit could accelerate cooperation between East Asian countries and the three new participants—Australia, India, and New Zealand—and thus might lead to the redefinition of an appropriate geographical scope of regional integration and community-building for the countries in East Asia.

Concerns outside the Region

Some observers outside the region consider preferential trade agreements an obstacle to global trade liberalization and thus question their efficacy both in general and in the East Asian context.[28] Another concern, particularly in the United States, is that East Asian regionalism has an anti-Western or anti-American bent that will create an exclusive bloc and undermine the achievement of global free trade.

Others argue that East Asian regionalism will have little substantive effect if it excludes the United States, the most important provider of markets, capital, technology, and political stability. Moreover, the proliferation of bilateral FTAs would constitute a step away from regional coherence. In their view, APEC is a better and more natural forum for achieving regional liberalization. Furthermore, the interests of the three major powers—the United States, China, and Japan—may not be compatible with each other, and Japan would not play an important role in the development of the regional order.

The following analysis puts these arguments to rest. If anything, East Asian regionalism complements and promotes globalism and has merit distinct from APEC. The proliferation of bilateral FTAs is not a sign that the region can never cohere but a necessary intermediate step toward a seamless integration into a pan-regional framework. And interaction among Japan, China, and the United States does have bearing on the path of East Asian regionalism.

Another of Washington's concerns, expressed in mid-2004, was that the idea of a separate East Asia summit circulating at the ASEAN + 3 meetings was designed to enhance the influence of China.[29] Because the decision to hold the summit was made somewhat abruptly and the difference between its purpose and that of the existing ASEAN + 3 leaders meeting was not made clear, some suspected that the true aim might be to exclude U.S. influence in the region and that China might use it as a forum to dominate the region. In fact, earlier in the preparation, Beijing had apparently tried to take the initiative in the East Asia summit by proposing to hold its first or second meeting in Beijing. China recognized, however, that Chinese overpresence not only was not welcome in the region, but also detrimental to its own interest because it could stimulate the sense of a China threat. Hence, Chinese officials became intent on emphasizing that ASEAN should play the leadership role.[30] Indeed, most countries of the region appear dedicated to the guiding principles on East Asian community-building articulated in an EAVG report, such as equality among countries and avoidance of duplication of the work of other related organizations. They understand that East Asian cooperation can only succeed if conducted in accordance with the agreed guiding principles. Now that the leaders have agreed to hold the East Asia summit annually, Australia, India, and New Zealand have a channel to voice their concerns about East Asian community building.[31] With these countries in the game, it has become even more unlikely that East Asian regionalism will become a vehicle of dominance of a particular power.

How Regionalism Complements Globalism

As just mentioned, regionalism, particularly in the form of a preferential trade agreement, should not be considered detrimental to global liberalization. If part of a multilayered structure of international economic institutions, it can contribute to both liberalization and rule making, as can be demonstrated by exploring two issues: the effect of preferential trade agreements on multilateral liberalization and rule making and the openness East Asian regionalism can achieve compared with similar frameworks around the world.

Why the WTO Is Not Enough

To reiterate, the concept of regionalism casts no doubt on the desirability of global solutions through the WTO. With its broad membership (which has risen to 148 after starting with 77 in 1995) and unique dispute settlement mechanism, this organization provides the largest degree of global welfare and the best ultimate solution to trade issues.[32] Rather, the question to consider is whether regional agreements can complement the WTO.

A large problem for the WTO today is how to keep pace with globalization and technological progress in promoting trade liberalization and addressing new issues. The organization spent seven years on the GATT Uruguay Round (UR) of trade negotiations. Furthermore, the scope of the resulting global trade regime is so broad that it has more difficulty keeping up with new issues and devising new rules to apply to them. The setback of the negotiations on a proposed Multilateral Agreement on Investment is a case in point.[33] It also has little time to establish rules on mutual recognition of the assessment of conformity to technical standards, a task left to bilateral, plurilateral, or regional agreements, or to prepare a comprehensive set of international rules to govern electronic commerce. These new issues are now being handled through FTAs such as the North American Free Trade Agreement (NAFTA) or the separate agreements Singapore has signed with Japan and the United States.

Admittedly, progress toward a free trade world is bound to be slow. Even so, there should be some means of recognizing that integration may be more urgent in some regions than in others. East Asia's dense production networks, for example, operate under a tight schedule and a low inventory and have parts and components going back and forth among factories in the region for numerous processing and assembly tasks before being shipped to the final markets. They have a keen interest in seeing streamlined and standardized customs procedures across the region, and in reducing the costs of business transactions. Governments in the region eager to attract foreign direct investment (FDI) are becoming sensitive to these concerns.

PTAs offer a pragmatic way to address regional problems in a timely and focused fashion and to generate policy innovations that might eventually be adopted at the global level. Although issue-specific agreements separate from PTAs could do the job, they are more effective in combination with PTAs. Such arrangements can enhance negotiating flexibilities. For example, developing countries might be more open to accepting constraints on their domestic industrial policies in a bilateral investment treaty if they get in return improved market access for their exports via an FTA. Another likely benefit would be greater attention from political leaders, which would help overcome domestic resistance to increased international competition arising from these agreements.[34]

The Uruguay Round also left the tariffs of developing countries relatively high and thus could not substantially reduce the margin of discrimination of existing preferential trade agreements, even as new PTAs rapidly proliferated and further widened the margin of discrimination in the 1990s. This situation was partly due to the fact that developed countries having FTAs with developing countries did not have a strong incentive for tariff reduction of their FTA partners. The prospect of East Asian regionalism can provide a new impetus to trade liberalization of middle-income countries that belong to FTAs with developed countries as well as help reinforce the rules on regional trade agreements.

FTAs: Building Blocks or Stumbling Blocks?

Whether preferential trade agreements help or hinder multilateral liberalization and rule making seems to depend on individual circumstances. In some cases, a PTA might create new vested interests that would benefit from trade diversion and therefore resist further liberalization.[35] In others, it might reduce the political weight of less competitive industries that stand in the way of liberalization.[36] Although PTAs could divert scarce policy resources away from multilateral negotiations, the "bicycle theory" suggests that the unavailability of ongoing trade negotiations in periods between major trade negotiations could strengthen the hands of those seeking protection.[37]

Bilateral and regional agreements are also used to increase leverage to promote ongoing multilateral negotiations. The George W. Bush administration explicitly adopted the strategy to "create a competition in liberalization" by "promoting free trade globally, regionally and bilaterally" and not to "permit any one country to veto America's drive for global free trade."[38] Such a strategy could foster global and regional economic interdependence by capitalizing on defensive motivations of other countries. Furthermore, FTAs might build momentum for liberalization in a way the WTO does not. By improving relations with particular countries they could generate domestic support to overcome resistance to liberalization and thus prompt a country to liberalize trade in some goods or services it had never considered before, although sensitive items might have to be excluded because of the difficulty of not just reducing but eliminating the tariffs on them. For these and other reasons, leading analysts argue that PTAs can be both beneficial and detrimental to multilateral liberalization, the outcome "determined not by theory but by the policies of the main players," notably the United States and the European Union.[39] However, the policies of East Asian economies should also matter, especially in designing an East Asian regionalism conducive to liberalization and globalization.

How East Asian Regionalism Can Promote Globalism

Most East Asian economies, being export-oriented and dependent on extraregional markets, are likely to maintain a strong incentive to promote global liberalization. Some evidence to this effect is their policy shift following the financial crisis of 1997–98, when they decided PTAs could help improve their economic performance. Recognizing the limit of the global institutions and inspired by the regionalism in Europe and the Americas, they became intent on reforming domestic policies, preparing for future liberalization, and building capacity to make bolder moves. They knew that the more they could offer, the more influential they could be in trade negotiations. Thus none of them pursued FTAs from protectionist (much less anti-Western or anti-American) motives, such as using PTAs to avoid further liberalization or to create an inward-looking bloc. Rather, it was Europe and the United States that tried to give neighbors preference over East Asian exporters, as President Clinton made clear when he said "NAFTA would help American firms to compete better with their (excluded) Japanese competitors."[40]

Indeed, there is a large difference between the FTA strategies of East Asia and the United States, though they may look similar on the surface in that both pursue liberalization on multiple fronts.[41] East Asia's goal is not just to open up foreign markets but also to energize domestic political constituencies. By contrast, the United States, whose "barriers are already very low" (albeit with some remaining sensitive items), is not concerned with stimulating domestic reform.[42] As the bicycle theory suggests, the primary domestic effect of lowering foreign barriers would be to contain domestic protectionist pressure to undo prior liberalization.[43]

Why East Asian Regionalism Matters

Since 1990 Washington's attitude toward East Asian regionalism has evolved from strong objections to benign neglect. While there is no official explanation, many observers point out that nothing significant happened over these years, and there seemed to be no need to worry. Critics further argue that there is only so much East Asians can do without the United States, their biggest market and an important source of investment and technology, and that is why APEC is the appropriate regional forum in which to look for significant achievements. They cite the proliferation of bilateral FTAs as evidence that East Asians cannot cohere and achieve regionalism.[44]

The proponents of East Asian regionalism would not deny that access to U.S. markets and technology is important to East Asian economies and that they value U.S. involvement in the region. Indeed, a number of countries are keen to conclude bilateral FTAs with the United States. Rather, the point is that regionalism could address issues of less concern to the United States, some of which the APEC process made clear. The United States has shown little interest in development cooperation in East Asia, for example, yet the

wide developmental gaps in the region require attention, particularly to prepare less-developed countries for trade and investment liberalization. This is
where regionalism could play an important role. By reducing the costs of
cross-border business and associated service links (in transportation,
telecommunications, information technology networks, and administration), it could help less-developed economies participate in production
networks and strengthen the manufacturing sector so important to their
economies.

Developing countries would liberalize trade and investment if they thought
it would attract foreign investors, but they also need to recognize that other
aspects of the business environment—both the physical infrastructure and
institutional capabilities—are just as important in this regard. Trade negotiations alone cannot make Asian production networks more efficient and
competitive. After all, extraregional investors such as American and European firms rely on these networks to enhance the efficiency of their global
operations while facilities in their home countries are not necessarily integrated into those operations.

If anything, U.S. interest in regional economic cooperation in Asia has
focused narrowly on Asia's trade and investment liberalization and limited
areas of trade and investment facilitation. It would be unrealistic to expect the
United States to worry enough about Asian economic development becoming stable and sustainable with a holistic perspective to contribute its policy
and financial resources to the seemingly time-consuming task of building
Asian cooperation. That is why East Asian frameworks are indispensable
channels of cooperation in adequately addressing important regional issues
that other forums ignore.

Why Not Just APEC?

As detailed in chapter 5, APEC cannot do everything. After becoming the
primary regional forum in Asia, it rapidly expanded its membership before
solidifying its core objectives—which should be to promote WTO negotiations and provide a forum for sharing information and developing
guidelines (where feasible) for facilitating trade and investment as well as
improving market-economy institutions. As important as these objectives
are to East Asian economies, they do not encompass all the issues requiring attention in the region. East Asian regionalism and APEC, each with its
distinct values, must therefore be seen as essential parts of a multilayered
structure of international economic institutions that complement the
WTO.

How Bilateral FTAs Can Lead to Pan–East Asian Regionalism

As should be clear by now, East Asia's strategy for achieving regionalism is to start with what is doable. The current proliferation of bilateral FTAs is a necessary intermediate step to the eventual integration of separate FTAs into a pan-regional framework. In their early negotiations of bilateral FTAs, however, the economies of the region did not share a common goal, have a definite sequence of actions or clear criteria in mind, or know whether their moves could lead to the desired outcome. Their approach can be described as "strategic opportunism," exploring which FTAs are doable and beneficial and reacting to other countries' moves on an ad hoc basis.[45]

Such an approach tends to give rise to overlapping FTAs with different rules of origin and thus can add to transaction costs.[46] Although the business sector may not necessarily be worse off—since it need not be trapped by the rules of origin of particular FTAs (if the additional costs from those rules were larger than the benefit of preferential tariff elimination, multinational corporations would give up on the preference and simply pay MFN tariffs)— the so-called spaghetti bowl effect of such overlapping rules would nullify the efforts to reduce transaction costs through FTAs.[47]

Today there are more grounds for optimism about regionalism since East Asian economies have a clear incentive to reduce transaction costs and enhance the competitiveness of production networks in the region, thereby increasing each country's attractiveness. The competitive dynamics would not last long in the face of inconsistent FTAs, which could wipe out the cost savings to be gained from their preferential tariff reductions and lead countries to seek actual reductions in the cost of cross-border operations. Now that they are more experienced in FTA negotiations, East Asian capitals are becoming more familiar with each other's priorities and preferences and thus better able to work out regional solutions to different issues that are acceptable to all of them.

Regionalism as East Asian Consensus

Despite complaints that the ASEAN + 3 meetings are creating visions with no immediate relevance and that the institutional outcome has been modest, East Asia is expected to conclude a regionwide FTA. The ASEAN + 3 summit will remain "the main vehicle" of "East Asian cooperation and community-building" while the East Asia summit, with Australia, India, and New Zealand, will complement the ASEAN + 3 summit.[48] The East Asian dream is that the region's nations—which share geographical proximity, many historical experiences, challenges, and complementary resources—will one day overcome political rivalries and historical animosities and fulfill the large potential for cooperation. The natural desire for peaceful and friendly neighborhoods, previously brushed aside as naive, can be reinforced by a nascent sense of regional identity. Already, the growth of urban middle-class markets has opened up "the possibility for the construction of market-oriented national and regional cultural identities," which can provide a broader social foundation for East Asian regionalism.[49] "Integration," asserts U.S. ambassador Howard Baker, "does not mean that we have to choose one culture over the other," but that citizens of the world, who are still citizens of various countries in Asia, may still be citizens of Asia.[50]

Although, as the EAVG has observed, "the pace of building an East Asian community is uncertain, the direction is clear and the trend currently underway is irreversible," with political and business leaders turning more attention and resources to giving more concrete shape to the regional enterprise.[51] Even if the recent surge of Sino-Japanese tension temporarily dampens enthusiasm, the incidents reinforce the need for stable mechanisms for regional cooperation and do not detract from the long-term vision.

The Crucial Role of Japan, China, and the United States

In large part, the shape of East Asian regionalism will be determined by the interaction of the policies of Japan, the United States, and China, not just those of the last two, as some analysts suggest.[52] Japan-U.S. relations have had a large impact on the evolution of East Asian regionalism. After joining the WTO, China started to play an increasingly important role and created new competitive dynamics with Japan and the United States. Without healthy Sino-Japanese relations and benign (if not positive) U.S. attitudes toward East Asian cohesion, East Asian regionalism will not make significant progress.

At the same time, the policies of the three powers are under the influence of the ASEAN countries and South Korea, occasionally making groundbreaking proposals but acting mainly as a mediator. Although some of the more developed among them, notably Singapore and Thailand, have (not just proposed but actually) initiated bilateral arrangements with external powers independent of ASEAN and set off competitive dynamics in and outside the region, Japan, China, and the United States have the largest influence on the direction and pace of East Asian regionalism. Needless to say, their interests are not necessarily compatible, but they have come into a historic alignment that makes a breakthrough in East Asian regionalism possible.

The United States

Although the United States has made an immense contribution to the region's peace and prosperity and can influence and even shape the regional order with its long experience in market-economy institutions and liberal democracy, the engine of East Asian cooperation must reside within the region. The United States is interested in Asia only insofar as it can affect U.S. global strategy. Particularly since the terrorist attacks of September 11, 2001, its major concern has been the war on terrorism and the situation in the Middle East and will likely remain so. Its resulting benign neglect of East Asia's move toward regionalism has, in fact, led the capitals in the region to be less concerned about U.S. reaction to each step they make in that direction. At the same time, the added security and counterterrorism burdens on U.S. shoulders across the world might prompt the United States to recognize the strategic value of a more integrated and mature Asia as a source of global growth and a force for global stability.

China

The rise of China has added significant momentum to East Asian regionalism. Its economic dynamism restored confidence that East Asia could become the center of global economic growth. Although there is some fear about its continued military buildup, military threat to Taiwan, and anti-Japanese sentiment in its schools and media, China's increasingly reassuring foreign policy postures have helped allay the persistent anxiety about its strategic intentions among some neighbors, who now think they can achieve a genuine mutual trust if China finally overcomes its sense of vulnerability and starts focusing on improving the welfare of its people. On the other hand, Beijing's justification of the violence against Japanese interests during the anti-Japanese violent demonstrations in major Chinese cities in April 2005 suggested that China does not have confidence in its domestic political stability and is not yet ready for the rule of law.

At present, China has two primary goals: to pursue domestic development and to increase its geopolitical stature, thereby achieving a favorable balance of power. The first entails the daunting task of governing and transforming a huge country. Hence the insight and determination of China's reform-oriented leaders cannot instantly translate into institutional capabilities that shape the reality on the ground, such as the quality of the rule of law. The second goal distracts China from securing a peaceful international environment that would allow it to focus on development. Moreover, to realize its ambition to become a great power and leader of Asia, China must command the region's respect and admiration, which ultimately depends on whether its own people can enjoy an attractive living environment with economic and political freedom. China has great promise and a long journey ahead.

Japan

Despite the relative decline of its economic weight, Japan has the most advanced technology in East Asia, not to mention a large and sophisticated consumer market, which is a breeding ground for new innovative goods and services. It also has an effective legal system and strong capabilities for designing institutional frameworks.

Its emphasis now is on economic restructuring, driven by the business sector's efforts to shed excess capacity, focus on core competitiveness, and explore new opportunities. In doing its share, the sector has become increasingly vocal about public policy, especially after consumers' rejection of unsafe products supplied by fraudulent firms amply demonstrated that shielding producers from competition, the ultimate discipline for corporate management, will not help them survive. Recent stagnation has also made business and consumers much less tolerant of regulations and protections that add to the business and living costs without achieving their stated purposes. With the pressure growing for real change, Japan's policy toward economic integration in East Asia is first and foremost aimed at revitalizing its economy by improving access to its neighbors' markets and production facilities while making it an attractive location within the business networks in East Asia and in the world. Japan's initiative has great potential to transform the region into a more open and transparent business environment with integrated markets.

With developmental success and the growth of an urban middle class in Asia, people in the region have a new sense of affinity that extends beyond national borders. This should help the Japanese public become more open and welcoming to its neighbors, even though Japan's wartime legacy has got in the way of community building in East Asia (if not economic calculations involved in FTA negotiations). As a former adversary, Japan was unable to play an active role in formulating the postwar world economic order or in formulating regional frameworks in Asia until recently. By then, Japan's postwar record of peaceful contributions had made the regional political environment much more open to an active role for Japan. Since the end of the cold war and proliferation of technologies that permit the instant sharing of information worldwide, however, Japan's history is raising public emotion anew.

Today, Asian people are freely expressing their concerns about Japan's recognition of history issues, and some are calling for compensation for their wartime sufferings. Government-to-government settlement of war-related claims would not guarantee public support for reconciliation, upon which the ultimate solution of this problem depends. Since trust is central to it, many Asian policymakers have pointed out that Japan needs to articulate its national strategy and the role it is willing to play in the region if it hopes to gain the confidence of its neighbors.

Sino-Japanese Relations

At the end of the 1990s, against the backdrop of China's economic rise, Japan's stagnation, and the de facto integration of their economies, many in Japan saw China as an economic threat. When exports to China expanded and the profitability of investments in China improved, attitudes changed, with Japan now focusing on the economic opportunities that China could provide. Still, there has been a growing uneasiness about the increased military expenditures that China is able to fund, together with issues related to Taiwan, the activities of Chinese research ships in Japanese waters, the competition for energy resources, and China's anti-Japanese thrust in education.

China, on the other hand, blames Japanese views of its history and the Taiwan issue for nurturing grass-roots suspicion of Japan, thereby justifying Beijing's repeated demands for Japan's apology, which in turn provokes Japanese public resentment. China also worries that the U.S.-Japan security alliance is part of a U.S. strategy to encircle China. At the same time, Beijing appreciates that the U.S. security presence in the region prevents Japan's rearmament. Since China aspires to be Asia's future leader, as already mentioned, it has tried to check Japan's political leadership in the region as well as in the global arena (for example, by not supporting a possible seat for Japan on the United Nations Security Council).

The danger is that hardliners in both countries may be tempted to use regional integration against each other, with Japan trying to sustain its influence in the face of a rising China, and China trying to isolate Japan within the region or solidify its influence. Alternatively, China might want to postpone institutional arrangements in the region until it becomes predominant and can formalize a new balance of power. Asian neighbors worry that the geopolitical competition between Japan and China would put pressure on them to choose sides, prevent regional capitals from focusing on substantive aspects of cooperation, and stall the development of regionwide institutions.

Historic Alignment

Despite the foregoing concerns, regionalism's chances of success are greater than ever because three major powers have come into "a historic alignment."[53] That is to say, Japan has finally started to reform its economy, driven by corporate restructuring and supported by changes, albeit not systematic, in government policies. The United States has become much more proactive and less negative toward East Asian economic regionalism, even pursuing bilateral FTAs with ASEAN countries and South Korea, and thus providing new impetus to regionalism. Now focused on domestic development and on ensuring that the international environment is conducive to it, China is developing a more open economy and more sophisticated foreign policy. Despite thorny Sino-Japanese relations and China's growing power and military buildup, each of the three powers, albeit without collaboration, is contributing to the building blocks for future regionwide frameworks.

This is a historic opportunity to promote East Asian regionalism as a prelude to pan-regional integration, including a regionwide free trade area. To this end, Japan should conclude ongoing FTA negotiations with South Korea and the ASEAN countries and integrate them into a comprehensive regional multilateral FTA. Through these negotiations, Japan should demonstrate that it is able to liberalize sensitive sectors such as agriculture and undertake systematic regulatory reform to make each sector more efficient and meet the public policy goals more effectively. For its part, China should honor its WTO commitment as well as its FTA with ASEAN, so as to boost the confidence of neighbors in its will and capacity to enforce international rules and to promote domestic reform. It could also explore the model elements of a comprehensive regional FTA, including high-level investment rules. Both Japan and China should work to improve bilateral relations and the political atmosphere surrounding East Asian regionalism. The United States could explore how parts of its FTAs with ASEAN countries could be combined with East Asian FTAs and expand its capacity-building support for developing countries in East Asia. Needless to say, the WTO's Doha negotiations are crucial to keeping regional frameworks more open to the outside.

Driving Forces and Impediments

In the past two decades, East Asian regionalism has been shaped by different forces. Although initially driven by defensive motivations, it has been largely shaped by an intraregional desire to deal with common concerns. Intraregional competition, which stimulated the launch of some bilateral FTA negotiations, on balance has promoted cooperation rather than conflict in the region. Although various obstacles remain—such as the aforementioned developmental gaps, the fear of economic dominance by China, U.S. opposition to East Asian–only forums, and hesitation about institutionalization—the countries in the region are gradually overcoming them.

Driving Force 1: Defensive Regionalism

Defensive regionalism refers to defensive reactions to extraregional pressures of two main kinds, one being discrimination caused by PTAs in other regions such as the European Union (EU) and the Americas (for example, via NAFTA).[54] Although preferential trade agreements do not always have an adverse effect on nonmembers (under certain conditions, trade creation can surpass trade diversion and enhance the welfare of nonmembers), regionalism in Europe and the Americas put steadily increasing pressure on East Asian capitals to compensate for welfare losses.[55] Hoping to strengthen their negotiation leverage against existing blocs and frustrated with the apparently unstoppable trend toward increasing regionalism in the world, East Asia has responded with proposals such as Malaysia's suggestion for an East Asian Economic Group (EAEG). Initially conceived as a trade bloc to countervail European and American blocs, it was soon transformed into a consultative forum.

The region's economies have also been frustrated by U.S. unilateral actions and "market fundamentalism," also known as "the Washington consensus."[56] In the late 1980s, East Asia, in concert with Australia, decided to address this problem by asking the United States to form a common front—APEC—to help manage their frictions. After the WTO was established in the mid-1990s, however, the legal protection against unilateral sanctions and various forms of protectionism was eventually provided by the WTO, not by APEC.

In this case, the causative factors are particular events (such as trade frictions with Washington or the initial mishandling of the Asian financial crisis) rather than regionalism in other areas. These events create an impetus for structural solutions to the underlying problems: for example, trade frictions with the United States prompted East Asian countries to stimulate domestic demand and eliminate trade barriers so they can trade more with each other and rectify the excessive dependence on the U.S. markets. Another significant event, the Asian financial crisis, reflected the region's overdependence on short-term capital flows, especially from outside the region, to fund local projects, and motivated them to develop Asian bond markets.

Although defensive motives gave impetus to regionalism in its early stages by awakening countries to the need for their own cooperation, they do not necessarily suggest what policies to pursue.[57] The most straightforward form of defensive reaction to the European Union and NAFTA, for instance, would be an East Asian FTA, which has not yet been viewed as a realistic short-term goal. Instead, East Asian economies have pursued a series of bilateral FTAs, not only among themselves but also across regions such as Korea and Chile or the United States and Singapore. Cross-regional FTAs are supposed to counter discrimination and therefore represent a more direct response to PTAs that exclude East Asian economies, but by definition they do not fall under East Asian regionalism.

Up to now, defensive regionalism has had limited effect in combating the regionalism in Europe and America because of a lack of cohesiveness and U.S. opposition. This suggests that when the region is enjoying strong economic growth, it may be less concerned about gains and losses in relation to other regions. The surge of interest in regionalism in the wake of the 1997–98 Asian financial crisis seems to add weight to this suggestion, although the idea did not fade away after recovery from the crisis, indicating a new balance between the driving forces and obstacles.

Instead of going on the defensive, East Asia could draw on regionalism in other parts of the world for its positive effects.[58] For example, the observation that Europe and North America, which had steered multilateral liberalization under GATT since the end of World War II, had also pursued regional liberalization inspired confidence that pursuing regionalism does not necessarily mean turning away from multilateralism.[59] Regionalism in Europe and North America also provides "a positive inspiration" that it can substantially enhance a region's productivity, as European integration has prompted mergers and acquisitions to capitalize on economies of scale available in a single market, or help lock in domestic reform, as NAFTA has done in Mexico.[60] According to many empirical studies of PTAs in Europe and North America, regionalism has had a positive impact on members' welfare, and there is every reason to expect similar benefits in East Asian economies.[61]

Whether defensive regionalism can achieve its intended outcome depends largely on the extent to which intraregional economic interdependence is promoted. East Asia, as discussed in chapter 3, is so dependent on extraregional markets that if it threatened to become a self-sufficient bloc in response to NAFTA and the European Union, turning inward-looking and protectionist, it would be suicidal (and in any case not credible). A region with a significant trade surplus has little room to use trade diversion to compensate for lost export opportunities (lost because of regionalism elsewhere). Regionalism's usefulness as a defensive mechanism therefore lies in the potential to make its united voice heard in international economic policymaking and to help alleviate the root cause of protectionism in other regions—its overde-pendence on extraregional markets—by stimulating regional domestic demand. To what extent those voices are heard will depend on the region's cohesiveness on various issues, while regional domestic demand can only be created by facilitating intraregional economic interdependence and stimu-lating growth. Anti-Western and anti-American sentiments thus appear to have played no role in the actual development of East Asian regionalism.

Driving Force 2: Intraregional Economic Interdependence

The desire of states to have an effective mechanism for cooperation—to pro-mote de facto integration, to manage various problems brought about by economic interdependence, and to deal with other common challenges—can be referred to as *intraregional economic interdependence*. This force creates an incentive to reduce transaction costs in existing trade and to strengthen economic linkages with high-growth areas in the region. Also, intraregional economic interdependence provides an incentive to improve the economic performance of the region as a whole and persuade its devel-oped countries to help their less-developed neighbors deal with such challenges as rapid industrialization and the institutional transition from developmental states to more market-oriented economies. Similar concerns lead countries with similar—therefore competing—economic structures to share their experiences. Furthermore, there is a political incentive to invite less-developed neighboring countries to participate in the network of eco-nomic interdependence, so as to promote their economic development and political stability and to maintain harmonious diplomatic relations with them. Whereas political factors help determine the boundary of a particular region to be covered by an institutional framework, the intensity of eco-nomic interaction contributes substance and depth and thereby a basis for institutionalized intergovernmental cooperation, including preferential trade agreements.

Intraregional economic interdependence did not bring about a pan–East Asian regionalism in a single leap. It first stimulated regionalism in ASEAN, where the private sector prompted the member governments to adopt more effective ways to promote intra-ASEAN integration, which eventually led to the ASEAN Free Trade Area (see chapter 3) in the early 1990s. Around that time, Japan and ASEAN, albeit without preferential trade agreements, started cooperating in promoting intra-ASEAN integration and improving ASEAN's business environment. Intraregional economic interdependence also shaped the APEC agenda, although it soon became narrowly focused on trade liberalization.

After the financial crisis, Japan and South Korea turned their attention to FTAs for the first time, and the ASEAN countries became receptive to the idea of FTAs other than the AFTA, including ones between individual members and non-ASEAN powers. The crisis had occurred just when information technology was spreading and revolutionizing ways of managing and optimizing global business operations. In short order, China emerged as the world's favorite site for assembling and producing parts. The post-crisis environment stimulated interest in regionalism in two ways. First, increasingly finer specialization within East Asia awakened businesses and governments in the region to the need for a more systematic approach to addressing various problems that compromise the efficiency of cross-border business operations—reducing tariffs, administrative procedures, testing requirements, and other transaction costs—and to improving the protection of intellectual property rights and the transparency and predictability of government regulations. As already noted, the WTO lacks speed and flexibility in taking up new issues. Second, China's rapidly growing markets and its accession to the WTO sparked investors' confidence in its business environment, prompting regional economies to strengthen economic linkages with China and making East Asian regionalism more attractive as a long-term enterprise.

As a result, East Asian governments started taking a multilayered approach, pursuing various channels to see what would work best for different issues. At the moment, most action is focused on bilateral FTAs because of the speed and ease of concluding agreements, particularly given the developmental gaps within East Asia. Aiming for seamless markets, however, governments are still trying to integrate separate bilateral FTAs into a broader regional FTA. Since this could be a complicated task, countries concluding FTAs should be trying to establish a common basis, with some variation as necessary. Given the concentration of production networks in East Asia, regional capitals will eventually try to conclude an East Asian FTA. These and other measures to reduce transaction costs are likely to spread to APEC as a whole or individual countries such as India, if all economies involved are willing to dismantle their barriers and have their own (sub)regional preferential arrangements absorbed in a broader regional arrangement. Because some barriers may only be negotiated at the global level, economic regionalism can be viewed as an intermediate step toward the ultimate goal of global integration. In East Asia alone, regionalism will provide a valuable foundation for promoting economic reform and building mutual trust.

Driving Force 3: Intraregional Competitive Dynamics

The concept of competitive dynamics cannot be understood without examining the types and objectives of economic competition. The first, known as competitive liberalization, focuses on liberalizing a country's own trade and investment regimes. The term was coined in the mid-1990s to describe the rush to liberalization by "so many countries, in so many different parts of the world, with such different economic systems, at such different stages of development" at that time.[62] Unilateral liberalization moved especially quickly in East Asia as developing economies competed with each other for FDI and export earnings. Once an influential country decides to make itself more attractive to foreign investors and more competitive in export markets (because of lower tariffs on imported inputs for manufacturing goods to be exported, for example), others are prompted to follow and thus offset its advantages. As Fred Bergsten points out, it is fairly easy to reduce very high tariffs at the outset "because they put few dents in the real level of protection and thus can often be implemented unilaterally," but most countries quickly find that "they must apply the traditional political economy approach," that is, "insist on reciprocity," "to engineer the later phases of the process."[63]

The second type of competition arises in connection with FTAs. Once an FTA is introduced, nonmembers are pressured to overcome the discrimination it has created, preferably via the *multilateral scenario,* meaning multilateral liberalization undertaken to reduce the margins of discrimination of various PTAs. The second-best way, the *bandwagon scenario,* is to join the FTA to get the preferential benefits. Next best is the *wedging scenario,* which means concluding an FTA with some of its members to partly offset the discrimination. If that is not feasible, nonmembers may try the *counterbalance scenario,* joining forces to conclude a separate FTA so as to improve negotiation leverage and prompt liberalization on a larger scale.

The term "competitive liberalization" (or "competition in liberalization") now applies to these two categories alike as both are based on the competitive impulse to offset the advantages other countries enjoy.[64] However, the two are still differentiated by whether the emphasis is on liberalizing a particular country's *own* trade and investment regime or on getting better access to foreign markets.

A third type of competition is driven by political rather than economic incentives. The political significance of FTAs between other countries often prompts a regional economy to conclude an FTA of its own. When political motivation is strong, the choice of FTA partners may be more important than the specific design of the FTA. Also, countries may compete for political influence not only by liberalizing but also by providing economic assistance.

A line must also be drawn between *global* and *intraregional* competitive dynamics, since they differ in their impact on regionalism. Global competitive dynamics are not always directly relevant to regionalism and can be further divided into scenarios: a multilateral scenario, which will lead to global liberalization; a bandwagon and a global wedging scenario, which will produce cross-regional FTAs; and a counterbalance scenario, which is a form of defensive regionalism. By way of example, global wedging was a driving force in the South Korea–Chile FTA and the Japan-Mexico economic partnership agreement (EPA) but has had little direct effect on East Asian regionalism. Of course, it may indirectly promote East Asian regionalism by accelerating domestic reform in South Korea or Japan, preparing them better for FTAs within the region.

By contrast, *intraregional* competitive dynamics have a direct impact on regionalism in all four of its scenarios: the multilateral scenario will lead to a pan-regional FTA; the bandwagon scenario will cause the membership of the initial FTA to expand; the wedging scenario will produce overlapping bilateral or subregional FTAs, such as the Japan-Singapore EPA, South Korea–Singapore FTA, or China-ASEAN comprehensive economic cooperation (CEC); and the counterbalance scenario will generate competing FTAs such as the Japan-South Korea EPA and China-ASEAN CEC.

Impediment 1: Lack of Cohesiveness because of Diversity and Distrust

A major obstacle in creating an institutional framework for East Asian regionalism is the lack of cohesiveness in this part of the world. Countries differ greatly in their stages of development, political systems, and cultural and religious background, not to mention historical antagonism and political rivalry.

In fact, gaps in development have not always hindered regionalism. As a World Bank report points out, a marked feature of the 1990s was "the advent of trade blocs in which both high-income industrial countries and developing countries are equal partners."[65] NAFTA was the most significant example of a North-South PTA, while the European Union added to it, concluded association agreements, and entered into a customs union with less-developed countries. However, the gaps in development among the partners of these agreements were much smaller than those within East Asia today. The U.S. per capita income at the beginning of 1994, when NAFTA was concluded, was 6 times that of Mexico.[66] Similarly, Luxembourg's per capita income in 1986 was 6 times that of new European Community member Portugal. The EU started to conclude agreements with less-developed countries only after it had established solid institutional frameworks. In 1993, when Bulgaria concluded an association agreement with the European Union, Luxembourg's per capita income was 32 times larger. And when Turkey and the European Union entered into a customs union at the beginning of 1996, Luxembourg's per capita income was 16 times larger than that of Turkey. In East Asia, by contrast, Japan's per capita income is 120 times larger than that of Cambodia, a difference comparable perhaps to that in the proposed FTAA where U.S. per capita income is 100 times larger than that of Haiti. Although complementary economic structures based on developmental gaps have been instrumental in promoting de facto economic integration in East Asia, the differences in institutional capabilities are expected to make it difficult for East Asian economies to agree on and enforce institutional frameworks at the same pace. To help less-developed economies build a capacity to participate in regional agreements at a faster pace and facilitate the economic convergence that regionalization promotes, East Asian countries incorporate developmental assistance in their regionalism.

Another challenge in East Asia is how to bring differing political systems into harmony. Regionalism in Europe and the Americas is at least based on shared values such as democracy and market economy concepts. Needless to say, countries with different political systems have joined the WTO, and the United States recently concluded several bilateral FTAs with countries that are not yet full-fledged democracies. Given these precedents, differences in political system do not seem to be a decisive factor any more. More crucial is the quality of the rule of law. Authoritarian regimes, in particular, are likely to reject such constraints on their behavior "internally and internationally," but they may accept intrusive international arrangements if such a move can enhance their competitiveness and attractiveness as investment destinations and thus help strengthen their authority.[67]

Eventually, the most serious obstacle to East Asian regionalism may be the mutual distrust between Japan and other countries of the region, particularly China. Whether increased interdependence between these two countries will lead to domestic coalitions and bilateral relations powerful enough to assuage such distrust remains to be seen. But there are grounds for cautious optimism.

In the case of South Korea, President Kim Dae Jung's bold offer of reconciliation in 1998 moved the Japanese public and made it more sensitive to the history problem. Although the reconciliation is not complete and anti-Japanese sentiment is still alive in South Korea, if diluted, both countries recognize the value of neighborliness, as demonstrated by their co-hosting of the World Cup soccer games, launching of bilateral FTA negotiations, and appreciation of each other's pop culture. While territorial disputes over the Takeshima (Tokdo in Korean) Islands inflamed the Korean public in the spring of 2005, the two governments have managed to prevent such incidents from harming their overall relations.

Also positive elements in Sino-Japanese relations aroused the hope that Sino-Japanese rapprochement, while still premature, may indeed be possible some time in the future. The popularity in Japan of Chinese articles published a few years ago that advocated for improved Sino-Japanese relations suggested how weary the Japanese had grown of the tense relations with their biggest neighbor and its anti-Japanese sentiments.[68] While those articles were severely criticized in China, the fact that they were published anyway seemed a sign of a more liberal policy debate in Beijing. Bilateral relations have experienced new tensions since the spring of 2005, however, stimulated by differences over history recognition and Japan's quest for a permanent seat on the United Nations Security Council. In view of China's domestic situation, particularly the lack of channels for airing public grievances and of freedom of speech or political campaign, fundamental changes in Sino-Japanese relations will not come soon. The pace of regionwide community building will remain slow until the two can ease these tensions.

Trust is a serious concern for the ASEAN countries as well as for China and South Korea, which recall all too well the suffering they experienced at the hands of stronger powers. Therefore when a particular power tries to dominate the region, it tends to stir up disunity and prompts other countries to oppose that power's initiatives. And if countries rely on external powers such as the United States to counterbalance the influence of a particular power in the region, this only strengthens the second major impediment: extraregional dependence.

Impediment 2: Extraregional Dependence

East Asian economies recognize the importance of accommodating their biggest customer, since they need its security presence, technology, and capital. East Asia's defensive regionalism sits in a precarious balance with this dependence on the United States and is thus greatly affected by U.S. policy. That is to say, the momentum for Asian-only forums through defensive regionalism is likely to decrease or increase in proportion to U.S. policy's consideration of East Asian common interests and strong commitment to regional stability and prosperity. Had it not been for the North American (or

Western Hemisphere) regionalism and the U.S. inclination toward unilateral actions against East Asian economies, Malaysia might not have proposed the EAEG in late 1990 after GATT's failed ministerial meeting or might not have evoked as much sympathy in other countries in the region. If the United States had taken the initiative to increase Asian quotas in the International Monetary Fund (IMF) in accordance with Asia's weight in the international capital flows, and if it had been more forthcoming with assistance when Asian countries were coordinating a package to support currency stabilization at the early stage of the 1997–98 crisis, Japan would not have proposed the Asian Monetary Fund.

Impediment 3: Hesitancy about Institutionalization

Although East Asian countries are serious about solving their problems, they are leery of rigid, top-down institutions.[69] ASEAN countries tend to prefer consensus building to confrontation. This approach, the so-called ASEAN way, is not so much the result of "an Asian culture" that values harmony but of "conscious political programs [designed] to dampen adversarial conflict internally and externally."[70] ASEAN applied this approach selectively on limited occasions when it needed to exhibit unity, so as to preempt the interference of external powers and enhance its leverage in negotiations.[71] ASEAN was cautious not only about rigid institutions, which could deny flexibility needed for future consensus building, but also about other regional forums that could minimize ASEAN's role or weaken its unity. This hesitancy had more to do with its membership than with the level of institutionalization or legalization.

By the time the Asia-Europe meeting was proposed in 1995, ASEAN countries seemed to have overcome the fear of dilution by larger forums. The fear of disunity, however, was evident when Singapore, without other ASEAN members, was about to start FTA negotiations with New Zealand in 1999.[72] Many were also hesitant about institutionalization because some economies lacked the commitment or capacity to follow through with politically unpopular measures. As a result, they still tend to avoid institutionalization in favor of easier, more flexible, and (occasionally) less fundamental solutions.

This hesitation offsets the impact of intraregional economic interdependence. It also changes over time, depending on the nature of the problems being faced and the availability of alternative solutions. Before the financial crisis, for example, the strong economic performance of East Asian economies made them confident of their growth dynamics, which did not depend on regional legal frameworks.[73] After the crisis, they grew less self-assured. When countries are faced with serious regional problems that cannot be resolved by other forums, institutionalization seems to gain momentum, possibly resulting in legally binding agreements that constrain sovereignty and may have discriminatory effects on nonmembers. As East Asian economies began to appreciate that institutional agreements could give political momentum to domestic reforms, they overcame automatic rejection of institutionalization and started choosing the most effective ways to solve particular problems. Nevertheless, the lack of willingness or capacity to thoroughly implement tough measures will slow the pace and dilute the substance of future institutionalization efforts.

3

The State of Regionalization

As mentioned earlier, world attitudes toward East Asian regionalization, especially Japan's role in it, have changed drastically since the late 1980s. As market processes pushed economic integration along, a primary concern was that the region might turn into a closed economic bloc, with Japanese firms replicating "their domestic system of networking in the region" and U.S. and European multinational corporations (MNCs) being "gradually squeezed out by the increasingly tight and exclusive nature of this highly competitive Japanese production alliance."[1] By the end of the 1990s, Japan was in a state of prolonged stagnation and the United States on an upswing, with information technology (IT) firing up U.S. productivity and U.S. firms dominating the IT sector. Once a formidable competitor, Japan was now of little consequence and even a risk to the global economy. With U.S. and European firms actively investing in East Asian economies, the fear of Japan's domination of Asia disappeared. Before long, China loomed large as a new center of growth, overshadowing Japan and stimulating the idea that Beijing aspired to restore a Sino-centric order in Asia.

While it is tempting to focus on the geopolitical implications of these developments, more important to this discussion are the factors motivating East Asia's economic entities—both business and government—to engage in regional cooperation as well as to search for advantageous positions and in turn create new complementarities. Since regionalization created the common interests and competitive dynamics that moved East Asia in this direction, this chapter is devoted to its evolution, mechanisms, and impact on regionalism.

Response to Globalization

Regionalization in East Asia is a direct result of economic competition under the pressures of globalization and technological progress. Global businesses have an economic incentive to choose the most suitable locations for particular operations in order to make the entire production process more efficient. Their freedom of choice in this regard has expanded greatly as a result of technological progress in transportation, information, and communications, which has made it easier to integrate and manage various steps in production networks at a distance from their headquarters. Individual talent and capital are also freer to go wherever they can maximize their value. Furthermore, business is freer to shun unattractive locations, leaving industries there hollowed-out and talent being drained away. Host governments, in turn, have come under strong pressure to compete with each other for foreign direct investment (FDI) as well as for productive resources such as individual talent and capital to spur economic growth and development. At the same time, they seek complementary relations so as to gain from each other's growth. Meanwhile global institutions such as the WTO and the IMF have been pushing host governments to liberalize their economies. These conditions, while not unique to East Asia, paved the way for the growth of the production networks that spawned regionalization. This wave of globalization began gathering momentum in the mid-1980s with a surge in FDI.

Surge in FDI in the Latter Half of the 1980s

Despite some earlier intraregional trade (predominantly of a bilateral nature with Japan), regionalization received its first strong boost from the sharp appreciation of the yen after the Plaza Accord of 1985. This accord changed East Asia's economic landscape. Japanese firms rushed to relocate their labor-intensive production processes to lower-cost countries in order to maintain competitiveness in export markets such as the United States and Europe, and export-oriented FDI poured into other East Asian countries. Between 1985 and 1989, total Japanese FDI grew at an annual average rate of 51 percent, while its FDI to East Asia (Indonesia, Malaysia, the Philippines, Thailand, Singapore, South Korea, China, Hong Kong and Taiwan) grew 52 percent.[2]

As striking as they are, these figures do not capture FDI's immense impact on individual countries. Between 1985 and 1988, the annual growth of Japan's FDI averaged 162 percent in Thailand and 70 percent in Malaysia; between 1986 and 1989 it jumped to 108 percent in the Philippines; and between 1989 and 1992, it reached 44 percent in Indonesia. Responding to trade frictions with the United States and the subsequent appreciation of their currencies

Figure 3-1. The Surge in FDI to Five ASEAN Countries after 1985
Billions of current U.S. dollars

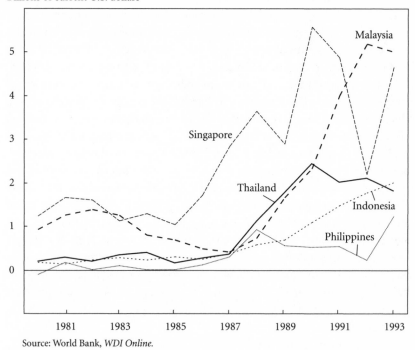

Source: World Bank, *WDI Online.*

against the U.S. dollar, manufacturers in newly industrializing economies (NIEs) such as South Korea and Taiwan followed suit and invested in ASEAN and China.[3] As a result, total net FDI inflows to ASEAN countries rose sharply; averaging 72 percent in Thailand (between 1985 and 1990), 65 percent in Malaysia (between 1987 and 1992), 327 percent in the Philippines (between 1985 and 1988), and 37 percent in Indonesia (between 1986 and 1996) (figure 3-1). This surge in FDI caused important structural changes in ASEAN countries—particularly Thailand, Malaysia, Indonesia, and the Philippines—that were a crucial factor in regionalization and regionalism in East Asia.

Impact of FDI on ASEAN Policies

This massive infusion of FDI came just as ASEAN governments, particularly in Thailand, Malaysia, the Philippines, and Indonesia, were being pressed to redesign their policies.[4] They had already made some moves to attract export-oriented FDI in the early to mid-1970s, by setting up export processing zones (EPZs) and providing inducements such as tax incentives, duty refunds on imported materials and components, and relaxed restrictions on foreign ownership. In those days, however, domestic manufacturers still enjoyed considerable protection under import-substitution policies that shielded home markets from foreign competition and imposed various requirements on foreign investors relating to local content, joint ventures with local firms, and export obligations, among others. The reverse oil shock and the fall in commodity prices in the early 1980s brought import-substitution policies to a dead end and prompted governments to liberalize their economies. The surge in export-oriented FDI at this juncture precipitated several structural changes, which reoriented business interests and government priorities and, in turn, affected the configuration of domestic coalitions in host countries.

First, FDI helped these countries accumulate manufacturing capacity and thus shifted the engine of economic growth from the state to the private sector. Between 1986 and 1991, value added in manufacturing as a percentage of gross domestic product (GDP) rose from 23.9 percent to 28.2 percent in Thailand, from 19.3 percent to 25.6 percent in Malaysia, from 16.7 percent to 21.4 percent in Indonesia, and from 24.6 percent to 25.3 percent in the Philippines. Machinery industries, in particular, grew rapidly. In the same period, machinery and transport equipment as a percentage of value added in manufacturing increased from 6.3 percent to 23.6 percent in Thailand, from 20.3 percent to 33.8 percent in Malaysia, and from 6.5 percent to 14.3 percent in the Philippines.[5]

The accumulation of manufacturing FDI contributed significantly to the expansion of trade and country economies. Between 1986 and 1991, dependence on international trade measured by trade as a percentage of GDP (trade-GDP ratio) surged from 49.2 percent to 78.5 percent in Thailand, from 105.0 percent to 159.3 percent in Malaysia, from 40.0 percent to 49.9 percent in Indonesia, and from 48.7 percent to 62.2 percent in the Philippines.[6] With the inflow of FDI, these countries quickly recovered from the recession of the early 1980s and entered a phase of strong growth in the latter half of the decade (figure 3-2), which continued in most of them until the Asian financial crisis.

Because of this powerful FDI-led economic growth, local firms no longer saw foreign investors as "competitors for small domestic markets" but as "potential partners to expand and diversify their business."[7] It also made ASEAN governments more responsive to requests from the private sector and less wary of the role of foreigners in domestic markets.

Second, the FDI-led boom brought wage hikes, labor shortages, and infrastructure bottlenecks in the more developed members of ASEAN, driving labor-intensive firms to less-developed economies.[8] This created both challenges and opportunities.

Figure 3-2. GDP Growth Rate of Five ASEAN Countries, 1980–2002

Percent per year

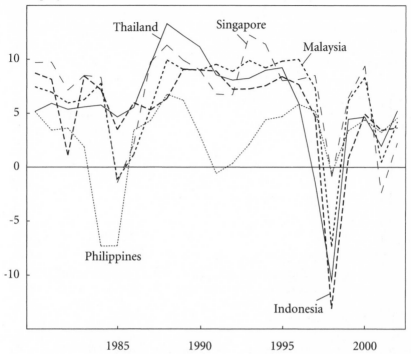

Source: World Bank, *WDI Online*.

One challenge was the new competition from lower-cost countries such as China and Vietnam (figure 3-3). FDI to China accelerated especially after Chinese leader Deng Xiaoping made public his support of special economic zones in his South China tour in January 1992. Between 1991 and 1994, FDI to China from all over the world grew at an average rate of 98 percent a year, and by 1993 had overtaken the FDI flow to ASEAN as a whole. Vietnam, too, started to attract FDI in the 1990s, a few years after introducing its Doi Moi (renovation) policy of market-oriented economic reform in 1986.[9] Between 1990 and 1994, the FDI to Vietnam increased at an annual rate of 232 percent, overtaking FDI flows to Thailand and the Philippines. The emergence of China and Vietnam added to the impetus to upgrade the industries of more developed ASEAN countries.

As economies expanded, domestic demand increased and opened up new prospects for middle-class markets (which, however, also widened the gaps between urban and rural areas, thus creating a new policy priority that further

Figure 3-3. Emergence of China and Vietnam as FDI Destinations, 1980–2001
Billions of current U.S. dollars

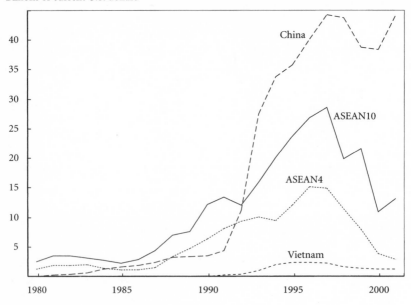

Source: World Bank, *WDI Online.*

helped develop the middle-class). As the boom hit emerging economies in the region, opportunities arose to provide higher value-added products or business services such as finance, telecommunications, and logistics. Local firms became keen to develop business networks with these economies, and governments tried to encourage economic linkages with them as well. Hoping to exploit these opportunities, local and foreign firms alike found that domestic protections were impediments to their businesses and advocated economic liberalization.[10]

Third, the FDI-led boom also affected the trade balance in many countries, turning the surplus of the mid-1980s into a deficit, even in oil-producing Indonesia.[11] Because of the widening deficits, not to mention competition from emerging economies, ASEAN governments were keen to see more robust backward linkages with foreign affiliates, stronger supporting industries, and more competitive import-substituting producers. However, little progress could be made in this regard even after governments lifted various restrictions on export-oriented foreign firms as long as import-substitution policies remained in place. These policies only served to weaken local suppliers' competitiveness. When foreign affiliates did procure parts and components locally, they were likely to avoid inefficient local import-substituting suppliers and rely on suppliers from the home country or other foreign countries. Local downstream producers also complained about the disadvantages of procuring from local import-substituting upstream producers. As Theodore H. Moran demonstrates, "the relationship between the foreign plant and domestic suppliers appears to be particularly robust, containing dynamic transfers of many kinds, when the parent's own competitive position in international markets depends upon the quality, reliability, timeliness, and up-to-date characteristics of the inputs that flow through the affiliate."[12] Conversely, affiliates whose parent could not integrate them into its strategy because of the host government's interference offered less extensive backward linkages, "with fewer efforts on the part of the investor to provide coaching to domestic suppliers in the newest or most sophisticated business practices."[13] Under the circumstances, ASEAN countries soon woke up to the importance of integrating broader domestic activities into global business networks in order to gain better access to cutting-edge technologies and business practices.

Thus in the early 1990s ASEAN countries began moving their economies "in an outward-oriented direction, towards a more neutral balance of incentives."[14] They first reduced some tariffs on an MFN basis, though most of them kept some margin of preference for the ASEAN Free Trade Area (AFTA) Common Effective Preferential Tariff (CEPT).[15] Thailand, for example, lowered the average applied MFN tariff from about 30 percent in 1994 to 18 percent in 1999 and 14.7 percent in 2003; Malaysia from 15.2 percent in 1993 to 8.1 percent in 1997 (but increased it to 9.2 percent in 1998); Indonesia from about 20 percent in 1994 to 9.5 percent in 1998, and to 7.2 percent in 2002; and the Philippines from 25.6 percent to 10.1 percent in 1999.[16] However, most ASEAN governments did not promote economic liberalization as a matter of principle or because of neoclassical belief. They did so only insofar as big local companies showed support for such a move—which they did when the benefits from the resulting new opportunities would outweigh the loss of rent under the old regime.[17] Therefore the "legacies of old import-substitution policies" still lived on in many ASEAN countries.[18]

Impetus for ASEAN Integration

The surge in FDI also had a strong impact on intra-ASEAN cooperation. As just mentioned, rising wages and competition from emerging economies forced ASEAN governments to consider upgrading their industries. Since import-substitution policies seemed to be taking their economies nowhere, they renewed their interest in promoting integration of their fragmented markets to attract global businesses eager to realize economies of scale.[19] They also paid more attention to the needs of the private sector, thereby giving long-time foreign investors in the region an opportunity to influence the policy environment.[20] Among the most active were Japanese automobile manufacturers, notably Mitsubishi Motors Corporation (MMC), which lobbied for a program to facilitate the exchange of components and realize economies of scale.[21] In 1984, in search of a more realistic program than previous efforts such as the ASEAN Industrial Complementation (AIC) and the ASEAN Industrial Joint Venture (AIJV), MMC developed a plan for intracompany trade to export passenger cars produced in Malaysia to Indonesia and in return bring commercial vehicles produced in Indonesia to Malaysia.[22] At the time, MMC was preparing for the production of subcompact passenger cars for Malaysia's national car project and for the production of engines in Indonesia.[23] This plan never got off the ground, however, because the two governments could not agree on the specific division of work. Each regarded the automobile sector as its strategic industry and tried to develop a full set of manufacturing capabilities. Eventually, MMC gave up on the export of completed cars and focused instead on trade in parts and components. In December 1987, at the Third ASEAN Summit in Manila, it came up with a new proposal, the Brand-to-Brand Complementation (BBC) scheme, which granted local content accreditation and a minimum 50 percent margin of tariff preference to specified parts or components of particular vehicle models ("brands") that met certain requirements. ASEAN economic ministers finally approved the scheme in October 1988.[24] Its first participants were Malaysia, the Philippines, and Thailand, joined by Indonesia in September 1994.[25] Capitalizing on the program, Japanese automakers invested in key components such as engines, transmissions, and steering gears in multiple ASEAN countries.[26] Restrictions imposed on the BBC (it was limited to the automobile sector and to the same "brands") were subsequently relaxed under the ASEAN Industrial Cooperation (AICO) scheme, introduced in 1996 to achieve ASEAN integration in intra-industry trade (IIT).[27]

In 1992 ASEAN moved beyond these sectoral arrangements by agreeing to establish the AFTA, a comprehensive agreement for preferential trade liberalization. Although political factors played a part in this shift, as discussed in chapter 4, the key reason was the new attitude toward foreign investors and sense of urgency to present ASEAN as an attractive investment destination.

scribe to the establishment of the ASEAN Free Trade Area (AFTA) simultaneously so as to create within the time frame of 15 years a truly liberalized ASEAN market with the Common Effective Preferential Tariff (CEPT) in the range of 0 to 5 percent for manufactured products."[104] At the Fourth ASEAN Summit held in Singapore in January 1992, ASEAN leaders signed the CEPT agreement for the AFTA, clearly a milestone in the association's efforts to promote interdependence among its members.[105] Behind this move was a strong sense of urgency to maintain ASEAN's relevance as well as political competition among its members. Since the end of the cold war, China and the countries of Eastern Europe had emerged as competitors for foreign direct investment. Another concern was that APEC could dilute and absorb ASEAN. Intra-ASEAN integration therefore had to be deep enough to make it as attractive as its competitors and fast enough to stay ahead of APEC. When Malaysia had proposed the caucus, Indonesia and Thailand thought that intra-ASEAN integration should be given higher priority than additional extra-ASEAN frameworks, so Thailand proposed the AFTA. To the surprise of many observers, Indonesia, opposed to ASEAN liberalization more persistently than most, proposed the CEPT to check both the Malaysian-led EAEC and the Thai-led AFTA.

As the first comprehensive preferential trade agreement in East Asia, AFTA had a significant impact on the subsequent development of regionalism there. Once it agreed on AFTA-CEPT, ASEAN became more confident of its ability to stay ahead of APEC and thus felt more positive toward the forum. Six months after the AFTA was signed, State Department counselor Bob Zoellick was appealing to ASEAN to strengthen U.S.-ASEAN relations, forge NAFTA-ASEAN linkages, and solidify APEC:

> As AFTA and NAFTA develop, we need to consider whether they might complement one another. I also hope we can advance the Pacific trade liberalization agenda within APEC. US-ASEAN cooperation has been fundamental to turning APEC from an idea into an institution.
>
> The U.S. offers the largest fully integrated market in the world. We want it to be a competitive, global market, not part of a bloc. . . . On the international side, we will press for free trade and open markets on all fronts—globally, regionally, and bilaterally. If some say no, we'll look for those who want to join our vision of greater trade and stronger growth. We want ASEAN and APEC to have a special place in this future.[106]

Conclusion

The APEC ministerial meeting in September 1992 marked a major break-through in institutionalizing APEC and liberalizing regional trade. ASEAN members had become remarkably more flexible. Only a year and a half earlier, they had been calling for gradual and pragmatic institutionalization. Now they recognized that "institutionalization could further strengthen APEC's role and enhance its efficiency in promoting regional economic cooperation" and agreed to set up a secretariat in Singapore.[107] Furthermore, the ministers agreed to establish the Eminent Persons Group (EPG) "to enunciate a vision for trade in the Asia Pacific region to the year 2000" and to make trade liberalization "a central focus" of the next year's meeting in the United States.[108]

Even after APEC was established, U.S. policymakers maintained a steady interest in bilateral or regional FTAs with the Asia Pacific economies. This was a natural consequence of Washington's multitrack strategy, especially when APEC was still in its infancy and not operational as a regional front of trade liberalization. In September 1992, President George H.W. Bush explicitly proposed to develop a network of FTAs with Latin America, Czechoslovakia, Hungary, Poland, and countries in the Pacific, also mentioning "the possibility of a connection between NAFTA and the ASEAN FTA or AFTA" and U.S. interest in closer economic ties already expressed by leaders in Australia and Korea.[109] Although the president made these remarks during a campaign and did not follow through on them, they left some APEC members worried. Australia's prime minister P. J. Keating responded immediately to the reference to his country: "Australia does not prefer an approach where Washington seeks to negotiate a series of separate bilateral (free trade) deals on the hub-and-spokes model of its security relationships in the Pacific."[110] Washington's counterargument would have been that "the spokes could connect and make a circle. Consistent FTAs among members of a hub system would regionalize the approach without multilateral regional negotiations which at first seemed very difficult if not possible to arrange."[111] In any case, the concern over U.S. hub-and-spoke FTAs in the region subsided with the lack of progress in that direction, as U.S. eyes were focused on APEC for the time being.

Indeed, by the end of the first stage of regionalism's evolution, it had become clear that APEC was likely to prevail, with NAFTA, AFTA, and the Australia–New Zealand Closer Economic Relations Trade Agreement (ANZCERTA) being mere subsystems of APEC. The simultaneous participation of China, Chinese Taipei, and Hong Kong in APEC in 1991 greatly enhanced its importance.[112] The EAEC proposal apparently persuaded Washington that APEC was the way to prevent Asian-only frameworks from gaining momentum. Also, AFTA made ASEAN more confident. Other frameworks were either never launched, as in the case of EAEC, or, like the idea of extending U.S. bilateral FTA networks to Asia Pacific countries, remained largely conceptual at this stage. For one thing, Washington was preoccupied with the Uruguay Round and the NAFTA negotiations; for another, it hoped APEC could be a more efficient channel of regional trade liberalization than a series of bilateral FTAs.[113] All the same, it saw APEC and bilateral FTAs as compatible entities.

In this first period, the main driving force was defensive regionalism (not in the form of responding in kind but) in the sense that Western Pacific economies had joined forces in an Asia Pacific forum hoping to restrain the United States from taking unilateral actions and expanding bilateral FTA networks. The EAEC proposal was a typical defensive response, but it did not fly because of a powerful obstacle: U.S. objections. The launch of an ASEAN Free Trade Area was also a defensive move designed to prevent ASEAN from being marginalized by larger regional associations such as APEC, and also to enhance its attractiveness as an investment destination. However, ASEAN is too small to be self-sufficient, its integration does not pose a threat to other regions, and therefore it does not invite counteractions. Although the growing intraregional economic interdependence made clear the need for some form of cooperation to deal with common challenges, at this point it did not play a large role in bringing to light substantive issues. Competitive dynamics within East Asia were evident only within ASEAN. Moreover, three obstacles—the lack of cohesiveness, U.S. displeasure over an Asian-only framework, and the avoidance of institutionalization—still stood in the way of major developments.

Hence regionalism during this period consisted of little substance despite an impulse to get together. In the absence of a regionwide framework, the tendency was to try to find a single formula that would accommodate all of these forces. Competing proposals were viewed as inconsistent with each other despite the emergence of multilayered thinking in the United States and Singapore.[114] Even Washington had not applied its multilayered policy to frameworks that did not include it. This explains why the countries involved were focused on the membership of each framework rather than on its core objectives or specific measures. As a result, there were no systematic efforts to sort out different motivations and assumptions of APEC members; one camp took a holistic approach to securing stable growth in Asia, whereas the other was narrowly focused on promoting liberalization; one tried to promote liberalization on an MFN basis and the other on a reciprocal basis; and one attached importance to consensus and called for patience to nurture the members' willingness to liberalize, while the other favored a structured approach to put pressure on the members to move forward with liberalization. These differences became clearer when APEC turned its attention from institution building to implementation, and they affected its sense of community.

5

The Primacy of Asia
Pacific Economic Cooperation

The second phase of Asia Pacific regionalism saw Asia Pacific Economic Cooperation (APEC) emerge as the primary vehicle for regional cooperation. The period essentially began with the 1992 APEC ministerial meeting, followed by the inauguration of William Jefferson Clinton in the United States in 1993 (the Clinton administration would soon define APEC's course). The period ended in mid-1998 when the consequences of the financial crisis in East Asia unfolded.

Although the George H. W. Bush administration had became more proactive in strengthening APEC since 1991, it was the Clinton administration that focused directly on Asia and the Pacific, announcing that no region in the world was more important to the United States and that "the time has come for America to join with Japan and others in this region to create a new Pacific community."[1] President Clinton emphasized that his outlook departed from that of his predecessors: "In years past, frankly, some Americans viewed Asia's vibrancy and particularly Japan's success as a threat. I see it very differently. I believe the Pacific region can and will be a vast source of jobs, of income, of partnerships, of ideas, of growth for our own people in the United States—if we have the courage to deal with the problems, both of our nations have within and beyond our borders."[2]

This initial focus on Asia significantly enhanced U.S. influence on APEC. President Clinton proposed and hosted the first meeting of APEC leaders in November 1993, "to discuss what we can do to continue to bring down the barriers that divide us and to create more opportunities for all of our people."[3] Clearly, the Clinton administration was positioning APEC as a vehicle of liberalization, and also "as the greatest opportunity to place a Clinton stamp on

U.S. trade policy," "not hand-me-down policies from Republicans."[4] Economically, the Clinton administration had a "mercantilist framework" and was "committed as none before it to increasing U.S. exports" (the administration described it as "export activism") and therefore quite naturally concentrated on the rapidly growing Asian markets.[5] Clinton also shifted U.S. trade and investment policy toward East Asia from a bilateral to regional focus (except for Japan and China) as it moved to change APEC "from an informal consultative mechanism to a more formal organization promoting trade liberalization within the Pacific region."[6]

Regional Trade Liberalization: A Process under Constant Tension

Thanks to U.S. activism and ASEAN's growing confidence, APEC's trade liberalization agenda made significant progress after the first leaders' meeting in Seattle with some bold new visions based on a report of the Eminent Persons Group (EPG). However, the political commitment and institutional capabilities to follow through on these ideas were still lacking. In addition, there was constant tension between those eager to promote regional trade and investment liberalization in APEC (the United States, Australia, New Zealand, Canada, Singapore, Hong Kong, and also Indonesia, after the adoption of the Bogor goal in 1994) and those with different priorities (Japan, South Korea, China, Taiwan, and the ASEAN economies other than Singapore). Another debate ensued between those insistent on reciprocal liberalization (the United States) and those opposed to preferential arrangements for APEC (most other countries, though some, such as Singapore and New Zealand, were flexible). They managed to paper over these tensions in successive leaders' meetings until they began considering the Early Voluntary Sectoral Liberalization (EVSL) proposal.

When the Eminent Persons Group announced its recommendations in October 1993, it presented APEC's members with a fundamental dilemma:

> The members would set a goal of achieving free trade in the region and indicate that they prefer to do so through further global liberalization but *would pursue a regional path, on a GATT-consistent basis,* if the favored strategy were not achievable. This would *operationalize APEC's concept of "open regionalism"* or "open economic association" *in a new and effective manner.*
>
> APEC would in essence seek to *"ratchet up" the process of global trade liberalization:* push for a maximum multilateral accord, then *work out new regional agreements* that incorporate both items that failed to win

global approval and new issues that were not yet attempted in the GATT, and complete the cycle by putting its own agreements on the global agenda for multilateral adoption.[7]

While adherence to "open regionalism" and "opposition to an inward-looking trading bloc" had become APEC mantras, they meant different things to different members so had little clear substance except for condemning customs unions. Apart from Singapore, Asian countries were against turning APEC into a preferential trade agreement (PTA). They tended to equate PTAs with trading blocs and defined "open regionalism" as regional economic integration through nondiscriminatory liberalization. Ever since the ASEAN Free Trade Area (AFTA) was launched, the purist definition of open regionalism had become somewhat awkward even in Asia. Nevertheless, most Asian countries, whether fundamentally against any PTA (as were Japan, South Korea, and China) or ready to allow for exceptions (as was most of ASEAN), were still opposed to an APEC FTA. But the United States, with the negotiating leverage of its large domestic markets, was not ready for APEC liberalization if it gave Europe a free economic ride.[8] Washington therefore embarked on "the artful use of the fear of exclusion," which is the essence of its multitrack strategy.[9] Also, to quell some criticism, it asserted that NAFTA was not a trading bloc because that would be equivalent to a customs union, which was not the case. In Washington's own definition,

> Open regionalism refers to plurilateral agreements that are nonexclusive and open to new members to join. It requires first that plurilateral initiatives be fully consistent with Article XXIV of the GATT, which prohibits an increase in average external barriers. Beyond that, it requires that plurilateral agreements not constrain members from pursuing additional liberalization either with nonmembers on a reciprocal basis or unilaterally. Because member countries are able to choose their external tariffs unilaterally, open agreements are less likely to develop into competing bargaining blocs. Finally, open regionalism implies that plurilateral agreements both allow and encourage nonmembers to join. This facilitates [a] beneficial domino effect.[10]

The EPG report supported Washington's understanding of the concept, finding "only one real economic bloc: the EC."[11]

At their November 1993 meeting, APEC leaders "envisioned a community of Asia Pacific economies in which . . . [w]e continue to reduce trade and investment barriers so that our trade expands within the region and with the world, and goods, services, capital and investment flow freely among our economies."[12] Specific ways of establishing regional trade liberalization were not mentioned, however. Instead, APEC members focused on successfully concluding the GATT Uruguay Round negotiations in the next month. According to the EPG, the contemplation of regional trade liberalization in APEC "helped persuade other countries to cooperate in strengthening the global system."[13]

While they could not reach a consensus on pursuing an FTA, the EPG and the leaders' meeting appeared to overcome bureaucratic resistance to an ambitious agenda. The 1994 EPG report's major recommendation for the next leaders' meeting was that APEC should set a timetable for deciding and achieving free trade and investment in the Asia Pacific region.[14] Meeting in Bogor, Indonesia, in November 1994, the leaders adopted the goal of liberalization in APEC by 2010 for developed economies and 2020 for developing economies.[15] Given the fact that among ASEAN members Indonesia had been the most cautious about liberalization, this was a surprising development. However, not all members were satisfied with the Bogor announcement, the details of which were to be worked out in Osaka in the next year. Malaysia specifically argued that APEC liberalization should proceed on an unconditional most favored nation (MFN) basis, that the Bogor target dates should be nonbinding, and that the decision of APEC should be based on consensus.[16] This suggests that by then APEC had departed from the original principles on which ASEAN had agreed to participate in it.

The 1994 EPG report also recommended clarifying "open regionalism" in order to bridge the gap between those against PTAs and those insistent on reciprocity, essentially calling for an APEC FTA. This would induce nonmembers to move toward liberalization while allowing individual members to extend the liberalization to nonmembers (in other words, APEC would not turn into a customs union):

> We recommend that APEC adopt a non–mutually exclusive four-part formula to implement its commitment to open regionalism:
> —the maximum possible extent of unilateral liberalization,
> —a commitment to continue reducing its barriers to nonmember countries while it liberalizes internally,
> —a willingness to extend its regional liberalization to nonmembers on a mutually reciprocal basis, and;
> —recognition that any individual APEC member can unilaterally extend its APEC liberalization to nonmembers on a conditional or unconditional basis.[17]

Because in reality domestic politics would require reciprocity in the liberalization of sensitive sectors and APEC, with its large markets, collectively commanded significant negotiation leverage, the EPG "rejected the concept of unconditional MFN treatment of nonmembers as the sole means of implementing open regionalism." To emphasize APEC's outward orientation, it also insisted that the extension of FTA benefits should not altogether be denied to nonmembers ("even though all three subregional arrangements within the APEC area themselves follow this approach" of standard denial) and concluded its formula was "a healthy basis for moving ahead."[18]

While many observers identified the EPG recommendations with Washington's drive for APEC liberalization, the Clinton administration reportedly found them unrealistic, though it valued the EPG "as a cheerleader."[19] At the Bogor meeting, it was decided that APEC liberalization would reduce barriers for nonmembers and the idea of an APEC FTA was not adopted. Liberalization on a reciprocal basis was not retained either as it could stimulate liberalization by nonmembers and thus could lead to "the actual reduction of barriers . . . between APEC members and non-APEC members."[20]

In its final report of 1995, the EPG responded to the leaders' direction "to review the interrelationships between APEC and the existing sub-regional arrangements . . . and to examine possible options to . . . promote consistency in their relations."[21] The report asserted that extending existing subregional trading arrangements, such as AFTA, ANZCERTA, and NAFTA, to other APEC members within the principles of "open sub-regionalism"—which were identical to those on which APEC open regionalism was to be based—would "be constructive and supportive of the overall APEC process" and represent a fallback mechanism with which to realize the Bogor declaration.[22]

In November 1995 APEC leaders agreed on the Osaka Action Agenda (OAA) as the mechanism for achieving the Bogor goal.[23] Two issues were hotly debated at this time. First, how comprehensive should APEC liberalization be? Washington and Canberra insisted there should be no exception, whereas many Asian countries argued for flexibility to protect sensitive sectors. In the end, the OAA's general principles called for both comprehensiveness and flexibility, leaving the relationship between the two to be clarified. Second, how was liberalization to be implemented—through individual members' voluntary actions or through collective actions based on members' prior agreements? The OAA suggested that tariffs be reduced individually by each APEC economy. At the same time, the individual action plans were subject to the consultation process, which "will be an ongoing collective effort of a confidence-building nature in order to facilitate exchange of information on progress in the preparation of Action Plans, ensuring transparency and contributing toward attaining the comparability of respective Action Plans." In other words, APEC members would put pressure on each other but ultimately decide on their own plan, after considering what others would do. Thus the leaders designated the individual action plan—or the "concerted liberalization" approach—as the primary channel of liberalization, despite its delicate nature. This meant its success hinged upon their "own continuing efforts, strong self-discipline, and close consultation."[24]

On the issue of whether to liberalize on a nondiscriminatory or reciprocal basis within APEC, the OAA adopted a principle of "nondiscrimination" on a best-effort basis.[25] At the same time, the guideline on tariff reduction states, "Each APEC economy will consider extending, on a voluntary basis, to all APEC members the benefits of tariff reductions and eliminations derived from sub-regional arrangements."[26] Thus APEC could not come up with a new discipline on subregional arrangements.

The EVSL Setback

The vague wording regarding how to proceed with APEC liberalization had an adverse impact on the U.S.-sponsored Early Voluntary Sectoral Liberalization (EVSL) initiative and raised questions about APEC's role in regional trade liberalization in general. Unhappy with OAA's decision on this matter, Washington worried that the momentum of further liberalization might be lost if left to voluntarism. Also, if Washington was to take positive measures, uncoordinated unilateral actions would not work. It needed to show concessions by other countries in order to persuade Congress to move forward.[27] In fact, the OAA already contained the seeds of the EVSL initiative in that one of the collective actions it recommended was to "identify industries in which the progressive reduction of tariffs may have positive impact on trade and on economic growth in the Asia-Pacific region or for which there is regional industry support for early liberalization."[28] Inspired by the success of the Information Technology Agreement (ITA) concluded in December 1996 and enacted in July 1997, Washington promoted the EVSL initiative, which was launched in 1996 and given a concrete form in 1997.[29] To ensure that the EVSL would support a balanced and mutually beneficial package as well as the APEC principle of voluntarism, its framers called for "the development of appropriate agreements or arrangements for market-opening and facilitation and economic and technical cooperation measures," based on existing proposals in certain sectors.[30]

Although Japan did not block the initiative at the outset, it did not participate in the fishery and forestry sectors in the 1998 final package.[31] It had initially agreed to do so on the assumption that the text referring to "voluntarism" meant APEC members were free to choose what to do in each sector from among "market-opening and facilitation and economic and technical cooperation measures" and therefore could opt out of liberalizing sensitive sectors. When the Japanese delegation stated it had difficulty in forestry and fishery, proponents such as the Canadian hosts and the Australians persuaded Japan not to pull out of these sectors just then, suggesting it could invoke voluntarism later.

Three days later, the leaders agreed that APEC's liberalization would proceed on a voluntary basis in fifteen sectors, "nine to be advanced throughout 1998 with a view to implementation beginning in 1999." This package was deemed to be "mutually beneficial and to represent a balance of interests."[32]

As it turned out, Washington did not share Tokyo's interpretation. Major powers such as Japan, it argued, always had to participate to achieve the critical mass needed to launch the initiative. Since all the agreed sectors constituted a package, none could be dropped. Furthermore, Tokyo had agreed to the text of the declaration, specifying that all agreed the package was mutually beneficial and represented a balance of interests. The particular phrase, however, was introduced without prior notice or explanation at the leaders' meeting, and Japan did not know the text would mean Japan could not have the flexibility others enjoyed. When for various reasons conditions did not exist for liberalizing certain sensitive sectors or items under a particular framework, the pressure of negotiations alone would not usually produce a large concession. A negotiation framework that leaves room for misunderstanding or entrapment makes it all the more difficult to prepare and persuade domestic constituencies. This is how Japan's painful process of damage control started.

Despite the term "voluntary," the initiative was designed to negotiate a package of sector-specific liberalization in APEC, which most of the Asian members did not fully recognize at the outset and actually had reservations about. Washington tried to change the mode of trade liberalization in APEC from voluntarism with peer pressure to negotiations based on reciprocity. Having managed to exclude sensitive U.S. sectors such as textiles from the package, the administration adopted the "strategy of isolating Japan" to put pressure on it from its Asian neighbors.[33] At Washington's urging, all the resisting economies except for Japan met the requirements, which allowed considerable flexibility for developing countries.[34] At the trade ministers' meeting in Kuching in June 1998, the Japanese minister refused to endorse a statement clarifying Washington's design to the effect that "participation in the 9 sectors and all three measures (trade liberalisation, facilitation, and ecotech) in each sector will be essential to maintain the mutual benefits and balance of interests" established in Vancouver. To maximize participation, "flexibility would be required to deal with product-specific concerns raised by individual economies in each sector. Such flexibility would generally be in the form of longer implementation periods. In principle developing economies should be allowed greater flexibility."[35]

Although Japanese officials considered the process unfair, they sought ways to go along with other members. Meanwhile Washington insisted on complete liberalization of Japan's tariffs on items in two sectors (fishery and forestry) and rejected any possibility of Japan's partial concessions. Unlike developing economies, it argued, Japan only had flexibility in the phasing-in period and had to accept the package as a whole. Though Tokyo explained that it was willing to negotiate at the World Trade Organization (WTO), Washington was not ready to wait for the multilateral negotiations.[36] The initial lack of transparency about the interpretation of "voluntary" had enraged Japanese domestic constituencies, making it all the more difficult to persuade them to make any concessions. When officials discovered there was no middle ground in this dispute, they had to turn to fellow APEC members to win sympathy for Japan's situation. Finally, the other members agreed to maintain their offers without Japan's participation in the liberalization in the two sectors and to send the package as it stood to the WTO process. Oddly, Japan was saved by its neighbors, when they expected it to spearhead the efforts needed to revitalize the region after the financial crisis.

Although other Asian members supported the package, they were not happy with its framework. For one thing, they felt the APEC principles of consensus and voluntarism were being compromised and APEC processes paralyzed by a U.S.-Japan disagreement. It was as if "the Americans and Japanese had brought their perennial trade war into APEC. It was like the bad old days when the U.S. fought tooth and nail to get Tokyo to open up its citrus and beef markets."[37] For another thing, they were disappointed by Washington's unwillingness to cut tariffs unilaterally, which in any case made it imperative to bring the package to the WTO before implementation.[38] Washington's "less than enthusiastic promotion of fast-track negotiating authority" further undermined their confidence in U.S. leadership.[39] As a result, many APEC members came to think that, after all, the WTO was a far more appropriate body through which to reach a binding trade agreement.[40]

Even those who had been supportive of the EVSL negotiations reached the same conclusion. As China's chief trade negotiator Long Yongtu pointed out (China had insisted on the principle of voluntarism), "It is logical that APEC submit difficult issues to the WTO.... Do not blame APEC too much, as it has never and will never become a vehicle for trade negotiations."[41] On the other hand, Australian prime minister John Howard, who had been supportive of the EVSL, noted, "I think at one stage people had unrealistically high expectations.... People shouldn't expect that [APEC is] going to solve every economic problem in the region."[42]

Euphoria Ends, Realism Sets In

By now it was clear that APEC had failed to fulfill the expectations that different members had held at the forum's inception.

Unfulfilled Expectations

As already mentioned, the United States had been frustrated in its attempt to use APEC for reciprocity-based negotiations. Although regional liberalization finally became a major priority of the APEC agenda, the EVSL showed that for both Japan and the United States the only way to liberalize highly sensitive items *on an MFN basis* was to negotiate through the WTO. They could liberalize on a preferential basis, but a PTA requires comprehensive coverage when developed economies are involved. If APEC as a whole is to produce results independent of the WTO process, its members will have to accept an APEC FTA, which is difficult to do because of its diverse membership. The remaining option is to give up on simultaneous progress for the entire APEC membership and instead pursue subregional FTAs. This partly explains the surge of interest in FTAs among APEC members in the next period.

Despite the considerable institutionalization and activism of APEC, it was unable to check the momentum for regionalism in North America, not to mention Europe. In December 1994 leaders in the Western Hemisphere agreed to construct a free trade area of the Americas (FTAA) in which barriers to trade and investment would be progressively eliminated, and to complete negotiations for the agreement by 2005.[43] Clearly, even the establishment of the WTO could not reverse the trend toward regionalism (though it did check unilateralism). In announcing its "policy of open regionalism," Washington felt it was laying a foundation for "the development of open, overlapping plurilateral trade agreements as stepping stones to global free trade" on "principles of openness and inclusion consistent with the GATT." By helping to improve access to foreign markets and easing trade tensions, it was creating "models for future multilateral liberalization through the WTO in areas such as intellectual property rights, services, investment, and environmental and labor standards." The end result would be a world with "several overlapping, open plurilateral arrangements, with the United States playing a leadership role in North America, Asia, and Latin America, rather than two or three competing blocs."[44]

Gradually, Asian policymakers began to recognize that regionalism was an unfolding phenomenon they could not stop. Instead, they had to live with it and, where possible, manage it to their benefit. For its part, Washington, since the first Bush administration, had emphasized that NAFTA could strengthen pan-Pacific ties, despite the widespread fear (or rather, because of the fear, in order to alleviate it) of U.S. trade distortion effects among Asian developing economies competing with Mexico.[45]

Also, Washington continued to express interest in extending NAFTA to Asia and the Pacific, but without any action in this direction under the Clinton administration. For example, U.S. Trade Representative Michael Kantor talked about connecting U.S. FTAs to Asia in the context of APEC.[46] Singapore responded eagerly, as in the first period, although the May 1994 caning of an American teenager for a crime apparently clouded the overall negotiating atmosphere for the time being, and the FTA initiative was stalled. Since the WTO dispute settlement mechanism offered the U.S. unilateral trade sanctions no option, Washington renewed its interest in FTAs as a policy tool to improve overseas market access.[47] As the Clinton administration shifted its attention to plurilateral trade agreements or "broad regionalism," it became less keen on pursuing small bilateral FTAs.[48] At the same time, some within the administration appeared to be sending mixed signals about "the best guarantors of progress in trade relations."[49] Bilateral agreements, done correctly, they argued, could "resolve issues expeditiously and also serve as proving grounds for rules and standards that are later adopted on a wider scale. Thus, the United States will continue to negotiate reciprocal free trade agreements with individual nations in the Asia-Pacific. Australia, New Zealand, and Singapore are a few of the possible partners in this respect."[50] Despite the lack of progress in this period, the exposure to Washington's multitrack strategy gradually led Asian policymakers to prepare to adopt their versions of it.

Asian countries also had to adjust their expectations for cooperative projects (as opposed to trade and investment liberalization). From the beginning, developing countries argued that the APEC agenda had to be balanced between liberalization and facilitation, on one hand, and cooperation, on the other. However, Washington was among the least enthusiastic about this idea, instead keeping its eye fixed on liberalization and on using "APEC and other forums at our disposal in order to open up more and more markets in Asia."[51] For developing economies, however, liberalization is not an end in itself but a means to achieve economic development. The fact that APEC could not provide a wide range of developmental assistance—as could international financial institutions or bilateral donors—did not mean that it could ignore other aspects of economic development. To reinstate the balance, the 1995 Osaka Action Agenda established the concept of "economic and technical cooperation," making it one of the two pillars of APEC action plans.

The OAA also clarified the objectives of project cooperation and the procedures for developing policy and evaluating projects. It set up a framework comprising "common policy concepts" (which include goals, basic principles, and priorities in each specific area of cooperation), "joint activities" (such as the "compilation and sharing of data and information, surveys, training, seminars, research and technical demonstrations), and "policy dialogue" (on common policy concepts and joint activities as well as on each APEC economy's policies or activities).[52] The role of APEC cooperation was basically to disseminate information so as to improve members' analytical skills, policy planning, and implementation capabilities as opposed to, for example, infrastructure projects. Projects directly in support of liberalization and facilitation objectives were to receive high priority.

The remaining issue was how to improve the effectiveness of cooperation activities on the ground. With a rotating chair, there was a deluge of new project proposals every year but no systematic effort to follow up on them.[53]

Last but not least, "the sense of being one region" failed to take hold throughout Asia and the Pacific, in part because APEC could not reconcile the fundamental differences over the approach to liberalization between U.S.-led activists and Asian gradualists. It became a constant theme, reminding APEC members of the forum's lack of cohesiveness. In addition, APEC's inability to check the U.S. unilateral approach to trade frictions until the mid-1990s "added to Asian ambivalence about the United States."[54] Also, when tension between the United States and Asian countries concerning human rights and political freedom clouded APEC meetings, many Asian countries—even those that saw the merit of Washington's arguments—tended to view the U.S. role in APEC warily.[55] Because of these divisions in APEC, Asian members tended "to see their interests as distinct from those of the West, and its Western members to differentiate themselves from the East Asian."[56] There was an increasing sense that "it is more appropriate to conceive of APEC as *trans*-regional than as a regional body."[57]

APEC's fundamental problem was that it grew too fast without solidifying its core objectives, leaving its members at odds on what APEC should do. Rather than closing the gaps, it expanded the agenda, knowing that some issues would not be fully addressed. The lesson to draw from all this is that APEC cannot be expected to solve all the region's problems and should have complementary forums, consisting of a smaller number of members whose interests converge.

The Fruits of APEC

APEC's most significant achievement in this period was to add momentum to the GATT Uruguay Round negotiations. The conclusion of the Information Technology Agreement was another example of APEC's constructive role in the WTO. After all, its members hoped to promote multilateral trade liberalization. With the convergence of interests, this is what APEC can do best.

In fact, the EVSL setback was a blessing in disguise and helped APEC solidify activities around its core objectives: which were to issue collective messages to promote the WTO negotiations, to design and implement measures for facilitating trade and investment, and to provide economic and technical assistance so that developing members could implement such measures. More recently, APEC widened the scope of its policy discussions to cover such issues as structural reform, e-commerce, transparency, counterterrorism measures, and public health, as the member economies faced new challenges. Today, facilitating trade and investment should be interpreted as encompassing policy dialogues and cooperation to improve the efficiency and security of cross-border economic activities, whereas economic and technical cooperation should also aim at enhancing the quality of market economy institutions in the member economies and addressing the sources of instabilities for the regional economy. As important as it is to define the scope of activities, it is essential to identify the specific measures on which members have a strong incentive to cooperate.

Needless to say, APEC has incubated regional cooperation in Asia. It has brought government and business together in the region through many meetings and projects, making them aware of common problems, new measures for cooperation, and different priorities. Equally important, it has provided economies in transition with an opportunity to learn about market economy institutions.

Above all, the leaders' meeting has provided a precious annual venue for the heads of state to meet at least as a group, even when their bilateral relations with each other have not been cordial. In particular, APEC has enabled U.S. and Chinese leaders to see each other every year, as long as they participate in these meetings. In addition, APEC countries can conveniently organize bilateral meetings at the margin of the leaders' meetings without visiting other countries. Thus APEC has become a forum not only for economic discussions but also for political and security dialogues beyond its formal agenda.

All these experiences laid the groundwork for the next period in the evolution of East Asian regionalism. First, Asian countries came to recognize that APEC is part of a multilayered structure of international economic institutions and cannot be expected to solve all the problems left by the WTO, and that they need to be creative in identifying the right agenda for APEC and in exploring other possible layers as appropriate. Second, APEC revealed the limitations of the voluntary approach to trade liberalization and added impetus to exploring the FTA as a policy option. Third, APEC discussions on trade and investment facilitation have stimulated interest in more concrete measures involving smaller or bilateral groups, thereby providing a richer basis for economic partnership agreements that combine liberalization and broader cooperation.

ASEAN as a Hub

During this period, ASEAN continued to strive to be a viable organization independent of APEC by accelerating the schedule of AFTA and taking the initiative in creating forums centering on ASEAN (in addition to the post-ministerial conferences that had existed since the 1970s), such as the ASEAN Regional Forum (ARF) established in 1994 and the Asia-Europe meeting (ASEM) initiated in 1996. ASEAN also expanded dialogues with various countries in the "ASEAN +" format. For example, it agreed to start informal consultation with NAFTA and the Australia–New Zealand Closer Economic Relations Trade Agreement (ANZCERTA or CER).[58]

In addition, it developed a cooperative framework with Japan, beginning in 1992, when the ASEAN economic ministers (AEM) and Japan's representative from the Ministry of International Trade and Industry (MITI) began holding meetings on the fringe of AEM meetings. The chief objective was to help improve the investment environment of each ASEAN member and promote integration within ASEAN. MITI provided technical assistance to projects under this framework to complement existing assistance on a bilateral basis.[59]

Japan's MITI stepped up the integration effort. The third AEM-MITI meeting established the Working Group on Economic Cooperation in Indochina and renamed the Working Group on Economic Cooperation in Cambodia, Laos, and Myanmar (CLM-WG) after Myanmar's participation in the January 1995 working group and Vietnam's accession to ASEAN in July 1995. The group consisted of members from both the public and private sectors ready to support ASEAN countries' initiative to strengthen economic linkages with Indochinese countries.[60] In December 1997 the leaders of ASEAN and Japan agreed that CLM-WG would be restructured "for enhanced industrial cooperation, improvement of ASEAN's competitiveness and development cooperation to the new member countries."[61] Accordingly, ASEAN and Japan established the AEM-MITI Economic and Industrial Cooperation Committee (AMEICC). Japan's cooperation through these forums was aimed at helping new members become integrated into ASEAN and giving fresh impetus to intra-ASEAN integration, which neither bilateral frameworks between Japan and individual ASEAN members nor APEC could effectively undertake. The cooperation was initiated by ASEAN countries' specific proposals and focused on strengthening the institutional foundations of integrated ASEAN markets, such as improving legal systems and regulatory frameworks and developing human resources for both government and business.[62]

Sequel to the EAEC

In October 1993, almost three years after the original proposal was put forth, ASEAN members agreed on the specifics of an East Asia Economic Caucus (EAEC). It was to fall under APEC, initially managed and supported by the AEM. ASEAN's secretary general was to obtain the views of the caucus's prospective members (East Asian members of APEC) and report them to the AEM for consideration and decision.[63] The newly agreed modalities of EAEC as a "caucus within APEC" reflected Malaysia's compromise but nonetheless failed to win Washington's support.[64] According to Malaysia's prime minister, Mahathir bin Mohamad, the Clinton administration, unlike its predecessor, dropped the objection but stopped short of showing support, which would have invited other East Asian countries to lend their support.[65]

The situation remained vague until about a month after ASEAN's secretary general Ajit Singh from Malaysia gave "a thorough briefing on EAEC" at the twelfth U.S.-ASEAN Dialogue immediately after the bilateral summit.[66] Ajit Singh presented "a seven-page paper on the proposal" that "outlined the rationale of the concept, the modality, agenda as well as the composition of EAEC members."[67] U.S. officials were reportedly "stunned with detailed plans for an EAEC structure" far more elaborate and sophisticated than they had expected.[68] On June 7, 1994, the United States formally conveyed its opposition to EAEC's proposal to ASEAN and Japan, saying it would have a negative effect on APEC.[69]

"Six (Seven) plus Three"

This opposition from the United States disappointed ASEAN, because it appeared that the EAEC was going to "haunt" the association for a while, just as it became interested in adopting a multilayered approach to international economic cooperation.[70] In response, ASEAN apparently devised a two-track approach. On the one hand, it did not drop the EAEC proposal and let Malaysia continue its pursuit.[71] On the other hand, ASEAN started inviting Japan, China, and South Korea (but not Taiwan and Hong Kong, as envisaged in the EAEC proposal) to its informal gatherings, which had an open agenda but were separate from the controversial EAEC. On July 25, 1994, at the margin of the first ASEAN Regional Forum (ARF) in Thailand, ASEAN foreign ministers invited their counterparts from Japan, China, and South Korea to an informal luncheon meeting of "Six plus Three."[72] Malaysia apparently seized this opportunity, and, as secretary general Singh briefed, nine ministers agreed to continue consultations on the EAEC proposal and work to dispel the "misconceptions or misgivings" that other countries may have had of their intentions and to ensure that the caucus would not derail or compete with the APEC process.[73] A similar meeting (this time between seven ASEAN ministers and three Northeast Asian ministers) took place on July 31, 1995, but the discussion was mainly about the ASEM instead of the EAEC.

Things did not proceed as smoothly, however, when the ASEAN economic ministers (supposedly in charge of launching the EAEC) were involved. In September 1994, at the third AEM-MITI meeting in Chiang Mai, Thailand, Deputy Prime Minister Supachai Panitchpakdi, who hosted the meeting, invited MITI minister Ryutaro Hashimoto to a "Six plus Three" informal gathering of economic ministers at Phuket the following April.[74] MITI proposed that Thailand also invite Australia and New Zealand, in part to lock in Australia's drive for Asianization.[75] Incidentally, Singapore proposed an Asia-Europe meeting shortly after the Chiang Mai meeting, and the Asian side had to decide on its membership. Tokyo pushed for the participation of Australia and New Zealand in the ASEM as Asian members. Their participation in the Phuket meeting would open the door to their participation in the ASEM as well, thus linking membership of the two meetings. As for the proposed Six plus Three meeting of economic ministers, it was criticized as a "backdoor EAEC" despite the host's efforts to present it as a separate proposal.[76] Japan, site of an APEC leaders' meeting later that year, obviously did not want to complicate the task of hosting the Osaka meeting, which already had to deal with an extremely challenging agenda: to design a mechanism to achieve the ambitious Bogor declaration.[77] With Australia and New Zealand participating in the Phuket meeting, it would be easier to deny that it was a backdoor EAEC. In the end, Bangkok failed to persuade ASEAN to invite Canberra and Wellington. As had been expected, Japan decided not to attend, and the AEM met without any ministers from Northeast Asia.[78]

The cancellation of the Six plus Three left some ASEAN countries feeling bitter, notably Malaysia, a strong advocate of the EAEC, and Thailand, the host. Tokyo had sensed that while ASEAN had reached a consensus on moving ahead with the EAEC, not all the members were behind the idea. It was hoped that asking for the participation of Australia and New Zealand would not jeopardize Japan's relations with ASEAN. When MITI suggested that the two countries be invited, the Thai host consulted with other ASEAN members.[79] At the same time, Japan indicated that if Australia and New Zealand could not participate, Japan would not attend either.[80] This prompted ASEAN to demonstrate that it could manage its relations with CER countries without Japan as its "spokesman."[81] At the Phuket meeting, ASEAN economic ministers "proposed to hold a consultative meeting with their counterparts from the CER countries in September 1995," hoping to show that it could still have good relations with them even if they were not invited to a particular meeting, and that Six plus Three was just one of the various channels of ASEAN's external relations.[82] At an ASEAN-CER meeting on September 9, 1995, the two sides demonstrated they could arrive at an agreement, announcing they would cooperate in setting common standards.[83]

Even so, a senior cabinet minister of Thailand remained frustrated with Japan's refusal to attend the meeting unless certain conditions were met, noting that Japan should have come and made its case for including CER countries so that everyone in attendance could have discussed the issue and possibly come up with a formula for such situations. As he also pointed out, the Six plus Three was never meant to be an EAEC meeting, could easily deal with nontrade issues, and open discussion of this sort would "actually advance the course of ASEAN economic cooperation."[84]

Obviously Bangkok was also vexed because the Six plus Three was still in the shadow of the EAEC owing to their similar membership and the fact that the EAEC agenda was left to the members to decide. Malaysia's advocacy of the EAEC in relation to the Six plus Three made Bangkok's efforts to separate the two meetings more difficult. To complicate matters, there was a rumor that Japan would be reluctant to attend the Phuket meeting if the EAEC was going to be discussed.[85] In reality, Japan made no explicit requests regarding the agenda, only about the membership, which could, however, indirectly affect the agenda. Malaysia's trade minister Rafidah said ASEAN members refused to be intimidated "into restricting our area of discussion, limiting the freedom of speech."[86]

Shortly after the incident, Minister Hashimoto subtly intimated that he too saw the benefit in a neighborhood get-together in Asia, which should be allowed as part of "multilayered international relations" in which Asia was engaged, and hoped to find a way to realize it in a "harmonious" manner.[87] Others were more candid in their support of an EAEC, not from an exclusive Asian perspective, but from a pragmatic, post–cold war perspective. They called on Japan to "view its external relations in a multi-layered structure" because that is how the world was now ordered, with many overlapping circles of international relations (as opposed to concentric circles during the cold war period): "We have to stop thinking in terms of dichotomy. . . . We should not think that a neighborhood gathering will damage U.S.-Japan relations. The two just do not contradict each other."[88] This statement captured an emerging sense of pragmatism toward East Asian regionalism that later took root in Tokyo and elsewhere in the region.

In retrospect, ASEAN's drive for Six plus Three meetings was more of a campaign to recover, as a matter of principle, "the freedom of meeting" suppressed by the controversy surrounding the EAEC, to "diffuse the passions" sparked by the issue, and to show the rest of the world that the meetings were in fact harmless.[89] In time, the three Northeast Asian capitals implicitly came to share its goal. The question was how to achieve it.

Asia-Europe Meeting: Impact on East Asia

In July 1994, soon after the United States informed ASEAN of its objection to the EAEC proposal, the European Commission adopted a policy paper on Europe's Asia strategy that gave momentum to efforts to strengthen dialogue between Europe and East Asia.[90] In October 1994, at the Third Europe–East Asia Economic Summit organized by the World Economic Forum, the idea of a meeting of heads of East Asian and European governments was advocated by Singapore's prime minister Goh Chok Tong, who worked to obtain the support of ASEAN and the EC presidency (at the time, France).[91] In March 1995 Thailand confirmed that it would host the first ASEM.[92]

What captured the Asian imagination was Europe's view of Asia as a major region of the world, with "three major players, North America, Europe and East Asia."[93] This helped redefine APEC as a framework between East Asia and North America. The relation between Europe and East Asia was "the missing link" or "the missing side of the triangle which could be formed by North America, Europe, and East Asia."[94] The meeting could change Europe's perception of Asia from a threat to an opportunity. Also, the United States had no grounds to criticize the meeting because the purpose, far from being inward looking, was to strengthen the linkages with other regions.[95]

As noted earlier, some controversy arose over the Asian participants when ASEAN reached a consensus that seven ASEAN countries, along with Japan, China, and South Korea should attend, arguing that it would be "better starting with a smaller group" for the first meeting.[96] Chinese Taipei and Hong Kong were not included because of the political issues on the ASEM agenda. Japan pushed for the participation of the CER countries but, unlike its conduct toward the Phuket meeting, eventually accepted the ASEAN consensus and withdrew its insistence that the two countries be included in the first meeting.[97] Australia's foreign minister Gareth Evans went along with the decision as well, stating that Australia had been seriously focusing on its relations with East Asia for only ten years or so and that it had "a lot more time left in the future."[98]

Unlike the European side, which had elaborate processes for internal coordination, the Asian side had not worked as a group before and decided to meet in preparation for the summit with the Europeans. The ten East Asian economic ministers met for the first time in Osaka in November 1995 and again in Chiang Rai, Thailand, in February 1996.[99] In the run-up to these meetings, Malaysian officials joined other Asian members and avoided characterizing them as EAEC meetings. The Asian participants believed ASEM was of historical significance since it was "the first step for Asia and Europe to build a new relationship as equal partners" and "the first occasion for Asian countries to get together as one region and have dialogue with another region and thus provides a great opportunity for us to reflect on ourselves in Asia."[100]

ASEAN + 3 Summit

In 1995, prompted by Singapore's prime minister Goh, ASEAN leaders decided to complement their formal summits held every three years with an informal summit in 1996 or 1997 to deal with rapid changes. Goh also proposed to invite their East Asian counterparts to the first informal summit with a view to achieving the same harmony and prosperity in the region as was apparent in Europe today, even if it might take fifty or more years to do so: "If we start thinking about it now, and begin to take small but concrete steps towards it, Asia can achieve harmony and today's European standard of living in the mid-21st century, because we will be working towards a common vision."[101]

Although the three Northeast Asian leaders did not attend the first informal summit in Jakarta in December 1996, a meeting of ASEAN + 3 leaders was eventually held in December 1997 in Kuala Lumpur.[102] The decision was triggered by Japanese prime minister Ryutaro Hashimoto's suggestion that regular summit meetings be held by Japan and ASEAN members. ASEAN then decided to invite not only Japan but also China and South Korea to Kuala Lumpur for a summit meeting, and to hold three bilateral meetings with each of the three.[103] By October 1998 ASEAN economic ministers were no longer referring to the EAEC and had finally put its ghost to rest.[104]

Conclusion

In the second stage of East Asian regionalism, countries focused on two issues. The first was how to capitalize on APEC to give additional momentum to multilateral trade negotiations, while trying to reconcile APEC's ambitious goals with domestic realities. APEC's initial attention was on the Uruguay Round negotiations, which all members were eager to support. After the WTO was established, the United States led APEC to explore multilateral initiatives in selected sectors. However, the United States did not have fast-track authority and insisted on reciprocity if its offer was to be implemented. As a result, other members had no incentive to make concessions in APEC since they would be no worse off if they waited until the WTO negotiations started. In addition, the U.S. approach of isolating Japan—by allowing developing countries considerable flexibility and denying Japan any meaningful flexibility—squelched the small possibility that APEC could have induced some, if limited, liberalization of sensitive items through peer pressure. As a former U.S. official recalls, Washington was less patient with the pace of APEC development in this period than in the first period. It was less prepared to accommodate the region's diversity and allow for the time needed to build a sense of community before achieving the desired results.[105] While Asian developing members were able to live with the EVSL package because it did allow them some flexibility, they were unhappy with the APEC's narrow focus on liberalization, which prompted them to take a multilayered view of international economic institutions.

The second issue was how to make an East Asia–only framework a viable part of multilayered international institutions. As seen in chapter 4, the EAEC was a typical case of defensive reaction to European and American regionalism. The U.S. formal objection made in 1994 nurtured a new defensive impulse to recover "the freedom of meeting," or the freedom to design various layers of the networks they were involved in. To avoid the controversy caused by the EAEC, East Asia came up with ASEAN + 3, a formula without a name.

East Asia was so dependent, however, on extraregional markets that its threat to become a self-sufficient bloc, if NAFTA and the European Union became inward looking and protectionist, would be suicidal. Rather, the efficacy of East Asian regionalism as a defensive mechanism lies in its potential to make the voice of its members (if united) heard better in the decision-making process of international economic policies. It can also help alleviate its overdependence on extraregional markets (which stimulate other regions' protectionism) by stimulating regional domestic demand. Success in the first instance depends on whether the region can reach a cohesive position on various issues, and in the second instance on whether East Asian regionalism can facilitate intraregional economic interdependence, which in turn depends on the level of intraregional cooperation.

Despite the U.S. objection to an East Asia–only framework, East Asian countries continued their pursuit of it, prompted by the need for cooperation to facilitate intraregional economic interdependence, on one hand, and APEC's limitations, on the other (its narrow focus on trade and investment liberalization, the persistent differences among its members over the specific means of liberalization, and the resulting lack of attention to economic and technical cooperation or to trade and investment facilitation). As regionalization progressed, with China and Vietnam accelerating their reform and opening up, other Indochinese countries wanted to join ASEAN, and more diverse investors (not just Japan and the United States but also newly industrializing economies) developed their business networks in the region. In response to this changing environment, ASEAN revised its long-standing policy of rejecting lectures and interference from developed economies and, as seen in its willingness to cooperate with Japan, became keener to receive external assistance and advice in promoting ASEAN integration. Although East Asian countries were not interested in preferential trade agreements (except for AFTA) in this period, Japan (which envisioned a broad range of economic cooperation in APEC when it developed its proposal) as well as other Asian countries became more serious about pursuing economic and technical cooperation to improve their institutional capabilities and facilitate cross-border business. In this way, defensive reaction began to give way to intraregional interdependence as the driving force behind the interest in developing the ASEAN + 3 forums.

6

New Assumptions about Regionalism

East Asian regionalism passed into its third phase during the financial crisis of 1997, which dramatically changed the landscape and mind-set of regional economies. The crisis helped remove the taboos on free trade agreements (FTAs) and East Asian–only forums and encouraged East Asian capitals to experiment with various additional layers of economic institutions, in search of effective and feasible tools to complement global institutions. This period is much shorter than the previous two, ending in late 2000 when China began exploring FTAs.

The Impact of the Asian Financial Crisis

From the outset, the "contagion" of the currency crisis reminded the countries in the region of their interdependence.[1] In addition, almost all believed the United States and the International Monetary Fund (IMF), itself considered a tool of U.S. international economic policy, had exacerbated their hardship. This perception, combined with the fact that U.S. hedge funds substantially profited from the massive selling of Asian currencies, hurt the image of the United States in the region.

The argument went like this. First, the so-called Washington consensus prompted the premature opening of Asian capital accounts, which caused the destructive capital movements that triggered the crisis.[2] Second, the United States was not forthcoming when Asian countries were coordinating a package to support currency stabilization in the early stages of the crisis. Third, the IMF's initial prescription to induce economic contraction did not address the basic problem of the capital account crisis and thus led to a full-fledged economic crisis. Fourth, measures such as cutting subsidies on imported fuels had a significant impact on the life of the poor and damaged the political stability of Indonesia. The experience persuaded East Asian countries that they had to protect their own interests, since global institutions under U.S. leadership could not always adequately do so. As a result, East Asian countries began building up foreign reserves and initiating regional cooperation to promote financial stability in Asia. The Asian Monetary Fund (AMF), proposed in August 1997, did not materialize owing to the strong objections of the United States and lack of support from China.[3] In November 2000, however, the ASEAN + 3 countries agreed to establish a web of currency swaps to prevent future currency and financial debacles.[4] In this way, the crisis increased the momentum for East Asian regional cooperation in the currency area and later led to a more comprehensive concept of regional integration. A keener awareness of intraregional economic interdependence reinforced defensive regionalism in the countries' collective response.

Confidence in Asia's economic dynamism was now dwindling, and there was a growing uneasiness about the progress of regionalism elsewhere. The sense of crisis permeated the region and made countries less hesitant about institutionalization. Because the crisis had brought down regional domestic markets, it was important to secure stable export markets. Countries had a stronger incentive to overcome the discrimination caused by FTAs to which they did not belong by concluding agreements with the members of such FTAs, in the hope of strengthening their relations with major markets of the world not affected by the crisis (although these moves do not constitute East Asian regionalism).[5] This attempt in turn reminded economies—especially the small and medium-sized ones—that their bargaining leverage depended largely on the attractiveness of the entire region to which they belonged. As a result, the momentum for FTAs increased among neighboring economies.[6]

The crisis also aroused a sense of urgency regarding economic reform, especially in countries with strong political leadership. Furthermore, to obtain necessary financing from the IMF, those countries had to implement agreed-upon reform measures.[7] From the sidelines, foreign investors watched how far governments were willing to go. President Kim Dae Jung of South Korea, for one, was eager to promote structural reform in order to attract foreign investment and overcome the crisis.[8] The need to restructure domestic economies and attract foreign direct investment (FDI) heightened their interest in FTAs that would lock in domestic reform in legally binding agreements with foreign countries. This made institutionalization that accompanied FTAs more acceptable.

Another effect of the crisis was that it sharply reduced ASEAN's influence as a benign mediator, which had once been central in developing various regional forums. Whereas China's economic performance remained relatively stable throughout the crisis and FDI into South Korea surged, ASEAN suffered from the collapse of domestic demand and the slow progress of economic reform, which tempered the attractiveness of its member countries as investment destinations. The addition of four new members, compounded by the diversity of political systems, widened the intraregional economic gap and put a serious strain on ASEAN's cohesiveness. Economic stagnation in Indonesia fueled by political turmoil and weak leadership only made matters worse. As ASEAN members became more and more preoccupied with domestic economic problems, they had little energy left to devote to proactive ASEAN initiatives present before the crisis. With the decline of ASEAN's influence and the shift in gravity to Northeast Asia, Singapore decided to go it alone in strengthening relations with countries outside ASEAN. Singapore's move set off intraregional competition that further reduced any hesitation Asian countries may have had about institutionalization, paving the way for the fourth period.

In the wake of the crisis, the region's perception of Japan changed. Japan lost its attractiveness as an economic model, and the threat of its economic domination in the region vanished.[9] If anything, countries feared that Japanese businesses might reduce their commitment in Asia and that Japan's economic deterioration might deepen the regional crisis.[10] Japan's inability to take the initiative in revitalizing the Asian economy drew much criticism.[11] Senior officials from Asian countries as well as the United States called on Japan to take responsibility for supporting Asia's economic recovery.[12] In fact, from the outbreak of the crisis Japanese manufacturing companies tried to maintain their offshore operations in the region and retain well-trained local employees. In addition, the Japanese government took various measures to aid the crisis-hit countries, as well as Japanese companies.[13] For example, it pledged substantial financial assistance for a package (thus pushed for agreement on the package) to support currency stabilization at an early stage of the crisis. When the "currency" crisis turned into a full-blown "economic" crisis, the Japanese government provided significant financial assistance for economic recovery on a bilateral basis. Japan's actions since late 1997 in providing assistance in the midst of its own economic turmoil revealed its deep commitment to the region.[14] As much as this assistance was appreciated, its neighbors seemed to also expect Japan to expand imports through its own economic recovery and to shoulder responsibility for the region. Instead of resisting an increased role for Japan as before, countries now expected it to lead the region out of the crisis and spearhead regional efforts to create a stable economic environment. This change in attitude toward Japan made East Asia more cohesive in its pursuit of frameworks for regional cooperation.

Asian countries were disappointed that APEC was unable to play an effective role in dealing with the financial crisis. Frustrations ran high when it spent so much time and energy on the Early Voluntary Sectoral Liberalization (EVSL) initiative in the middle of the crisis.[15] It was not just a question of the right priority, however, but also of capability.[16] The crisis merely strengthened suspicions, present even beforehand, that, after all, APEC could not do everything.

From Washington's perspective, the depression in Asia dampened U.S. enthusiasm for the region's markets. U.S. trade policy in Asia thus shifted its attention to the negotiations on China's accession to the World Trade Organization (WTO). Disappointment with APEC as a vehicle of regional trade liberalization rekindled interest in the U.S. Trade Representative's 1997 proposal for FTAs with Australia, New Zealand, and Singapore. It was developed into a "P5 (Project 5)" initiative for an FTA among five "like-minded" countries (the United States, Chile, Singapore, Australia, and New Zealand).[17] These events, in turn, reinforced the growing conviction among Asian capitals that APEC need not be the only regional framework in Asia and that forums could be formed without the United States.

Although the impact of the crisis differed from country to country, the collective experience of rapid change in the region's economic and political landscape solidified the acceptance of and desire for a multitrack strategy (which had emerged during the second period) and triggered two major developments. First, as already mentioned, East Asia–only forums ceased to be taboo. Second, preferential trade agreements such as FTAs ceased to be taboo even in Northeast Asia. With these two constraints gone, there was enormous excitement to try various alternatives.

The Development of the ASEAN + 3 Forums

As the development of the ASEAN + 3 forums demonstrates, the Asian financial crisis was not the sole cause of East Asian regionalism. Rather, the crisis was the catalyst that made countries recognize the efficacy of multitrack approaches to international economic issues. In April 1997, even before the crisis erupted, ASEAN countries decided to hold an ASEAN + 3 leaders' meeting later that year. At that point, however, Asian countries were still very cautious about giving the impression of a high level of institutionalization. With the exception of the Asia-Europe meeting (ASEM), where the linkages with other regions made clear that it was not an inward-looking group, stand-alone Asian forums were presented as informal, ad hoc, and low-key gatherings. Although Ryutaro Hashimoto's call for regular summits between Japan and ASEAN led the association to hold ASEAN + 3 summits beginning in December 1997, it hesitated to make these regular events at first.[18]

In the third period, the ASEAN + 3 framework became more institution-alized, and member countries set about developing a future vision. They also made some progress in practical, functional cooperation. At the 1998 summit, East Asian leaders agreed that they would hold ASEAN + 3 summits every year in association with ASEAN summits.[19] At this meeting, Singapore's prime minister Goh Chok Tong reportedly advocated the concept of a new East Asia free trade zone, and Malaysia's prime minister Mahathir bin Mohamad told reporters that the ASEAN Free Trade Area (AFTA) could be extended to encompass China, Japan, and South Korea on a case-by-case basis.[20] Leaders freely entertained ambitious goals without worrying about their immediate feasibility or extraregional reactions. South Korea's president Kim Dae Jung proposed to set up an East Asia Vision Group to seek ways to revitalize the region, including the possibility of launching an economic community.[21] In November 1999 the ASEAN + 3 summit issued its first official statement, the Joint Statement on East Asia Cooperation.[22] It listed a wide range of eco-nomic, social, and political issues for the cooperation agenda, called for intensified coordination and cooperation with international and regional forums, and asked the relevant ministers to oversee its implementation. The leaders also decided to have their foreign ministers meet on the periphery of the ASEAN post-ministerial conferences (PMC).

Financial Cooperation

The most notable achievement of the ASEAN + 3 frameworks was financial cooperation. In May 2000 the ASEAN + 3 financial ministers agreed to develop a network of currency swap agreements through the Chiang Mai Ini-tiative.[23] As already noted, this initiative was based on an earlier proposal to set up an Asian Monetary Fund, which was modified to meet the objections of the United States and the IMF and to make it more workable given the lack of sufficient monitoring capabilities among the East Asian countries.

While some argue that East Asian financial cooperation is driven by Japan's desire to challenge the global financial regime or is based on anti-Western or anti-IMF attitudes, a closer look reveals that the need to address specific problems is what has shaped the different proposals and initiatives. Since some problems were later addressed by the IMF, East Asian countries shifted their focus to issues that were not dealt with by global institutions and found the solutions in regional cooperation.

For example, the main objective of the AMF proposal was to supplement insufficient financial resources available from the IMF. When Thailand turned to the IMF for financial support, the IMF told Japan that Thailand needed more than $10 billion (later found to be $14 billion), but the IMF could provide only $4 billion on the basis of Thailand's quota and asked whether Japan and the other Asian countries could shoulder the rest. To find a way out, Japan and the IMF co-hosted a meeting of supporters of Thailand on August 11, 1997, and put together a $17 billion financing package. To avoid a recurrence of this precarious operation in the future, Tokyo demanded an increase in Asian quotas in accordance with Asia's weight in the international economy. At the same time, to institutionalize the operation of self-help among the Asian countries during the Thai crisis, Tokyo proposed an AMF. However, the IMF introduced the Supplementary Reserve Facility (SRF) in time for the Korean crisis, enabling the fund to provide substantially greater financial support. In subsequent crises, the IMF, along with the World Bank and Asian Development Bank, was able to provide adequate financial assistance to the countries affected, and bilateral assistance took the form of a "second line of defense." However, to make themselves immune to future financial crises, the Asian countries built up huge foreign exchange reserves and also agreed on the Chiang Mai Initiative, which was intended to complement IMF assistance in future crises. Thus there was less need to create an AMF with vast financial resources.

In entertaining the idea of a regional facility, countries also tried to address the problems ensuing from inappropriate policy prescriptions and conditionalities set by the IMF during the crisis. For example, the fiscal policy prescribed for Indonesia at first was too contractional and made matters worse. Some of the structural conditionalities, such as the ones related to the national car project and the food distribution monopoly, were irrelevant and even counterproductive in the sense that the government's failure to implement these measures was interpreted as a lack of commitment to economic reform and caused a massive selling of rupiah, to the detriment of the fragile national economy. Recognizing these and other shortcomings, the IMF subsequently revised its advice on fiscal policy and also started to streamline the structural conditionalities, limiting them to those with macroeconomic relevance.

Since being launched, the Chiang Mai Initiative has been expanded as a regional self-help mechanism to complement IMF programs. A regional facility is no longer urgently needed because the problems the original AMF proposals tried to address have by and large been solved. Not all issues are being dealt with at the global level, however. For example, the development of bond markets in Asia, which would enable countries in the region to raise long-term funds in local currencies, is not something that the IMF would take up.

Inspiration from Mexico

While East Asia was consumed by the financial crisis, the global trend toward regionalism continued apace. The European Union, in response to the North American Free Trade Agreement (NAFTA) (EU-Mexico trade had declined significantly since NAFTA came into force), explored ways to strengthen relations with Mexico "as a link between the NAFTA countries and the other countries of Latin America."[24] The European Union and Mexico signed the Interim Trade Agreement in December 1997, which would allow the two parties to immediately start FTA negotiations.[25] The agreement went into force in July 1998. Around this time, Mexico's commerce and industry minister Herminio Blanco invited former MITI vice minister for international affairs and then president of JETRO Noboru Hatakeyama, a long-time friend, to explore the possibility of an FTA between Japan and Mexico.[26] Hatakeyama told his former colleagues at MITI about the situation and urged them to consider the matter. His suggestion immediately inspired some MITI policymakers to explore FTAs as a trade policy tool. This had occurred just after APEC's difficult discussions about the EVSL initiative, which caused them to think that Japan's passive posture had invited the problems and they had to create a framework of trade liberalization that would not prompt rejection but inspire willingness among domestic constituencies. Although a compelling case could be made for nullifying the additional discrimination created by the prospective EU-Mexico FTA, the large share (about 20 percent) of agricultural produce in Japan's imports from Mexico looked too challenging as a starter.[27] If Japan should start exploring an FTA at all, the first such endeavor would have to create a sense of political inevitability in order to overcome not only the resistance to liberalizing sensitive items but also the hesitation over preferential trade arrangements.

Japan-Korea FTA Study

It was the most unlikely couple at first sight that started the wave of bilateral FTAs in East Asia. During a visit to Japan in October 1998, South Korea's president Kim Dae Jung initiated efforts to overcome historical antagonism, telling Japan's prime minister Keizo Obuchi that the problems of the twentieth century should be resolved within the century.[28] The statement had wide popular appeal in Japan, and the visit marked a dramatic turning point in bilateral relations. Because the 1997–98 financial crisis had had a devastating effect on the Korean economy, Seoul hoped that improved relations would result in more FDI from Japan and help its economic recovery. Also, the North Korean missile crisis made it all the more important to strengthen cooperation between them.

Before President Kim's visit to Japan, hopes for renewed bilateral relations were high, and a proposal for a bilateral FTA was floated about as a symbol of the new relations.[29] A Japan-Korea FTA (JKFTA) seemed a very natural enterprise given their geographical proximity, OECD membership, and common values and interests. Even those opposed to preferential trade agreements (PTAs) could accept it as a special exception to their adherence to the most favored nation (MFN) principle, in the same vein as the U.S.-Canada FTA and the closer economic relations (CER) between Australia and New Zealand. A JKFTA would create the largest free trade area in East Asia, would include 170 million affluent people with a combined GDP of $5 trillion (about three-fourths of the entire East Asian economy), and would greatly appeal to domestic and foreign investors. An FTA between the only two OECD members in Asia, with advanced rules commensurate with their economic level, could set a standard for economic integration in the region. Businesses in both countries would enhance their competitiveness through industrial adjustment. It would also promote regional stability, allowing the two nations to overcome their historic animosity and forge relations as economic allies. If East Asia should embark on FTAs, the one between Japan and South Korea seemed to be the logical first step.

Although the FTA was not taken up in the leaders' meeting, serious consideration began soon after, prompted by South Korea's announcement on November 4, 1998, of its new policy to promote FTAs with major trade partners, Chile being the first candidate. Korea and Chile agreed to explore the possibility of an FTA at a separate bilateral summit later that month, started preparatory processes in April 1999, and launched negotiations in September 1999.[30] Korea, long insistent that free trade be pursued via an open and multilateral approach, had clearly taken a concrete step toward using FTAs as a policy option.

Because a bilateral FTA was a politically sensitive subject in both countries, Tokyo and Seoul adopted a cautious, incremental approach in order to avoid a backlash. In November, they agreed to launch a study on bilateral economic relations, which evolved into a feasibility study of a bilateral FTA.[31] In March 1999 Obuchi and Kim met again in Seoul and announced the Japan–Republic of Korea Economic Agenda 21, listing priority measures of bilateral cooperation.[32] These included negotiations for the bilateral investment treaty and cooperation on mutual recognition, standardization, and the protection of intellectual property. Although the agenda did not mention an FTA specifically, these measures were building blocks of bilateral institutions for economic integration.

Because the idea of a Japan-Korea FTA posed great challenges to both countries, it took them four more years to launch negotiations. Government-affiliated think tanks on both sides conducted studies on closer Japan-Korea economic relations and in May 2000 published their reports on the possible effects of a bilateral FTA.[33] They predicted that such an agreement would increase exports of sensitive items both ways, with Korea exporting apparel, leather products, and agriculture and fishery products to Japan, and Japan sending sophisticated machinery and metal and chemical products to South Korea. They also predicted that Korea's trade deficit with Japan would increase further, as Korea's average tariff rate on Japanese products was higher than Japan's average tariff rate on Korean products. Thus Koreans were particularly concerned that the FTA was not going to be a balanced deal. The history issue added to their hesitation. Nonetheless, the very debate in Japanese policy circles represented a sea change in Tokyo's attitudes toward FTAs and brought forth various ideas about possible FTAs and economic integration.

Singapore Spearheads the FTA Drive

Moves to explore bilateral FTAs intensified after New Zealand persuaded Singapore to use FTAs to boost APEC liberalization. In June 1999 New Zealand proposed a bilateral FTA with Singapore on the heels of the APEC trade ministers' meeting in Auckland, whose chair hoped to "catalyse APEC towards realizing the Bogor goals."[34] Singapore had already shown its willingness to go it alone without other ASEAN members by offering FTA negotiations with the United States, but this was its first realistic offer of an independent FTA. In September 1999 Singapore and New Zealand agreed to start FTA negotiations at the fringe of the APEC leaders' meeting in Auckland.[35] Singapore then agreed to explore the possibility of negotiating FTAs with Mexico and Chile and proposed a trilateral agreement with South Korea and Chile.[36] Eventually, New Zealand, Singapore, and Chile agreed "to work together to pursue the broader P5 free trade initiative."[37] On October 1, 1999, three weeks after the agreement with New Zealand, Singapore proposed an FTA between the AFTA and CER at a meeting of ASEAN economic ministers (AEM) and CER ministers in Singapore. ASEAN and CER ministers agreed to establish a high-level task force to study the feasibility of an AFTA-CER free trade area.[38] It was a significant accomplishment from Singapore's perspective, considering the initial backlash from other ASEAN members against Singapore's move to negotiate an FTA with New Zealand on its own. Though resented at first, this stimulated other ASEAN members to follow suit, which in turn added momentum to Singapore's drive for FTAs with non-ASEAN economies.

By this point, Singapore was pursuing a full-fledged multitrack strategy, with FTAs independent of ASEAN added to its toolbox. Urging East Asian countries to think of themselves as a region distinct from Europe or North America, Prime Minister Goh proposed holding ASEM and ASEAN + 3 summits and exploring an East Asia Free Trade Area. Before long, Singapore was pursuing FTAs with countries in the Asia Pacific and even with European countries.[39] Its "strategic opportunism" set the tone for East Asia's exploration of regionalism in this period.[40]

Japan-Singapore FTA

In the middle of this FTA boom, Singapore was surprised to find that Japan was no longer resisting the FTA idea. At the same time, it worried that Japan's commitment in Southeast Asia would ebb as its attention turned to Northeast Asia, where information technology (IT) manufacturing capabilities and markets were growing rapidly. While pursuing an FTA with New Zealand, Singapore unofficially sounded out the possibility of a bilateral FTA with Japanese politicians, businesspeople, and government officials, and eventually proposed exploring an FTA at a bilateral summit between Goh and Obuchi in December 1999.

Singapore's proposal presented Japan with an opportunity to negotiate a doable FTA (because Singapore did not have many sensitive exports) and to overcome two major obstacles to its multitrack strategy back home. One was the persistent skepticism toward preferential trade agreements as a matter of principle. The other was the political resistance to liberalization of sensitive items such as agricultural produce in forums other than the WTO. Japan had to stop treating sensitive sectors as sanctuaries and to start examining the possibility of liberalization on an item-by-item basis. Clearing these hurdles would not be easy but seemed worth trying. At least it was clear that unless Japan could conclude an FTA with Singapore, it could not arrive at any FTA. Singapore's advanced economic level would also allow the two countries to explore innovative measures to facilitate business activities. The prospects of policy innovation and the additional impetus to domestic regulatory reform to be gained from designing and implementing an agreement were important added benefits of an FTA with Singapore, an already free port in goods trade with small markets.[41]

An FTA with Singapore was not without its drawbacks, however. For one thing, it could alienate other ASEAN members and nullify years of Japanese support for ASEAN integration and unity. In any case, an FTA with ASEAN as a whole looked next to impossible. At the end of the day, Japan trusted Singapore's judgment that its move would stimulate other ASEAN members to follow suit. After all, Japan had to first overcome its own obstacles before being able to credibly propose an FTA with ASEAN as a whole. Singapore was the necessary first step.

A Japan-Singapore FTA could also be regarded as a precursor to an exclusive Asian trade bloc and might prompt other regions to lash back. Although the ASEAN + 3 summits became regular events, Tokyo was not yet completely free from these worries. Nonetheless, it decided that this risk would be manageable, especially since Singapore was one of the least likely candidates to promote exclusive, inward-looking arrangements. It had hoped to conclude an FTA with the United States for over a decade and was negotiating such an agreement with New Zealand, one of the strong advocates of APEC liberalization.

On October 22, 2000, Japan announced it would launch FTA negotiations with Singapore in 2001. As noted in chapter 2, this triggered a chain of competitive reactions. On November 16, 2000, U.S. and Singapore leaders unexpectedly announced their agreement to start negotiations on a bilateral FTA. On November 25, 2000, at their leaders' meeting, China and ASEAN agreed to set up an expert group to study how economic cooperation and free trade relations between them could be deepened. The door to a new era had obviously opened.

Conclusion

Once the financial crisis freed countries of the taboos on East Asia–only frameworks and FTAs, they were able to cultivate their interest in designing additional layers of the multilayered international institutions nurtured in preceding periods. The crisis reminded East Asian countries of their interdependence and of what they might do together to move toward recovery, prevent future crises, and promote stable growth in the region as a whole. It also dashed the confidence or even complacency prevalent in the region before the crisis. Many had thought that they could count on business activities and global institutions to keep their economies vibrant and did not need to bother with additional regional institutions or bilateral agreements. After the crisis, East Asian countries were eager to explore whatever would work to revitalize their economies. The crisis shifted economic gravity away from ASEAN to China and South Korea (after its sharp recovery) and prompted ASEAN to forge a closer tie with Northeast Asia. Furthermore, Japan no longer seemed to threaten East Asia with economic domination, making countries more comfortable with more institutionalized cooperation with Japan. The United States now became half-hearted in its enthusiasm and policy attention to Asian economies in general, as reflected in the U.S. Trade Representative's narrow focus on EVSL in APEC, which made Asian policymakers less worried about U.S. reactions to East Asian regionalism.

The crisis also added momentum to bilateral FTAs. First, it helped East Asian countries overcome their traditional aversion to preferential trade agreements and recognize the need for better economic relations with Japan. South Korea's developmental achievements of the preceding decades, which had qualified it for OECD membership, encouraged it to reach out to Japan and put an end to the bilateral animosity due in part to the history issue. Although the bilateral reconciliation was incomplete, these steps changed Japan's perception of South Korea and the nature of the bilateral relations. Second, the shift in economic prowess from ASEAN to Northeast Asia rendered a psychological blow to ASEAN countries and prompted Singapore to finally go it alone and conclude bilateral FTAs with non-ASEAN countries. Third, other Asian countries could propose FTAs with Japan now that the threat of its economic domination had subsided.

Admittedly, countries throughout the region resented the way in which the United States and the IMF had dealt with the crisis. Therefore it is often argued that East Asian regionalism is the result of anti-American sentiments at the time, but this is too simplistic a view. In fact, the defensive regionalism ensuing from the crisis, which prompted financial cooperation, most notably the AMF proposal, achieved its objective largely by inducing changes in IMF policy. The Chiang Mai Initiative is a regional self-help mechanism to complement IMF assistance in future crises.

In the area of trade, the crisis did not necessarily precipitate defensive regionalism. Its most important impact here was the new impetus to make crisis-hit economies more attractive to investors, through domestic reform and liberalization of trade and investment. They were driven not by defensive regionalism but by the desire to promote intraregional economic interdependence and stimulate growth. The establishment of the WTO dispute settlement mechanism had also solved the problem of U.S. unilateral trade sanctions and reduced the defensive motivations of East Asian regionalism. Having greater freedom to experiment with various forums, East Asian capitals could concentrate on the substantive issues assigned to each forum. Taking a realistic view of APEC, they became more proactive in creating frameworks for negotiating trade and investment liberalization that would better suit their situations. For practical reasons, then, they pursued bilateral FTAs rather than a pan–East Asian FTA.

This is not to deny that defensive motivations were at work in trade in this period, too. The greatest impetus lay in the growing regionalism, particularly the European Union's efforts to conclude FTAs with Mexico and other Latin American countries in response to NAFTA and the Free Trade Area of the Americas initiative. The actual measures, however, consisted of exploring cross-regional FTAs such as FTAs with Mexico and Chile and were not necessarily in the form of East Asian regionalism. For the most part, defensive regionalism played a symbolic role in making East Asian–only frameworks more legitimate.

In this period, the traditional obstacles to regionalism in East Asia were to some extent overcome. The financial crisis, experienced by all the countries, strengthened the region's sense of common interest and its cohesiveness. Although a sense of community may not yet be present, the countries are now much more willing to find ways to cooperate better. Another marked change occurred in U.S. attitudes toward East Asian cooperation. Once categorically opposed to economic integration, in the new environment Washington confined its opposition to the design of particular proposals. For their part, East Asian capitals have become more relaxed about U.S. reactions, feeling they can discuss problems with the United States as they arise and rectify them as appropriate. Above all, East Asian countries are far less hesitant about institutionalization and more comfortable with free trade agreements, albeit not with customs unions or currency integration.

7

The Race for a Free Trade Agreement

In the fourth period, the regional landscape changed yet again, this time owing largely to the rise of China. By the turn of the century, China had become an important link in the production network and its growing domestic demand was helping to regionalize the East Asian economy, also making it an indispensable member of the region's economic framework. At the same time, China had become an active player in promoting regionalism, and this activism accelerated intraregional competition.

Beijing's new attitude toward regional cooperation can be traced to a proposal by Premier Zhu Rongji at the ASEAN-China summit on November 25, 2000, calling for an ASEAN-China Expert Group on Economic Cooperation to look into the implications of China's accession to the World Trade Organization (WTO) and ways to further enhance ASEAN-China economic cooperation and integration, including the possibility of establishing a free trade area between the two. This proposal, put forward after completing major negotiations for its accession to the WTO in 2000, marked the start of a race for free trade agreements (FTAs). This period continues to the present, though the pace of new negotiations is likely to decelerate as the countries involved come to recognize that they need more domestic preparations (both political readiness and institutional capabilities) to go further.

Beijing's Catch-up Game

China's move to conclude an FTA with ASEAN was a result of its overall regional policy shift and the competitive dynamics that the FTA policy of Japan and Korea had set off. China had begun attaching more importance to its relations with neighboring countries since the early 1990s as a way to secure the benign international environment that would enable it to focus on its domestic economic development. In addition, the positive experience of participating in APEC processes helped China overcome its long-held fear that multilateral frameworks could reduce its freedom and damage its interests.[1] Its territorial disputes in the South China Sea and cross-strait tensions, however, reminded ASEAN economies that China's military might still posed a destabilizing threat to the region. China was sending them mixed signals.

All the same, since the financial crisis China had become more aware of the interdependence between itself and the outside world.[2] Moreover, it had become more confident and proactive. In mid-1998 China succeeded in projecting an image of a "responsible great power" by not devaluing the renminbi.[3] However, analysts argued that this was not a sacrifice because, under the particular circumstances, the devaluation was not in China's interest.[4] This episode made Beijing further confident in its ability to positively shape the regional environment. It actively participated in the ASEAN + 3 meetings since the first summit in 1997. At the same time, China, as well as Japan and South Korea, started a separate summit with ASEAN (ASEAN + 1), which in a joint statement emphasized "good-neighborly and friendly relations."[5] It reversed its initial cautious attitude to the Asian Monetary Fund (AMF) proposal and supported the Chiang Mai Initiative at the ASEAN + 3 meeting of finance ministers in May 2000.[6] Its accession to the WTO further heightened its sense of being a responsible great power.

China's efforts to improve relations with neighboring countries stemmed in part from its anxiety over the security environment, especially after the U.S. bombing of the Chinese embassy in Belgrade in 1999. The George W. Bush administration's initial policy of regarding China as a strategic competitor caused further alarm, prompting precautions against possible U.S. attempts to encircle and contain it.[7]

When it needed to improve relations with its neighbors, however, China sensed anxiety there as well. The Asian financial crisis and China's rise had left them much less confident about their economic future. With developmental stages close to those of China and overlapping export structures, many ASEAN countries viewed China's rise as a competitive threat to their economic welfare much more strongly than Japan or South Korea would.[8] An offer of an FTA between China and ASEAN, albeit not without the risk of further exacerbating the sense of China's competitive threat, would at least demonstrate China's willingness to let ASEAN gain from its economic growth.

This might help alleviate ASEAN's anxiety about China's rise, which was expected to accelerate after its accession to the WTO.[9]

In addition to China's overall regional policy, competitive dynamics prompted China to move toward an FTA with ASEAN. In the area of trade policy, it had warily watched Japan, South Korea, and other neighboring countries shift their focus to FTAs just when it was preoccupied with WTO accession negotiations.[10] The trend toward preferential trade agreements, which had spread even to Asia, was particularly worrisome for China, in view of the increased competition with imports after its accession to the WTO and the need to expand export markets. It should be noted, however, that intraregional competitive dynamics do not necessarily imply confrontational or hostile intentions to exclude other economies. Chinese officials often deny that "competitive" elements are behind their FTA moves and emphasize that they "reach out to ASEAN for its own reasons" as "part of Beijing's 'periphery diplomacy.'"[11] In fact, the competition in an FTA race consists of moving early on in order to secure more favorable positions in future larger FTA initiatives. This kind of competition does take place even between countries working toward eventual economic integration that would include them both. The developments in the third period convinced Beijing that it should also participate in the regional trend toward FTAs.

Actually, the offer came from the ASEAN side, when the ASEAN secretariat's October 2000 proposal to study economic integration among ASEAN + 3 members failed to win approval.[12] As an alternative, the chair of the ASEAN economic ministers meeting (AEM) proposed studying three bilateral FTAs (ASEAN-Japan, ASEAN-China, and ASEAN-Korea). Japan's Ministry of Economy, Trade and Industry (METI), under Takeo Hiranuma, was positive but not forthcoming enough to launch an FTA joint study. In contrast, China immediately "grabbed this opportunity."[13]

China chose ASEAN as its first FTA partner not only to ease tensions on the economic and security fronts but also to start with a doable deal. Unlike an FTA with a more developed economy such as Japan or South Korea, an FTA with ASEAN would be relatively easy and help China quickly catch up with the regional trend toward FTAs. If negotiations turned out to be difficult, China and ASEAN could invoke the "enabling clause" for developing members of the WTO, which would make their FTA exempt from the strict rule to cover "substantially all the trade."[14] Japan and South Korea have competitive manufacturing industries that state-owned enterprises (SOEs) in China would have difficulty competing with.[15] The resistance from politically sensitive agricultural sectors in Japan and Korea would also be difficult to overcome. Thus when China proposed a feasibility study of an FTA for China, South Korea, and Japan in November 2002, the idea met with a lukewarm reception.

China moved swiftly with a proposal to ASEAN. By October 2001 China and ASEAN had completed a joint feasibility study for an FTA, and in November 2001 China persuaded ASEAN to agree to establish an ASEAN-China Free Trade Area within ten years.[16] For ASEAN members, except for advanced economies such as Singapore, China's exports presented a competitive threat. Therefore China's offer to ASEAN members early on, of "special and differential treatment and flexibility to the newer ASEAN members" and "early harvest," where both sides would reduce tariffs on items of interest (agricultural produce), had apparently played an important role in persuading ASEAN to accept the FTA proposal.[17] In November 2002 China and ASEAN signed the Framework Agreement on Comprehensive Economic Cooperation, which would "serve as the fulcrum" for establishing the free trade area by 2010 for the older ASEAN members and by 2015 for the newer members.[18]

China also decided to extend most favored nation (MFN) treatment to the three non-WTO members (Vietnam, Laos, and Cambodia).[19] Initially, it intended to deal with ASEAN as a whole. In June 2003, however, China and Thailand signed a separate agreement to implement their early harvest measures and to eliminate tariffs on imported fruits and vegetables (108 edible vegetables and 80 edible fruits and nuts) from October 1, 2003.[20] To allow for separate bilateral or plurilateral agreements between China and individual ASEAN members, the Chinese and the ASEAN leaders agreed to amend the Framework Agreement to introduce an article clarifying the status of outside agreements.[21] The early harvest measures between other ASEAN members and China were implemented on January 1, 2004.[22] On November 29, 2004, two years after they signed the Framework Agreement, ASEAN and China concluded the Agreement on Trade in Goods under it.[23]

The implementation of the early harvest measures was not altogether smooth in the beginning. First, the agreed package was less substantial than expected, covering about 10 percent of all tariff lines but only about US$860,000 of actual trade between ASEAN and China in 2001.[24] Thailand, ahead of other ASEAN members, started the early harvest measure on vegetables and fruits under a separate bilateral FTA. According to the Thai ambassador to Beijing, China's "non-tariff barriers such as food safety and import licenses . . . had proved a major trade obstacle for Thai agricultural products."[25] To control the volume of imported goods, Beijing required importers to obtain its permission every time they brought in goods.[26] On the other hand, Thailand's imports of agricultural products from China increased 200 to 300 percent since the implementation of the early harvest measure in October 2003, and this had a major impact on Thailand's northern farmers.[27] It should be mentioned that Thailand expanded its export of vegetables and fruits to China, too, albeit less dramatically. According to customs statistics, between October and December 2003, Thailand's exports of vegetables and fruits to China grew 130 percent and 40 percent, respectively, while its imports of vegetable and fruits from China jumped 270 percent and 210 percent, respectively.[28] China's apparent reluctance to let the market decide the amount of import of particular items even after it eliminated relevant tariffs on them did not bode well for future FTAs. To address this problem, Thailand and China agreed to simplify the inspection and quarantine procedures by limiting fruits for export to each other to those from export orchards and packing houses registered with relevant authorities, effective from May 1, 2005.[29] How faithfully the new protocol will be implemented remains to be seen.

Japan's Incrementalism

Further promise of broad cooperation was present in negotiations concluded by Japan and Singapore in October 2001.[30] Although Japan drew criticism for excluding most agricultural produce, it did eliminate the tariffs on chemical, petroleum, and plastic products, as well as textiles and apparel. Also, the agreement did not just eliminate tariffs and liberalize trade (in trade in services, investment, and government procurement), it also included a broad range of economic cooperation to expand bilateral exchanges and to reduce transaction costs (pertaining to customs procedures, mutual recognition, movement of natural persons, intellectual property, facilitation of the procedures of accreditation and recognition of certification authorities of electronic signature, and the like). The measures envisioned in the Joint Study Group Report but not implemented with the agreement (such as cross-recognition of privacy marks) were deferred to future cooperation. The Japan-Singapore Agreement for a New Age Economic Partnership (JSEPA), named to reflect the aim of the agreement to promote comprehensive economic partnership, was signed in January 2002 and went into force on November 30, 2002.[31]

In October 2002, about one year after Japan completed negotiations for JSEPA, Prime Minister Junichiro Koizumi and President Vicente Fox Quesada of Mexico agreed that the two governments should start official negotiations for an FTA in November 2002.[32] Once Japan overcame its opposition to FTAs, it chose a non-Asian country with clear economic benefits. This time Japan would have to actually reduce agricultural tariffs. After missing their target for concluding negotiations within approximately one year, the two governments finally reached agreement in substance in March 2004 on the major elements for strengthening their economic partnership.[33] Japan agreed to reduce trade barriers on five sensitive agricultural items (pork, beef, chicken, orange juice, and fresh oranges) and liberalize more than 600 forestry, fishery, and agricultural products (such as pumpkin, broccoli, asparagus, mango, and avocado), as well as sensitive manufactured goods (such as leather and footwear items).[34] In return, Mexico agreed to liberalize steel and automobile items, together with other industrial goods that had had discriminatory tariffs on imports from Japan (because of the North American Free Trade Agreement and an EU-Mexico FTA under high MFN tariffs, 16 percent on average). In addition, the agreement introduced high-level rules on investment, the agreement on service sectors (with a negative list, for the first time for Japan), and the government procurement agreement rectifying the disadvantages for Japanese firms. The Economic Partnership Agreement (EPA) with Mexico was the first FTA in which Japan liberalized sensitive items in the agricultural sector and demonstrated that an FTA could help it overcome domestic political sensitivities if the benefits of the agreements were clearly articulated. The successful conclusion of an FTA with Mexico was indeed an important foundation for Japan's FTA negotiations with other Asian countries.

In March 2000, after more than three years of consideration by think tanks and a business forum, Japan and Korea agreed to start official discussions for a bilateral FTA.[35] Their Joint Study Group (comprising representatives from business, government, and academia, as in the FTAs with Singapore and Mexico) completed its report in October 2003.[36] The two governments finally agreed to launch FTA negotiations in the same month and started their talks in December 2003.[37]

While Japan had been considering FTAs with Mexico and South Korea since the late 1990s, its FTA talks in this period were broadened to other ASEAN countries. In January 2002, on a trip to ASEAN countries, during which he signed the JSEPA, Prime Minister Koizumi also proposed an Initiative for Japan-ASEAN Comprehensive Economic Partnership (CEP).[38] Shortly after, Japan and ASEAN started considering specific measures and by October 2003 had agreed on a framework for comprehensive economic partnership, with plans to start negotiations in 2005.[39] Unlike China, Japan was a developed country governed by the strict General Agreement on Tariffs and Trade (GATT) rules on FTAs, which require a high standard of coverage and cannot allow even less-developed economies to exclude a significant part of the bilateral trade. As a result, Japan had to take a one-by-one approach, identifying countries with good prospects for a successful conclusion of FTA negotiations. That is why it chose to negotiate bilateral FTAs with a few countries before launching FTA talks with ASEAN. Prime Minister Koizumi met Prime Minister Thaksin Shinawatra of Thailand, President Gloria Macapagal-Arroyo of the Philippines, and Prime Minister Datuk Seri Abdullah Ahmad Badawi of Malaysia separately and agreed to launch three bilateral EPA talks.[40] Talks on a Japan-Malaysia EPA (JMEPA) started in January 2004 and talks on a Japan-Philippines EPA (JPEPA) and Japan-Thailand EPA (JTEPA) started in February. On November 29, 2004, Prime Minister Koizumi and President Arroyo confirmed that both sides had agreed in principle on major elements of the bilateral agreement.[41] On December 13, 2005, Prime Minister Koizumi and Prime Minister Abdullah of Malaysia signed the bilateral agreement for an economic partnership.[42] These bilateral negotiations were to form a basis for subsequent negotiations with ten ASEAN countries for a framework agreement for Japan-ASEAN Comprehensive Economic Partnership, which started in April 2005.[43] These are by no means easy negotiations, with substantial liberalization of sensitive agricultural produce as well as of foreign skilled labor such as nurses and caregivers high on the agenda of some of the ASEAN countries.

Sino-Japanese Competition?

Although Japan had been considering FTAs with other ASEAN countries after negotiating one with Singapore, the decisive factor moving it in this direction was the China-ASEAN agreement.[44] It was only natural for Japan to take up the challenge posed by intraregional competitive dynamics, initially amplified by a geopolitical spin by both China and ASEAN, but for different reasons. China was playing the catch-up game and its initial success encouraged Chinese policymakers and observers to declare that its geopolitical standing in the region had markedly improved. Hence more and more statements were issued to show that it was a responsible great power and that its diplomacy had become more mature and self-confident.[45] For their part, the ASEAN countries saw geopolitical significance in the agreement with China and an opportunity to put pressure on Japan. One Singaporean official called the China-ASEAN FTA "a great coup" for it allowed China to start "entrenching" itself in the region. Japan, it was said, needed to respond just as swiftly "in this strategic game."[46]

Tokyo officials presumably capitalized on the urgency of the situation to persuade politicians at home that Japan's resistance to liberalization of sensitive sectors was holding it back in the new trade agreement race. Also, Tokyo did not have the option of invoking WTO's enabling clause for developing members. The pressure was on to make domestic constituencies ready for further liberalization, while getting business inputs to develop new rules and measures that would better address the problems in their business environment.

As Japan showed more signs of favoring an FTA with ASEAN, Singapore adjusted its pressure. A year later, Singapore's Trade and Industry minister George Yeo struck a positive note on Japan-ASEAN CEP, perhaps partly to encourage Japan further and partly to send a signal to Beijing not to relax, noting that "an FTA between Japan and Southeast Asia would be far more beneficial than one with China because the relation between Japan and Southeast Asia is more complementary than the one between China and Southeast Asia."[47] Yeo was also candid about ASEAN's interest in keeping Japan and China competing for relations with ASEAN:

On the question of East Asian FTA, it will be 3 + 10 rather than 10 + 3. The economic size of the three is much larger than the ten. ASEAN will be marginalized. Therefore, we prefer 10 + 1, in a position to deal with Japan, China and ROK separately. On the other hand, vis-à-vis North America, 10 + 3 is effective because we will have stronger bargaining power if we negotiate as East Asia as a whole.[48]

ASEAN's central dilemma is that it is too small to be self-contained and needs to strengthen linkages with non-ASEAN powers even when the intra-ASEAN integration is incomplete. On the one hand, its external relations could give some impetus to its internal integration. On the other hand, if the external powers are too strong, ASEAN could be divided and marginalized. Thus as long as ASEAN integration is incomplete, its strategic interest is to keep external powers competing with one another. In the keynote address at the ASEAN Business and Investment Summit in October 2003, Singapore's prime minister Goh urged ASEAN members to look at the reality of ASEAN integration on the ground:

On tariff reductions, we have done well. . . . But feedback from businesses is that we have not done enough. Traders have made limited use of the preferential treatment under AFTA. . . . [I]t is too costly to apply for preferential tariffs in some ASEAN countries. Companies would rather pay more, than put up with red tape and delays that they would encounter if they applied for preferential treatment under AFTA.

There also remain many non-tariff barriers. Products have to comply with a bewildering range of standards, which vary from one ASEAN country to another.

It is not our geography that holds them [MNCs] back. . . . The time taken for some ASEAN customs authorities to clear the consignments is uncertain. One leading electronics firm observed that identical components sometimes clear customs in one day, sometimes up to five weeks. Such uncertainties translate to higher inventories and higher working capital costs. It makes ASEAN uncompetitive.[49]

Meanwhile, China's new confidence was having a significant effect on its posture toward East Asian regionalism. Initially, as noted earlier, it was focused on the catch-up game. Reacting to the regional trend toward FTAs initiated by Japan and South Korea, China tried to catch up, with considerable success at first, which led it to boast that it would "be much faster than Japan in concluding our negotiations."[50] Such remarks helped boost its profile as a regional leader eager to promote "a multi-polar world" rather than one dominated by the United States.[51] For this strategy to be credible, however, there had to be signs of better Sino-Japanese cooperation. Indeed, China began emphasizing that it did not see itself "in any strategic or economic competition with Japan" and even joined ASEAN in urging Japan to move faster.[52] As Sino-U.S. relations improved after September 11 and Washington worked to secure China's cooperation in its fight against terrorism, however, China stopped using the term "multipolarity," substituting its version of pragmatic, multilayered thinking: "China accepts that while some countries in ASEAN may be close to the U.S., they are not anti-China. That's OK. It is not as if China wants the U.S. out of Asia altogether. . . . In the end, ASEAN does not have to align itself with China. It just does not have to align itself against China."[53]

Washington's Comeback

At the end of the third period, Washington, which had been inactive on the P5 initiative, increased its interest in an FTA with Singapore. When the respective leaders agreed to launch FTA talks, Asian capitals were surprised but no longer alarmed. Once Asian countries started their own FTAs, the fear of the U.S. hub-and-spoke approach subsided.

In the fourth period, under the George W. Bush administration, Washington paid closer attention to the region. China's rise, combined with its active regional economic diplomacy toward ASEAN, including its efforts to promote an FTA, while Japan—the primary ally of the United States in Asia—was stagnating, indicated a potential shift in the regional balance of power. At the same time, a weakened ASEAN invited security concerns, particularly that it might become a hotbed of terrorism. Responding to the moves for a China-ASEAN FTA and other FTAs in the region, the U.S.-ASEAN Business Council submitted a paper to the U.S. government calling for "initial steps toward the creation of a US-ASEAN Free Trade Area."[54]

Washington complied on several fronts. First, the U.S. Trade Representative stepped up its efforts to negotiate an FTA with Singapore, and in August 2002 the Bush administration obtained Trade Promotion Authority (TPA).[55] The U.S.-Singapore FTA achieved a high level of market access (covering goods, services, investment, and government procurement), as well as "ground-breaking" rules, which, in particular, incorporated U.S. digital trade policy agenda (for example, a permanent duty-free moratorium on e-commerce, liberalization of electronically deliverable services, improved protection of intellectual property rights in an online environment, and limited liability for Internet service providers).[56] The agreement was signed in May 2003 and entered into force on January 1, 2004.

Second, the U.S. Trade Representative started to explore other FTA opportunities in ASEAN. However, after looking into the idea of an FTA with ASEAN counterparts in a U.S.-ASEAN meeting of economic ministers held early in April 2002, Trade Representative Robert Zoellick concluded that it was premature to enter into negotiations with ASEAN as a whole and called for a "step-by-step approach."[57] Trade ministers therefore agreed to adopt a work program to further the trade and investment relationships between ASEAN and the United States, which covered areas such as "trade and investment, agriculture, intellectual property rights, information technology, customs and biotechnology."[58]

The United States also began to take concrete steps toward bilateral FTAs. During the same trip, Zoellick agreed with Commerce Minister Adisai Bodharamik of Thailand to begin work on a bilateral trade and investment framework agreement (TIFA) as "building blocks for trade partnership," and in October 2002 they both signed the TIFA.[59] In the same month, President Bush announced a new trade initiative with ASEAN: the Enterprise for ASEAN Initiative (EAI).[60] It established a roadmap to bilateral FTAs between the United States and individual ASEAN members: the United States would expect a potential FTA partner to be a WTO member, and to have concluded a TIFA with the United States. Also, FTAs with ASEAN countries were to be based on the high standards set in the U.S.-Singapore FTA. In essence, the initiative indicated that the United States would be willing to engage in FTA talks with more ASEAN countries, but, unlike China, it would be in no hurry to conclude FTAs if ASEAN countries could not meet U.S. standards. A year later, in October 2003, President Bush announced his intention to launch FTA negotiations with Thailand.[61]

The U.S. business community, however, is still concerned about Washington's relatively low level of attention to East Asia. Despite initiatives such as the EAI, Washington is still preoccupied with the war on terrorism, whereas, according to ASEAN's secretary general Ong Keng Yong, "China wants to be seen as cooperative, friendly and economics-oriented. . . . It qualitatively wants to change Southeast Asia's mindset about China, which is heavy, big and overwhelming."[62] The president of the U.S.-ASEAN Business Council observed: "I've never seen a time when the U.S. has been so distracted and China has been so focused. . . . China is focusing on Southeast Asia like a laser."[63]

More recently, however, Washington has been strengthening cooperation with its allies to demonstrate its role as a guarantor of the peace and stability of the region. In December 2004 it mobilized a massive military operation to provide tsunami aid relief and led an international Core Group that included Australia, Japan, India, Canada, the Netherlands, and the United Nations to coordinate the first stages of the international response.[64] On February 19, 2005, the U.S.-Japan Security Consultative Committee issued a joint statement on the strengthening of the bilateral security and defense cooperation.[65] On April 14, 2005, a State Department official announced that the United States would soon begin a strategic dialogue with the European Union on the general security situation in the Asia Pacific region, with an eye to limiting sales of military equipment to China that put regional peace and security at risk.[66] On May 4, 2005, Secretary of State Condoleezza Rice announced that the United States, Australia, and Japan had agreed to create a trilateral strategic dialogue at the level of foreign minister with the focus on regional security issues.[67]

The United States has also been strengthening economic cooperation with countries in East Asia. On November 17, 2005, U.S. President George W. Bush and seven ASEAN leaders held talks on the sidelines of the APEC summit in Busan, South Korea, and issued a Joint Vision Statement on the ASEAN-U.S. Enhanced Partnership and "agree[d] to work together to conclude a region-wide ASEAN-United States Trade and Investment Framework Agreement (TIFA)."[68] On February 2, 2006, the United States and South Korea announced their intentions to negotiate a bilateral FTA.[69]

Developments in the ASEAN + 3 Forums

Discussions at the ASEAN + 3 summits initially concentrated on long-term visions. In November 2000, as noted in chapter 2, the leaders proposed such ideas as an East Asian summit and a free trade area or a free investment area. In November 2001 the East Asia Vision Group (EAVG) proposed the formation of an East Asian community in a report submitted to the ASEAN + 3 leaders.[70] Its key recommendations included establishing an East Asia Free Trade Area (EAFTA) and liberalizing trade well ahead of the APEC Bogor goal, expanding the Framework Agreement on an ASEAN Investment Area to all of East Asia, establishing a self-help regional facility for financial cooperation, adopting a better mechanism for coordinating exchange rates consistent with both financial stability and economic development, and transforming the annual summit meetings of ASEAN + 3 into an East Asian summit.[71] The leaders asked the East Asia Study Group (EASG) set up in 2000 to assess the EAVG proposals.[72]

In moving outside the ASEAN + 3 framework, East Asian countries recognized that it was more realistic to focus on immediately feasible cooperation. In its November 2002 report to the ASEAN + 3 leaders, the EASG identified 17 concrete short-term measures for East Asian cooperation (for example, the establishment of an East Asia Business Council, a network of East Asian think tanks, and an East Asia forum) and 9 medium- to long-term measures (such as EAFTA, an East Asia investment area, a regional financial facility, a regional exchange rate mechanism, and an East Asian summit).[73] Economic ministers were asked to study and formulate opinions on the gradual formation of an East Asia free trade area.[74] In October 2003 the leaders endorsed the implementation strategy of the short-term measures of the EASG report.[75] The report concluded that the establishment of a free trade area would be a long-term goal carried out in steps to take into account the differences in social, economic, and cultural stages of development among East Asian countries. The East Asian countries plan to let the bilateral and subregional free trade areas take the lead outside the scope of the ASEAN + 3 forums and to eventually integrate them into a pan-regional free trade area.

In other words, the ASEAN + 3 framework is so far a vehicle not for trade liberalization but for economic and technical cooperation in various functional areas such as finance (in ASEAN + 3 finance ministers meeting), information technology, conformance to standards, the environment, energy, and human resources development for small- and medium-sized companies (as occurred at the ASEAN + 3 economic ministers meeting, which met for the first time in May 2000 in Yangon, Myanmar), and labor issues (discussed at the ASEAN + 3 labor ministers meeting). They hold functional ministerial meetings when particular issues become important for the region. In 2003, for example, the special ASEAN + 3 health ministers meeting on severe acute respiratory syndrome (SARS) was convened, and in June 2004 the ASEAN + 3 energy ministers meeting was held for the first time in Manila, the Philippines, to discuss cooperation on energy security in response to the surge in energy demand and oil prices. Some of these matters directly affect trade and investment. By way of example, the Asian Common Skill Standard Initiative for Information Technology (IT) Engineers would allow the countries in the region to share information on the development of IT engineer examinations and facilitate cross-border service trade in IT services. The Conformity Assessment Development Program in Industrial Standards would facilitate East Asian participation in arrangements for international mutual recognition. Courses for countries in the Mekong Basin on laws and practices pertaining to international trade and investment would help improve the quality of legal infrastructure in these countries.[76] Other elements are intended to close the developmental gaps among the members or to facilitate sustainable growth by addressing energy and environmental issues.

East Asia Summit

At the Eighth ASEAN + 3 Summit on November 29, 2004, the leaders agreed to convene the First East Asia Summit (EAS) in Malaysia in 2005.[77] However, they failed to agree on its concept and modalities, including the agenda, membership, and relationship with the existing ASEAN + 3 process, despite the fact that their foreign ministers had pointed out the need for a thorough consideration of these issues, especially since countries differed on these matters.[78] With respect to membership, for instance, Japan argued for including India, Australia, and New Zealand, and having the United States attend as an observer.[79] Malaysia was reportedly reluctant to invite Australia, while Indonesia endorsed Australia's participation.[80] Eventually, in April 2005, ASEAN countries agreed that participants would have to meet the following criteria: they must be a full Dialogue Partner, must accede to the ASEAN Treaty of Amity and Cooperation, and must have substantive relations with ASEAN.[81] Subsequently, the ASEAN + 3 foreign ministers agreed on India's participation and would include Australia and New Zealand if they signed the Treaty of Amity and Cooperation, but not the United States, which had not applied for participation.[82] On July 27, 2005, the ASEAN + 3 foreign ministers agreed that "the first EAS, apart from ASEAN, China, Japan and the Republic of Korea, will be participated in by Australia, India, and New Zealand."[83]

In December 2005 two regional summit meetings were held in Kuala Lumpur, each issuing a declaration. On December 12 the ASEAN + 3 leaders reiterated their "common resolve to realise an East Asian community as a long-term goal" and declared that "the ASEAN Plus Three process will continue to be the main vehicle in achieving that goal" and they would "continue to hold the ASEAN Plus Three Summit annually . . . to guide and provide political momentum to East Asian community building under the ASEAN Plus Three cooperation."[84] Two days later, at the First East Asia Summit, the 16 leaders shared the view that the summit "could play a significant role in community building in this region" and declared that "the efforts of the East Asia Summit to promote community building in this region . . . will form an integral part of the evolving regional architecture."[85] The two declarations did not clarify the specific division of work between the two processes, and how the East Asia summit will affect the course of East Asian regionalism remains to be seen. The participation of India, Australia, and New Zealand might point to the future membership of an East Asian community. Also, the leaders' agreement "that the East Asia Summit will be an open, inclusive, transparent and outward-looking forum in which we strive to strengthen global norms and universally recognised values" suggests that the summit could help remind East Asia of what the global community would expect of it.

Japan-China-Korea Trilateral Cooperation

The development of the ASEAN + 3 forums prompted the + 3 countries (Japan, China, and South Korea) to form a trilateral forum. The process began in November 1999, when three leaders had a breakfast meeting in the margin of the ASEAN + 3 summit, with President Kim's proposal for a joint study by think tanks from the three countries on how to strengthen their economic cooperation. In a 2002 trilateral summit meeting, China's premier Zhu proposed a feasibility study on a trilateral FTA, which was subsequently conducted under the framework of the joint think tank studies, with the understanding that a trilateral FTA was a long-term project. In 2003 the three leaders agreed to launch a joint study by their governments, businesspeople, and academic communities on the possible modality of trilateral investment arrangements to promote investment among them as a more immediate policy agenda than an FTA. The joint study group met for the first time in March 2004 and has since discussed possible improvements in the investment environment in the three countries and the elements of a possible trilateral investment treaty.[86]

In a second meeting, South Korea's contingent compared the Japan-Korea Investment Treaty and the Korea-China Investment Protection Treaty and proposed to use the former as a model for the investment rules, with a high degree of freedom in promoting investment among the three countries.[87] The joint study group recommended that a legal framework concerning investment be explored in a timely manner, noting that Japan and Korea had agreed on the need to consider entering into negotiations on the high-level trilateral investment agreement, whereas China stated it was still premature to enter into such negotiations given the different levels of economic development of the three countries.[88] Foreign ministers of the three countries met on May 7, 2005, in Kyoto and agreed to hold official consultations forthwith concerning a legal framework for investment among the three countries.[89]

Choice of FTA Route: Talking Regional, Acting Bilateral

The state of the FTA race just described can be summarized as "talking regionally, acting bilaterally." Inasmuch as "economic logic favors preferential arrangements among larger, more inclusive groupings," other things being equal, ideally East Asian countries should create an FTA that covers the entire region.[90] Indeed, integration of this extent became a politically correct, popular theme in East Asian capitals. However, actual progress in trade liberalization occurred in bilateral and subregional FTAs.

Forging an all–East Asian FTA in stepwise fashion through bilateral FTAs, rather than all at once, would help countries make the politically difficult adjustments necessitated by the liberalization of sensitive items in each deal. GATT Article 24 regarding developed countries stipulates that an FTA has to cover "substantially all the trade" among its parties. Although there is no standard interpretation of what would constitute "substantially all" trade, precedents under the WTO suggest that an FTA should cover 80 to 90 percent of existing trade. Because of this discipline, an FTA could exert strong pressure to eliminate (not just lower) the tariffs on particular sensitive items in a way that multilateral negotiations would not. This is a benefit of employing FTAs to complement multilateral trade liberalization. An all–East Asian FTA, however, would demand that all the countries in the region drastically liberalize politically sensitive sectors at the same pace (within 10 years).[91] Given the large gaps in the stages of economic development and levels of government capacity to enforce trade agreements, with some economies not even WTO members, a uniform treatment of all the members would be unrealistic.

In addition, a stepwise approach could focus more attention on solving the diverse problems in different countries and hence become a potential model for larger forums. In fact, there would be ongoing feedback among various forums at bilateral, subregional, regional, cross-regional, and global levels: bilateral solutions could find broader applications; and new ideas discussed in larger forums might become legally binding agreements among like-minded economies.

Furthermore, no decision has yet been reached on which economies should participate in an East Asia FTA. Hong Kong and Taiwan, both important nodes in Asian production networks, are members of APEC but not of ASEAN + 3. Similarly, there is no agreement on which extraregional but nearby countries should be considered for FTAs. Australia, New Zealand, and India, the three countries that participated in the East Asia summit of December 2005, are possible candidates. Although these countries are not (at least for now) tightly integrated into Asian production networks and therefore may not necessarily feel as pressed to reduce the various transaction costs of intra-industry trade, FTAs with them would at least help expand export opportunities for East Asian economies. Those more developed economies ready to conclude FTAs did not want to wait for an East Asian FTA to emerge, and individually went ahead with opportunities open to them. The flexibility provided by this stepwise process would allow other economies to strengthen economic relations with current members of ASEAN + 3 and thereby affect the pattern of the interdependence and sense of community in the region, potentially expanding the scope of "East Asia."

On the other hand, independent bilateral FTAs could produce many different rules of origin and other discrepancies, and hence higher transaction costs. Many East Asian capitals, aware of the needs of production networks, naturally have a strong incentive to avoid the "spaghetti-bowl effect," hoping to eventually merge separately negotiated bilateral FTAs into a regional FTA with regional rules of origin and other common rules. This issue is being considered in the design of the FTAs currently under negotiation.

Some might argue that countries with large markets such as Japan and China would have more leverage in a bilateral rather than a regional or multilateral context and thus should prefer bilateral routes. In reality, those two had no practical choice. Japan could not risk infringing the WTO rule or a breakdown of FTA negotiations. China was not ready for an FTA before its accession to the WTO. At the time it became ready, not many countries were in a position to conclude an FTA with it in the short run. In addition, the size of the market is just one of many factors affecting negotiating leverage. For example, a country that is excluded from an existing FTA would be more eager to conclude an FTA because it has a strong incentive to overcome the discrimination. The political dynamics of each bilateral FTA, however, are beyond the scope of this chapter.

Conclusion

In this period, intraregional competitive dynamics—particularly among Japan, China, and the United States—became the most conspicuous force in operation and accelerated the proliferation of bilateral FTAs. Japan's move to conclude FTAs with Singapore and South Korea prompted the United States to start negotiations with Singapore, which in turn persuaded even China to pursue a free trade agreement with ASEAN. China's move had a decisive accelerating impact on the FTA race. So far, the competition has not created conflicts among the three powers but has stimulated constructive responses to each other's moves. With the proliferation of FTAs, the business sector has grown concerned about the spaghetti-bowl effect and is expected to lobby various forums to make bilateral FTAs the building blocks of a pan-regional FTA.

Though overshadowed by the competitive dynamics, intraregional interdependence is now the dominant economic force in East Asia. With further regionalization, East Asian countries grew more interested in facilitating intraregional business transactions. Trade and investment within the region were greatly boosted by the rise of China, which became the factory of the world and an important node in regional production networks. As the intraregional specialization has become finer and the networks more tightly integrated, the need to address increasingly diverse problems concerning transaction costs and the investment environment has become more urgent. At the same time, the rapid growth of the Chinese markets and of complementary relations among East Asian countries has brightened the prospects for significant gains from East Asian regionalism in the future. Thus regionalism is now evolving along a pragmatic track directed at solving specific problems and promoting intraregional economic interdependence, as reflected in the trend toward bilateral FTAs and the choice of specific cooperation programs under the ASEAN + 3 framework. The East Asian countries have started negotiating FTAs with easier partners, so as to increase momentum for liberalization and become better equipped to deal with more difficult partners later on. In choosing cooperation programs, ASEAN + 3 members have identified where their diverse interests converge so that the programs will attract the attention and resources needed to achieve their purposes.

The rise of China also provided a political impetus to promote regionalism. Just when its potential to become the biggest power in the region awakened its neighbors to the risk of volatile transition processes, China's generally more conciliatory foreign policy posture, albeit without a clear indication of its intentions, helped reduce centrifugal forces in the region and build momentum toward a regional community for managing the transition period and integrating China firmly in a rule-based system at the regional level as well.

The role of defensive regionalism has now become less conspicuous or important, with attention focused on how to design and make the best possible use of new policy tools such as East Asian forums and free trade agreements. Also, the challenge of managing the rise of China has strengthened the desire for U.S. blessing and active support of this regional venture, which is still traveling an uncertain path in many respects.

What is the next stage? The FTA bubble could burst if trade agreements fail to realize significant liberalization or are not faithfully implemented, eroding investors' and regional capitals' confidence in East Asian regionalism. Conversely, the countries in the region could start taking practical steps to integrate the separate FTAs into a seamless, pan-regional framework.

Another possibility to consider is that a new fifth period could start (or, in hindsight, might have already started) in which East Asian regionalism might be reconfigured. The speed and impact of China's rise, combined with the recognition of the risks involved in its economic and political systems, has strengthened the desire of other countries to avoid concentrating economic activities in China and to create multiple growth centers in the region.[92] This also adds weight to arguments for forging economic arrangements with countries other than China, within and beyond East Asia. The move to invite India, Australia, and New Zealand to the East Asia summit in December 2005 might turn out to be a precursor to the expansion of community membership or to the creation of a new structural layer, different from either ASEAN + 3 or APEC.

As the preceding chapters have shown, economics and politics have worked hand in hand to shape East Asian regionalism. Even now, the geopolitical implications of China's rise and heightened tensions between Japan and China have renewed the sense that East Asia still lacks the cohesiveness required to put regionalism on a strong foundation. Therefore the role of three major powers—Japan, the United States, and China—would become crucial in determining the course of East Asian regionalism. Just what they could do to improve the economic and political conditions for regional cooperation in East Asia is the subject of chapter 8.

8

Major Powers and East Asian Economic Integration

As the preceding chapters suggest, the major powers that have shaped various frameworks for economic integration in East Asia have just begun to work on how to *actually* reduce transaction costs in the region. For a long time, they were bogged down in the more divisive issues (the membership of various forums or the approach to trade liberalization) instead of focusing on what they could immediately achieve, so as to allow them to build on successful experiences. Interest in substantive issues took hold only recently—in the wake of the Asian financial crisis in the case of Japan, South Korea, and members of the Association of Southeast Asian Nations (ASEAN); under the Bush administration in the case of the United States; and perhaps not yet in the case of China.

Why was it so difficult to focus on pragmatic cooperation until recently? How effective have recent efforts been? And how can the leading powers— Japan, the United States, and China—improve their policies? These are the central questions explored in this chapter. To answer them, one needs to look at the major policy problems for each country: for Japan, the lack of a grand strategy to support its policies; for the United States, its wary attitude toward East Asian regionalism; and for China, the lack of attention to implementation on the ground. Interestingly, their policies have in some ways been conducive to the development of East Asian regionalism and are now coming into a historic alignment that makes a breakthrough possible.

Why Japan, the United States, and China?

The shape of East Asian regionalism will be largely determined by the interaction of the policies of Japan, the United States, and China. As already discussed, Japan-U.S. relations have had a large impact throughout the evolution of East Asian regionalism. China started to play an increasingly important role after joining the World Trade Organization (WTO). The rise of China created new competitive dynamics with Japan and the United States. Without healthy Sino-Japanese relations and a benign (if not positive) attitude on the part of the United States, East Asian regionalism will not make significant progress. Japan and the United States have a common interest in integrating China into the rule-based system both regionally and globally. At the same time, Japan and China, as neighbors, share a keen interest in securing not only peace and stability but also sustainable development and prosperity in the region. With Japan's remaining power resources and its interest in using East Asian regionalism as an impetus to revitalizing its economy and earning due respect and trust in the region, Japan is well positioned to take the initiative in moving East Asian regionalism forward.

At the same time, ASEAN and South Korea can influence the policies of the three powers and facilitate their cooperation and interaction. Whereas ASEAN was a key player (together with Japan and the United States) in the earlier stages of regionalism's evolution in East Asia, after the 1997–98 Asian financial crisis, it became a balancer of other powers. Yet the norms of behavior—equality, mutual respect, pragmatism, and openness—that ASEAN has proposed in various regional forums have played a pivotal role in shaping the norms of East Asian cooperation. The collective impacts of ASEAN members' policies are largely predictable. All in all, ASEAN will continue to remind other powers of these norms, will help mediate and balance those powers, and thus dampen conflict and facilitate their cooperation. Its member countries will try to unite when dealing with external powers and stimulate competition among other powers for influence over ASEAN, so as to make sure none of them gain too much of such influence. They will try to alleviate the tension between the external powers to avoid situations in which they have to choose one over another. They will also compete with each other for the more prominent economic and political roles. ASEAN will show stronger cohesiveness over the issues of critical importance to the association as a whole, but otherwise its members will tend to focus on internal competition. While ASEAN can become more effective if it is more internally united, its role as the watchman and mediator will not change unless it becomes completely confident in one of the powers to lead it, or other powers recede into irrelevance.

South Korea has the resources to influence the interactions of the three powers, though it has not fully used them: its developmental achievements (a liberal democracy and membership in the Organization for Economic Cooperation and Development [OECD]—the only member from Asia except for Japan); its affinity to China; its disposition to balance the influence of China, the United States, and Japan; and its basic approach to the history problem with Japan since the Kim Dae Jung administration (which has been to criticize Japan's apparent lack of sensitivity toward its neighbors' concerns and emotions but to keep the issue from damaging overall bilateral relations).[1] With these resources, it has the potential to facilitate Sino-Japanese reconciliation, the positive involvement of the United States, and the improvement of the quality of rules incorporated in East Asian regionalism.

Japan

Japan's policy toward Asia is not easy to describe, largely because of the way Japan has presented it. Announcements have tended to list specific initiatives for geographical or functional areas without clearly defining a coherent national purpose—how Japan is going to survive the challenges facing it, what kind of country it aims to be, and what role it aims to play in the world.[2] Japan has not been explicit about its national purpose because its Asia policy was developed separately from domestic policies, in other words, without requiring significant adjustments of domestic economic structure and thus without much internal coordination. The inconsistency between domestic and external policies has been exacerbated by the fact that Japan is in the process of a major policy shift: from the postwar paradigm, which implicitly viewed the nation as a separate entity from the rest of Asia and dealt with Asia as a collection of bilateral relations, to a new one that aims to foster East Asian regionalism and embed Japan in an increasingly integrated Asia. Japan's policy toward East Asian regionalism needs to be understood in the context of this transition.

Old Paradigm

Japan's external policy in the postwar era, particularly its Asia policy, was initially shaped by the legacy of World War II. It returned to the international community as a "former enemy" and naturally became a regime taker. It concentrated on economic development under the U.S. security umbrella by expanding exports mainly to the United States, other industrial countries, and Asian developing countries. Japan's economic dependence on the West and trauma of defeat in the war led to two major characteristics of its post-war regional policy. First, Japan became a staunch but reactive multilateralist in trade policy. As in its prewar nightmare, regionalism meant discrimination against Japan in its major markets and therefore was something to be condemned. Second, Japan refrained from taking the initiative in formulating regional frameworks in general, "haunted by the failure of the Greater East Asian Co-Prosperity Sphere and World War II."[3] The understanding that Japan's prewar "Asianism" was "born of Japan's aversion to the West rather than compassion toward Asia" bred a notion that Japan's fascination with Asia would necessarily be anti-Western at bottom and contrary to its national interests.[4] The concern that "a coherent Asia policy could be mistaken for a resurgence of prewar 'Asianism'" apparently dominated the minds of Japanese policymakers.[5]

Japan's postwar economic relations with Asia started through reparations, later replaced by official development assistance (ODA), which financed government-led projects for infrastructure and natural resources in the recipient countries and provided markets for Japanese products and resource supplies for Japan. An important objective of Japan's economic policies toward these countries was to allocate and manage ODA and export credit on a bilateral basis. There was no economic necessity to deal with Asia or East Asia as a region.

Transition

The surge in foreign direct investment (FDI) following the Plaza Accord (described in chapter 3) fundamentally changed Japan's economic relations with Asia. Japanese firms developed production networks throughout the region and contributed to the expansion of intraregional trade—not just between Japan and other Asian countries but also between countries other than Japan. The exchange rate adjustments of currencies in newly industrializing economies (NIEs) that followed the yen appreciation prompted firms in those economies to invest in other Asian countries. Reducing transaction costs in the region thus became an important agenda of common interest there. Friction over the large trade surplus with the United States, which spread to other Asian countries, was another factor. The fundamental solution to this problem was to stimulate domestic demand-led growth in Japan and other Asian countries through deregulation and privatization, which was not a bilateral agenda but a common regional agenda. Thus the regionalization of the Asian economy turned Japan's economic relations with Asia from a collection of bilateral ties to a web of relations among Asian countries.

Japan's policy change lagged behind the economic reality. The halfway adjustment led to a policy that sent mixed signals, consisting in part of promoting Asian industrialization through ODA and encouraging Japanese FDI, on the one hand, and discouraging cheap imports in sensitive sectors where Asian countries had comparative advantages, on the other. Though it started to take a regional approach through Asia Pacific Economic Cooperation (APEC) and ASEAN-Japan forums, its external and domestic economic policies remained barely integrated. Policy measures implemented through these forums seldom required changes in domestic regulations. For example, while APEC provided an additional channel of external pressure on Japan for desired changes, Tokyo has yet to achieve a national consensus to transform its domestic economic structure through liberalization and deregulation of protected sectors. It remained reactive toward the APEC liberalization agenda, even though it had argued that Asian countries had an incentive to liberalize on a voluntary basis. If Japan could not bring much to the regional table, it could not expect significant progress in the regional agenda. As for ASEAN-Japan forums, while Japan helped provide a forum for government-business cooperation and helped less-developed countries build the capacity to facilitate intra-ASEAN integration, this did not provide much impetus to Japan's own efforts at liberalization and deregulation.

In the meantime, the controversy surrounding the East Asia Economic Caucus (EAEC) revealed the dichotomy between the tendency of older generations to see the EAEC proposal through a prewar prism and the views of younger generations, which wondered why Japan did not even try to persuade both the United States and other East Asian countries that Japan's participation in an East Asian forum was not anti-Western or would not lead to Japan's domination of the region—and why Japan was not yet free of the prewar obsession. This argument was deemed reckless and did not prevail in the early 1990s—shortly after the end of cold war, when there was a lot of uncertainty about the future of the U.S. security presence in Asia and U.S.-Japan economic frictions were becoming fierce, which could further dampen U.S. public support for its security commitment.

New Thinking

In the latter half of the 1990s, after the initial uncertainty about the U.S. security commitment in Asia was dispelled and the WTO provided the settlement mechanism that helped prevent disputes from being politicized, both Tokyo and Washington, perhaps to different degrees, seemingly became more relaxed about East Asian forums. There was a growing awareness in Japan that it would only be natural for the national interests and priorities of the two countries, each responsible to its own people, to be dissimilar. As a corollary, there was a sense that Japan should not remain reactive but start to be proactive and shape the international environment to secure peace and prosperity in the region, particularly by engaging the entire region in a web of economic interdependence. Somewhat counterintuitively, it seems Japan-U.S. relations can be more stable if Japan becomes a more mature and independently capable power. If basic goals are shared and there is trust between them, Japan should not have to worry about U.S. reactions and hesitate to participate in an East Asian forum.

In the late 1990s, seeing what the Asian financial crisis had done to Japan's markets and the high degree of economic interdependence in the region, the government decided to review its Asia policy, which had previously consisted of unilateral assistance and investment. It also saw that exports to the booming U.S. market were an enormous factor in the Asian recovery, regardless of what Japan had done to help Asian economies get over the worst of the crisis. Clearly, Japan's financial assistance could not make up for the economic stagnation at home. A turning point in Japan's view of its relations with the rest of Asia came in November 1999 when a report submitted to Prime Minister Keizo Obuchi emphasized the interdependence between Japan and the region and the importance of opening Japan if it was to revitalize its economy and society, and nurture Asia's confidence in it. The report urged the government to adapt to "the historical trend of globalization," marked by the mutually complementary movement of people, goods, money, and information: "If one of them stops, it creates large distortions in the others."[6]

In fact, opening Japan was not just a means of pulling its economy out of the recession but a much-needed strategy for improving its long-term welfare, which now depends on its capacity to gain from new opportunities in Asia. The rise of China has made these prospects even more realistic to the business community and general public, particularly since the "China threat" argument has been put to rest.[7] Businesses can substantially enhance their competitiveness by capitalizing on close and abundant cheap labor and other strengths available in the region, and thereby focus on higher value-added activities that can be sold globally as well as in rapidly growing regional markets. Consumers will gain from lower prices. Developing economies in the region can enjoy stronger growth thanks to increased export to Japan and, in turn, provide it with larger markets.[8]

If this strategy of positioning itself as a key link in Asian business networks is to be viable, Japan must help improve the efficiency of regional networks by reducing transaction costs not only between itself and other nodes in Asia but also between other nodes. Thus Japan should, on the one hand, accelerate domestic regulatory reform and trade liberalization and enhance the efficiency of the business environment at home. On the other hand, it should create a stable mechanism to improve business environments elsewhere in the region. The relevant policy measures are legally binding agreements at various—bilateral, regional, and global—levels to liberalize trade and investment, most notably through the WTO and free trade agreements (FTAs), as well as functional cooperation, using ODA as needed, to help developing countries build their institutional capabilities.[9]

Enabler

Can Japan formulate this line of new thinking into a coherent strategy and implement it? Despite the relative decline of its economic weight in the region, Japan still has several important advantages, beginning with its manufacturing competitiveness, particularly as the supplier of key components, high-tech materials and machine tools, technology, and capital. Therefore investment from Japan offers East Asian economies a promising vehicle to link up with globally competitive production networks. Second, its mature consumer market is still the largest and the most sophisticated in the region—a breeding ground of innovative goods and services. Third, its rule of law and institutional capabilities are indispensable in taking the initiative in designing institutional frameworks.

Constraints

However, Japan's external policy is constrained by the "dual structure" of its industrial sector: part is competitive and part protected and inefficient, with the former expected to earn national wealth to be distributed to the latter.[10] In the postwar era, this system helped develop domestic mass markets with little income disparity that nurtured domestic manufacturers. Increasingly, however, it created a high-cost business and living environment. Now the Japanese population is aging and shrinking, limiting the long-term prospects for the growth of domestic demand. High-performing firms, increasingly under competitive pressure, could shift more of their operations overseas at will, while inefficient firms would remain at home with limited prospects of contributing to the nation's welfare. The dual structure has become unsustainable as the costs of protecting the weak have become prohibitive in a low-growth environment. This structure prevents Japan from making bold offers, deprives it of negotiating leverage in global trade liberalization or FTAs, and limits its potential to gain better access to export markets.

Criticism of Japan's economic structure and its efforts to rectify it is nothing new. The Maekawa Report of 1986, for instance, advocated a shift from export-led to domestic demand-led growth through macroeconomic stimulus and deregulation.[11] Subsequent recommendations, responding to the persistent bilateral trade imbalance between Japan and the United States, appeared in a series of talks such as the Structural Impediments Initiative launched in 1989 and the Framework Talks started in 1993.[12] These initiatives had limited results in terms of restructuring the Japanese economy. Their focus was on the macroeconomic imbalances, to which the most direct remedy was macroeconomic stimulus to Japan (and the reduction of U.S. fiscal deficits). While sector-specific trade frictions as well as the Japanese government efforts to reduce business costs in the wake of the sharp appreciation of the yen in 1995 brought about significant achievements, such as deregulation in telecommunications, financial services, energy, retailing, and transportation, these efforts were mostly made to the extent necessary to manage external pressure and were not enough to transform Japan's economic structure as a whole.[13] Even if the political will is there, however, this structure cannot be changed overnight.

For a long time, Japan did not have (or need) adequate external markets in corporate resources, which led to a shortage of general managers and professionals required for corporate restructuring. In the absence of well-functioning labor markets, the skills of the unemployed failed to match the skills needed in new sectors, adding to the public's anxiety about losing their jobs. The Japanese political system has also tended to reinforce the status quo. Uneven voting power in favor of rural areas, where a significant proportion of voters are employed in protected, subsidized sectors, in addition to well-organized vested interest groups, has helped politicians who resist structural reform stay in power. The resulting inertia in economic, social, and political structures has made Japan's transformation all the more difficult and limited its ability to move decisively toward regionalism. Like dominos, new efforts to try new ways and change expectations have been falling to the wayside and will keep doing so until they reach a critical mass that will awaken political leaders to the need for a new national consensus.

Also important, Japanese firms, unlike their U.S. counterparts, have been slow to press the government for institutional solutions to their problems. Instead, they tend to negotiate and manage problems on an ad hoc basis.[14]

While such skills are valuable at the corporate level in adapting to the existing environment, they do not help shape new institutional frameworks at the government level.

Finally, the lack of political leadership in addressing lingering history problems and neighboring countries' distrust of Japan will eventually hinder its efforts to build a regional community. Since the end of the cold war, the nature of the history problem has changed. Asian people freely express their concerns about Japan's recognition of "history" issues and bring up individual claims for compensation for their wartime sufferings. Government-to-government settlement of war-related claims does not guarantee public support for reconciliations, upon which the ultimate solution of this problem depends. As many Asian policymakers have pointed out, if Japan hopes to gain the confidence of its neighbors, it needs to articulate its national strategy and the role it is willing to play in the region. To do so, it will have to undertake a long-overdue comprehensive review of its national strategy. Whether Japan can meet this historic challenge and earn trust and due respect from the international community and its neighbors, in particular, will have a great impact on the confidence and vitality of its citizens and thus its quality and attractiveness as a society.

FTAs as an Educational Process

FTAs have the potential to help Japan overcome these various constraints. First, although there is not yet a national consensus on dismantling the dual structure described earlier, the FTA could help the public become more aware of the structure's problems by scrutinizing the rationale for protecting various sectors and making the case that exposing weak sectors to competition will accelerate reform and strengthen the economy as a whole.[15]

The problem in the case of sensitive items is that the public is seldom aware of the cost of protection. While the multilateral trade negotiations through the WTO would be the most effective way to liberalize politically sensitive items on a nondiscriminatory basis, global negotiations take place only once in a while and take several years to complete. The process is so complex that the cost of being reactive and defensive is not clearly visible to the public.

In contrast, the cost of losing an FTA deal and the factors to blame are clearly visible; if Japan cannot liberalize certain key items, it will lose the deal and the other party will likely go ahead and conclude separate deals with some other countries, increasing discrimination against Japan. Each FTA deal has a different set of sensitive items. If the benefits of a particular FTA can be fully articulated, it will be possible to overcome resistance to them. The Japanese government has carefully chosen the countries with which to negotiate FTAs, the criterion being that perceived benefits are large enough to over-come political resistance involved in each deal. The agreement with Singapore was the first step to break the norm of treating sensitive sectors as a whole as sanctuaries and to start item-by-item considerations.[16] The agreement with Mexico was the first to eliminate tariffs on sensitive agricultural produce imported in large volume as well as to liberalize those not previously imported. It was an achievement unthinkable just a few years ago. The suc-cessful experience of relatively easy reforms could further change expectations and open up opportunities for more difficult reforms down the road. It could have an effect not only on eliminating sensitive tariffs (as discussed in the next subsection) but also on liberalizing services and allowing foreign profession-als to work in Japan.

Second, the process of designing and negotiating FTAs provides valuable training for government officials and businesspeople. While the WTO is slow to take up new issues in the negotiation agenda, FTAs can be designed flexibly once the other governments agree. As noted in chapter 7, Japan and Singapore strove to incorporate into their partnership agreement (JSEPA) a wide range of innovative policy measures to reduce transaction costs between them. The creative process of designing the JSEPA in close consul-tation with the business community gave Japanese officials new confidence that such an exercise would enable them to identify specific problems and practical solutions. Indeed, it provided new channels for the business com-munity to influence the design of the institutional frameworks that have a profound impact on their business environment. Such new opportunities in turn motivated businesses to give more systematic attention to the problems they face. The frequent contact between various agencies of government and business throughout the preparatory and negotiating processes could also help the policy thinking of different agencies converge, alleviating the problem of the stovepipe system.[17] The process helps government officials draw lessons from the policy "best practices" of other countries, understand their challenges better, and become more sensitive to their perceptions of and expectations for Japan and the region as a whole. In addition, it stimu-lates reflection on Japan's domestic rules and regulations, and on the attributes of rules and regulations that are potential models for other coun-tries or international rules. This will add to the internal drive necessary for microeconomic reform and the eventual dismantlement of Japan's dual structure.

Shifting Coalitions, Emerging Consensus

Since Japan started negotiating FTAs, the question of how to reform and liberalize agriculture has come to be discussed in a much more open and positive way, which shows that the efforts to conclude FTAs have had a transforming effect on Japan's domestic debate. Such discussions were stimulated by scandals such as Snow Brand Milk's food poisoning case in 2000 and the beef buyback fraud cases in 2001.[18] These incidents were vivid reminders that "the agriculture sector, however protected, would be doomed if it lost consumers' trust and support."[19] Afterward, farmers and food businesses made an all-out effort to become more market-oriented and impress consumers with the quality and safety of their products.

Agricultural policy protection not only weakened Japanese agriculture but also failed to win strong public support. In a public opinion poll on agricultural trade conducted by the Prime Minister's Office in July 2000, 82 percent of the respondents preferred domestic produce because of safety concerns, 78 percent expressed concern about the future of Japan's food self-sufficiency, 63 percent said agriculture should be reformed and strengthened enough to survive international competition, and 5 percent favored removing agriculture from protection.[20] Only 21 percent believed agriculture should be given a "handicap" to compensate for the disadvantages of natural and geographical conditions.[21]

Another factor affecting policy in this sector has been the rise in export opportunities. The sales of apples from the Aomori Prefecture and pears from the Tottori Prefecture to Taiwan, for example, have climbed and brightened the prospects for more sales to the high-end markets of increasingly affluent consumers in Asia.[22] The Ministry of Agriculture, Forestry and Fisheries (MAFF) renewed its efforts to help farmers explore and capitalize on new market opportunities in cooperation with the Japan External Trade Organization (JETRO) and local governments.[23] Since Japan's export of agriculture, forestry, and fisheries was less than one-twentieth of its import, expansion here could not immediately match import increases.[24] Nevertheless, the interest in exports has the potential to alter the mind-set of the agricultural sector in favor of competition and innovation. It could lead to a network of specialization in East Asia with Japan focusing on growing high-end produce, for example, and developing new seeds and saplings.

In recent FTA negotiations, Prime Minister Junichiro Koizumi sent a clear signal on agricultural reform and liberalization, and the importance of avoiding "an agricultural closed-door policy": "We have to face the reality that foreign agricultural produce flows into our markets. We should think about what kind of structural reform is necessary."[25] Indeed, FTAs are now more widely accepted in the sector's official circles, as demonstrated by MAFF's willingness to deal with them "positively and strategically."[26] Furthermore, the ministry has planned to devise a program for drastic reforms of its rice policy, deregulation of corporations' entry into agriculture, and reorganization of its item-by-item price stabilization scheme into one that would provide direct payment to professional, full-time farmers.[27] MAFF's position has apparently moved closer to that of more reformist elements in the government, as reflected in a senior official's clear support for a direct payment scheme and reduction in tariff protection. The old system not only dampened trade policy initiatives and put a heavy burden on consumers, but it also distorted incentives to produce high-cost rice well in excess of the demand at the expense of other produce and thereby failed to maintain Japan's self-sufficiency in food.[28] A shift to direct payment would meet strong political resistance, however, as it would mean denying subsidies to about 80 percent of all farmers, who are not dedicated, full-time farmers.[29] Although the cabinet approved MAFF's Basic Plan for Food, Agriculture and Rural Areas in March 2005, the plan had been diluted and the direct payment system designed to apply only to products (such as barley, soybeans, sugar beets, and potatoes for starch) that suffered from foreign competition with border measures too low to compensate for inferior production conditions.[30] Price props for rice will not be replaced by direct payment until the protection of rice is reduced enough to reveal the difference in conditions for production through WTO negotiations. In short, the FTA negotiations induced agricultural policy reforms but left the most difficult part to WTO negotiations.

Another significant development is that the business community is no longer reluctant to voice a critical opinion about agriculture for fear of alienating an important customer base.[31] Its more proactive attitude and willingness to do its share in shaping public policy go beyond agricultural issues. Since the late 1990s, the business sector has striven to shed excess capacity, focus on core competitiveness, and explore new opportunities. Persistent stagnation has also made business much less tolerant of regulations and protections that add to its costs without effectively achieving their stated purposes.

Long-Term Vision Left Open-Ended

The long-term vision for East Asian regionalism has not been clearly articulated. Regional capitals are more interested in what they can agree and cooperate on today rather than in the future. Tokyo has been slow to propose its vision. In January 2002 Prime Minister Koizumi called for the creation of a "community that acts together and advances together" (which later that year Koizumi referred to as "an initiative for a growing East Asian community") "through expanding East Asia cooperation founded upon the Japan-ASEAN relationship."[32] He expected the core members of this community to be "the countries of ASEAN, Japan, China, the Republic of Korea, Australia and New Zealand." To this end, he suggested making use of the framework of ASEAN + 3 and also listed trilateral cooperation between Japan, China, and South Korea; an ASEAN-China FTA; and economic partnership between ASEAN and Australia and New Zealand. These and other similar cooperative initiatives would contribute to the realization of such a community. Foreign Minister Yoriko Kawaguchi elaborated on Koizumi's proposal, noting that

> Japan does not intend to materialize East Asian regional cooperation by putting an institution first. We would like to accumulate functional cooperation such as the economic partnership that promotes the transition to market economy and cooperation on trans-border issues, and hope that the accumulated experience of such cooperation will lead to the construction of a community in East Asia, where its members share the sense that they should "act together and advance together."[33]

Neither Koizumi nor Kawaguchi specified the sequence of measures that would be used to build an East Asian community.

Clear FTA Strategy

Whereas Tokyo's vision of an East Asian community is vague on specifics, except to urge the region's countries to build on the ASEAN + 3 process as a central mechanism, its FTA strategy is clearly laid out. Its first priority is to negotiate high-standard agreements with South Korea and ASEAN.[34] Japan already has JSEPA, and Korea and Singapore also concluded an FTA (which entered into force in March 2006). By the time the three countries complete the bilateral FTAs, a regional standard could emerge that is applicable to higher-income countries. In the meantime, Japan and ASEAN have clarified the relationship between bilateral FTAs between Japan and individual ASEAN members, on the one hand, and an FTA between Japan and ASEAN as a whole, on the other:

> 1. Japan and ASEAN will start the consultations on the Japan-ASEAN CEP [comprehensive economic partnership] on the liberalisation of

trade in goods, trade in services, and investment, from the beginning of 2004 by discussing the basic principles of Japan-ASEAN cumulative rules of origin and customs classification and collecting and analysing trade and custom[s] data.

2. Japan and ASEAN will initiate a negotiation on the CEP Agreement between Japan and ASEAN as a whole, taking into account the achievements of bilateral negotiations between Japan and each ASEAN Member State, and the further progress of the ASEAN integration process. Such Agreement should be consistent with the WTO Agreement.

3. During the negotiation, those ASEAN Member States that have not concluded bilateral Economic Partnership Agreement ("EPA") with Japan will negotiate concessions bilaterally. Schedules of liberalisation concessions between Japan and those ASEAN Member States that have concluded a bilateral EPA should not be renegotiated in the negotiation of the Japan-ASEAN CEP Agreement. All schedules of liberalisation concessions will be annexed to the Japan-ASEAN CEP Agreement.[35]

In short, bilateral FTAs are modules with common rules that are supposed to become parts of the Japan-ASEAN CEP once the latter is agreed on (bilateral schedules not agreed on before the CEP rule is established will be negotiated according to it).

As noted in chapter 3, one of Japan's policy objectives, which it has consistently pursued since before it started to explore FTAs, is to promote intra-ASEAN integration, which will enhance the competitiveness of Japanese (as well as other) production networks involving various ASEAN countries. This also informs Japan's policy for an FTA with ASEAN, the aim of which is to add impetus to the integration of ASEAN economies. The problem is that East Asian countries are so diverse and burdened with political resistance that an all–East Asian FTA is not immediately feasible. The issue therefore is how to balance the three policy objectives: first, to apply incremental pressure on domestic reform with doable FTAs; second, to avoid the proliferation of ad hoc, mutually inconsistent rules through overlapping bilateral FTAs (the "spaghetti-bowl" effect); and third, to make sure that the resulting frameworks can earn the trust of investors with their quality, arrived at through high-standard, transparent, and enforceable rules that prompt the governments to strengthen the rule of law.

Japan's answer was to first focus on stimulating domestic reform through doable FTAs. When it has brighter prospects for overcoming domestic resistance, it could extract common elements from the FTAs with more advanced economies and develop a proposed set of regional rules, which should have two parts: core elements that will apply to all the economies in the region, on the one hand, and add-on elements to be adopted as economies in the region become more developed and ready for them, on the other. Japan is also prepared to address capacity building and other relevant needs so as to accelerate the efforts of less-developed economies to establish solid market economy institutions and the rule of law, and to liberalize their trade and investment.

By the time bilateral FTAs have converged into a Japan-ASEAN FTA, it is also hoped that the Japan-Korea FTA will share common rules and structure so that the liberalization schedules agreed between South Korea and ASEAN members can in turn become part of a regional FTA between Japan, South Korea, and ASEAN. Thus the conflict of different rules of origin will only be temporary. Also, while there is a risk of the spaghetti-bowl effect, the business sector, as noted in chapter 2, can avoid it by giving up on preferential tariffs and sticking with most favored nation (MFN) tariffs. The problem of the rules of origin is more important in an environment with high MFN tariffs. Global trade liberalization will eventually rectify the spaghetti-bowl effect and provide an additional incentive for Japan to promote WTO negotiations.

Some argue that Japan should pursue a customs union instead of overlapping bilateral FTAs in order to eliminate complex rules of origin and make the regional markets indeed seamless.[36] A customs union, however, requires the participating countries to adopt common external tariffs. With Singapore's tariffs at 0 percent except for a few alcohol products, the external tariffs of an East Asian customs union would be 0 percent for the most part—which is essentially the same as complete liberalization on an MFN basis. Although a customs union theoretically provides an attractive alternative, it does not yet seem to suit the situation in the region. If East Asian countries one day achieve 0 percent MFN tariffs, however, it will then be feasible for them to adopt a common market approach by harmonizing standards and eliminating various procedures at national borders to further reduce transaction costs. On the other hand, countries participating in the common market initiative will have to accept rules and regulations unified at the regional level and thus the associated loss of autonomy in trade negotiations with nonmember countries. There is a trade-off between achieving a seamless business environment within the region and flexibly adopting new models of rules and regulations in and outside the region.

As for a possible partnership with China, Japan's position on whether and when to start actual negotiations will probably depend on "such factors as the quality of China's implementation of the WTO agreements, the condition of overall Japan-China relations, and the progress in its EPA/FTA with ASEAN and [Korea]."[37] Seoul seems to share the same sequential approach, although powerful minorities in business and academic groups argue that South Korea should first conclude an FTA with China.[38] In a newspaper interview in February 2004, Lee Jong-seok, deputy secretary general of the National Security Council, expressed hopes to see South Korea and Japan conclude an FTA and visa exemptions within the next year so as to promote economic and private exchanges. Subsequently, "China and North Korea, which started its transition to market economy, will participate in the joint efforts. The year 2005 should be the starting point."[39]

Economic logic dictates that China will eventually be indispensable to East Asian cooperation. It is by far the largest country in size and population. It has been Japan's largest source of imports since 2002, became Japan's largest trading partner in 2004 if combined with Hong Kong, and will eventually become the biggest economic power in the region. In a survey of businesspeople asking for Japan's high-priority FTA partners, 55 percent of the respondents named ASEAN, 53 percent the United States, and 49 percent China.[40] Another survey of corporate managers of Japan, China, and South Korea found that 70 percent of Japanese managers, 64 percent of their Chinese counterparts, and 75 percent of Korean managers believed an FTA among Japan, China, and South Korea was necessary.[41] In time, China will fully implement the WTO rules and become ready for additional rules such as FTAs. While many worry about a severe impact on agriculture and labor-intensive industries in Japan, most of Japan's tariffs are much lower than those of China.[42] A large volume of imports, with significant cost advantages, has overcome the existing tariffs and flowed into Japan anyway, whereas China's tariffs still remain high after its WTO accession. Therefore Japan stands to gain more than China does from eliminating the tariffs. Because eliminating nontariff barriers is important to achieve the desired outcome and it is more urgent to rectify problems encountered by Japanese firms already operating in China, however, Japan has proposed that Japan, South Korea, and China conclude a trilateral investment agreement.

Economic logic does not always dictate the choice of FTA partners, however. After all, FTA partners give special favor to each other beyond the MFN treatment under the WTO. When China fully implements the WTO and no economic logic stands in the way, the overall bilateral relationship will become the most important factor. At that point, Tokyo will need to garner public support for an FTA with China that is strong enough to overcome the remaining resistance to further liberalization and the lingering concern about forging a special relationship with a country with which it has a deep-seated mutual distrust.

Membership of a Regional Community

Japan's long-term vision for an East Asian community is open-ended not only in terms of its core objectives and agenda but also its membership. Prime Minister Koizumi proposed that its core members be the countries of ASEAN, Japan, China, South Korea, Australia, and New Zealand, but he also advocated making the best use of ASEAN + 3, which does not include Australia and New Zealand. As for FTAs or economic partnerships, Japan's first partner choices are Korea and ASEAN. Recognizing the increasing cooperation between ASEAN and India, some have speculated it may even prove possible "to create an expansive, pan-Asian economic area, extending from East to South Asia."[43]

Underlying this open-endedness are pragmatic considerations. As discussed in relation to APEC in chapter 5, it is difficult to designate a primary forum in the region and put it in charge of all the agenda. By contrast, a multilayered system allows various countries, with their different interests and priorities, to cooperate flexibly. After all, regionalism is not an end in itself but a means to achieving peace and prosperity in a way that complements global frameworks.

The reduction of transaction costs, for example, should eventually be achieved at the global level inasmuch as regionalism is adopted to accelerate and improve the global process. It does this by stimulating domestic reforms and increasing the region's voice in the global process, while reaping the benefits of deeper integration early on wherever economic reality has given high priority. How broad the region of deeper integration should be depends on the degree of potential gains. The most important factor to consider is the level and nature of de facto economic integration (not just in terms of the share in the total value of trade but also the level of coordination necessary to sustain the drive for higher efficiency in the business activities operating there). In the case of East Asia, governments hoping to have their economies integrated in and gain from the production networks have a strong incentive to reduce transaction costs and improve the performance of the entire network, where parts and components go back and forth among factories in close proximity for numerous processing and assembly tasks, with a tight schedule and low inventory, before being shipped to final markets. Other important considerations are the current level of transaction costs and the potential of future economic integration. In a region as dynamic as Asia, where new linkages are constantly being explored and developed and the geographical frontier of tightly knit business networks is expanding, it makes economic sense to leave the membership of regional arrangements open-ended. For example, Australia, New Zealand, and India, which are close to but not in East Asia, are not yet fully integrated into Asian production networks. Nevertheless, they may be part of a broader Asian community in the future, as indicated by their participation in the East Asia summit of December 2005.

If the problems have geographical or other unique regional aspects, the regional frameworks devised to address them will have a more permanent nature. For example, the ASEAN + 3 processes deal with not only the reduction of transaction costs but also potential sources of instability such as energy, environment, and transportation safety failings, though some of these issues might as well be addressed within broader forums. Regional frameworks will continue to explore and identify specific problems suitable for them to solve. However, the ASEAN + 3 does not cover all of East Asia. Most notably, it does not include Taiwan and Hong Kong, both APEC members and important nodes in the East Asian business networks, because of Beijing's objection. Given the importance of these economies, the solutions derived at the ASEAN + 3 frameworks may need to be expanded to take these economies into account. In the future, countries and economies that are geographically in East Asia but not included in the ASEAN + 3 processes will eventually participate in them.

A regional community is based not just on economic considerations but also on a sense of community and desire to ensure peace and stability in the neighborhoods. The region's vision of an East Asia community also has a broader political perspective, which Japan shares, namely, that economic cooperation should ensure less-developed economies are helped to integrate and converge with the rest of the region. Japan also shares with other East Asian countries the understanding that ASEAN + 3, albeit not perfect, offers the best foundation on which to build an East Asian community. The lack of participation of Australia and New Zealand is not likely to alter Japan's willingness to deepen cooperation under the ASEAN + 3 framework, where the middle powers of South Korea and ASEAN hope for a stable relationship between Japan and China, the two regional powers with unstable political relations.[44] ASEAN + 3 therefore offers an important vehicle that Japan and China can use to deepen functional cooperation and solidify economic interdependence even when their political relations are not conducive to deepening cooperation on a bilateral basis. Of course, regional forums are no substitute for the political will the two powers need to improve their bilateral relations. In the final analysis, prospects for East Asian regionalism depend on the relations between Japan and China.

Japan's Grand Strategy behind East Asian Regionalism

The essence of Japan's grand strategy is, first, to maintain and strengthen, as necessary, the security alliance with the United States, and, second, to capitalize on East Asian economic growth to revitalize its economy and eventually build an East Asian community to secure peace, stability, and prosperity in the region, in the interest of Japan's own economy and security.

These are compatible goals. While it is often pointed out that American public support "for the continuing U.S. security role in Asia depends partly on their sense of whether the U.S. is treated fairly economically," promoting East Asian regionalism not as a closed, inward-looking bloc but as part of the multilayered international economic institutions, where the WTO takes precedence, should not be interpreted as unfair economic treatment for the United States.[45] On the contrary, East Asian cooperation will make the region more economically dynamic and its markets more robust for the United States and the rest of the world. It might possibly even help rectify the large current account imbalance between the United States and East Asia. It will certainly help Japan revitalize its economy and earn trust in the region, making it a more valuable ally for the United States. If East Asian regionalism succeeds in promoting peace and stability, that will also help reduce the U.S. security burden in the region. Japan's strategy is to use an East Asian community as a force for positive changes in the region.

Prospects

Though Japan's FTA policy has been incremental and prudent, and has been given high priority, it is not supported by an articulated grand strategy or long-term vision for the region. This stems from the fact that Japan is still in transition from its old paradigm, of having the competitive sectors shoulder the burden of creating national wealth while shielding the weak sectors from international competition, to a new paradigm, of opening and reforming its economy and actively developing complementary economic relations with its neighbors. Without a grand strategy to bolster its policy for developing East Asian regionalism, Japan cannot decisively undertake economic reforms at home or eliminate the causes of neighboring countries' distrust.

Despite the limitations, Japan has finally started visibly restructuring its economy, driven by corporate restructuring and supported by policy changes, though not yet systematic in nature. With consumers becoming more critical of the effectiveness of government policies in providing public health, safety, and economic security, there may be less political support for policies that protect inefficient sectors of the economy under the name of those objectives. The country as a whole is coming to recognize that doing nothing will make it uncompetitive and irrelevant, whereas East Asian regionalism will help revitalize its economy and earn Japan due respect in the international community.

The United States

U.S. interests in Asia, said to be "remarkably consistent" over time, have focused mainly on "peace and security; commercial access to the region; freedom of navigation; and the prevention of the rise of any hegemonic power or coalition."[46] Another consideration has been "to spread value systems preferred by Americans."[47] Of these interests, "peace and stability" may well be the ultimate goal, and the others "fundamental principles to guide American policy in the region . . . as the surest way to preserve peace and stability in the region."[48]

The security-centered character of U.S. policy toward Asia was spelled out in a 1995 Department of Defense report noting "security comes first," and "the American security presence has helped provide this 'oxygen' for East Asian development."[49] Until recently, the United States had not tried to actively shape the regional economic order, leaving the management of economic issues in Asia to their bilateral relations and the global institutions.[50] Although the Clinton administration tried to turn APEC into a major vehicle of its export promotion policy, after the financial crisis it concentrated on negotiations for China's accession to the WTO. The George W. Bush administration regained a regional perspective by introducing the Enterprise for ASEAN Initiative (EAI) in response to China's FTA initiative with ASEAN and other moves toward regionalism in East Asia. It also renewed its interest in APEC as a forum to spur global trade negotiations, facilitate trade and investment, and help reduce transaction costs in the Asia Pacific region. However, the Bush administration has been largely preoccupied with the war on terrorism since the September 11 terrorist attacks and has given Asian economic affairs only intermittent attention.

U.S. FTA Policy under George W. Bush

Though overshadowed by other policy priorities and not systematically presented, the Bush administration's approach to regionalism in East Asia is markedly different from that of its predecessors. It seems to conclude FTAs with East Asian economies to drive an institutional wedge through East Asian regionalism, and thereby ensure that East Asia will not become a customs union, and to nullify the discrimination arising from FTAs in East Asia.[51] At the same time, Washington has avoided simplistic reactions in kind to the progress of other FTA initiatives in the region. It decided not to pursue an FTA with ASEAN as a whole and instead moved to bilaterally negotiate an FTA with individual members ready to live up to American standards. It presented a roadmap and specific procedures to prepare potential FTA partners in the Enterprise for ASEAN Initiative. In April 2002 U.S. Trade Representative Robert Zoellick declared Washington intended to avoid the exchange of "grandiose goals that are not met by facts on the ground" and to look at an FTA between the United States and ASEAN "step by step."[52]

Another significant move on the administration's part, though not yet implemented in East Asia, was the introduction of development assistance, in cooperation with international and regional financial institutions, to help developing countries prepare, negotiate, and implement their FTAs with the United States and to facilitate the transition to free trade. For example, in pursuing FTAs with Morocco and Central American countries, it introduced new measures to help build trade capacity and reform sectoral structure.[53] This shows that Washington had become more willing to pay attention to developmental concerns when serious about getting a deal and making desired changes happen. As noted in chapter 4, this was a significant departure from its early approach to APEC. It could show the same willingness in implementing the EAI.

In addition, the Bush administration has refrained from criticizing East Asian regionalism merely because the United States is not a member. In April 2002, Zoellick clearly signaled a change in U.S. views on this point when asked about U.S. reaction to ASEAN's efforts for East Asian regionalism:

> We have no problems with that at all and we think the more countries that seek to expand free trade in the world—as long as it's not diverting trade—that's a good thing.... Frankly, I wish the United States would have moved more quickly on its own free trade agreements. One of the reasons that we are seeking our trade promotion authority from the Congress is so that we can, frankly, catch up.
>
> But we're not mercantilists. We would like to have a stronger trade relationship with the ASEAN countries. . . . But if, at the same time, ASEAN can improve its free trade relations with others, that's all to the better. . . . If we don't catch up, that's our problem—not anybody else's.[54]

He even suggested that stronger demand in East Asia would help provide additional balance in exports, much of which currently goes to the United States.[55] Although this statement suggests a new open-mindedness toward economies of the region, it could simply be stopgap rhetoric from a belief that East Asian regionalism would not go far.

Either way, the new pragmatism—the pursuit of WTO negotiations and bilateral FTAs in East Asia, as well as the hands-off posture (or benign neglect) with respect to East Asian regionalism—seems to serve Washington's Asia policy goals much better than its earlier trade policy "stalemate" and displeasure with East Asian regionalism.[56] Applied diligently, this policy could promote U.S. economic interests. It would improve commercial access to the region for not only U.S. firms already operating in Asia that can benefit from East Asian regionalism but also those exporting from the United States through its bilateral FTAs in addition to liberalization on an MFN basis via WTO negotiations. Some criticized, however, that the United States should give a higher priority to large trading partners such as South Korea.[57] Also, U.S. bilateral FTAs could suggest rules for East Asian economies to follow, although Washington is just focusing on its own bilateral FTAs and APEC at the moment and not the way FTAs are evolving in East Asia or how different FTAs could converge and avoid the proliferation of different rules. Without harmonizing effort, East Asia may not benefit from the stimulus of U.S. policy innovations. Needless to say, open-mindedness will help avoid a negative political impact on U.S. relations with Asian countries, not to mention a defensive response in East Asia, with countries wanting to "gang up against the United States."[58]

Enablers

Can Washington sustain this new pragmatic approach and successfully shape the East Asian economic order in concert with its goals? As the only superpower, the United States has many resources that would help it shape the regional economic order. The first is U.S. economic power: through its markets, technology, and capital. An FTA with the United States would provide preferential access to U.S. markets and help attract U.S. investors. The second is the high quality of a U.S. FTA, both in its content and implementation, which would boost world investors' confidence in the business environment of U.S. FTA partners. The third is U.S. influence on the international rules. The rules in U.S. FTAs are more likely to become global standards than those of other countries' FTAs. Last but not least, U.S. military preeminence and East Asian confidence in the U.S. role as an important stabilizer of regional security enhance the value of an FTA with the United States as a symbol of good relations with the superpower.

Constraints

At the same time, the United States may have difficulty pursuing its policies in Asia. One large problem resulting from globalization, which it has promoted, is the domestic adjustment needed in certain negatively affected sectors even as the economy as a whole has benefited. Ironically, this has made it more difficult for Washington to continue a leadership role in trade liberalization.[59] The issue is not new. Especially since the 1970s, the U.S. economic structure has undergone a drastic change, exposing more American producers and workers to foreign competition and the hardships of adjustment, which tend to receive greater attention in the domestic political arena than the thinly spread benefits from more open trade. In the 1980s, the relative decline of the U.S. position in the world economy, in addition to ballooning trade deficits (although the fundamental problem was not in trade but in macroeconomic imbalance), made free traders more vulnerable to protectionist pressure at home. With the end of the cold war, the "security glue" among Western allies that had prevented trade frictions from jeopardizing their security cooperation finally dissolved, and the United States became less willing to bear the heavy burden of maintaining and strengthening the world economic order.[60] More recently, the anxiety about job losses intensified as new information and communications technologies facilitated the offshore outsourcing of white-collar jobs such as professional services and back-office operations.

Although the problem is solvable through effective policies, "nothing was done to overcome the domestic stalemate over globalization that plagued the United States throughout the 1990s and underlay the stagnation of trade policy."[61] When, for the first time in eight years, Congress finally gave the president trade promotion authority in 2002, "it was thanks only to a series of protectionist concessions on the part of the Bush administration."[62] According to observers, "the only long-term strategy for achieving domestic consensus . . . is to improve education and raise the overall skill level of the population" while, "in the short term, effective government assistance to workers who are displaced by increased trade flows" is provided through "stronger safety nets to cushion the transitional costs of job displacement, and more effective training and other adjustment programs to help workers qualify for new positions." [63]

A second concern is that Asia is not a natural priority for the United States. Because America is a global superpower before it is "a Pacific power," its policy will remain "subject to the distractions of responsibilities and crises elsewhere in the world."[64] Also, its global involvements have put "very real limits on the resources that the U.S. government could or would make available for this region."[65] This seems to explain, at least in part, its occasional impatience with the gradual nature of institutional changes in Asia. The United States is, above all, a Western Hemisphere power. Its neighboring areas necessarily weigh heavily in its strategic calculations because problems there will be felt more strongly than problems elsewhere in the world. As a result, Washington has been pursuing economic integration within its hemisphere. Its responses to regional currency crises have been different, too. The stark contrast between its massive and immediate assistance to Mexico in the 1994 crisis and its decision not to contribute to the rescue package for Thailand in 1997, whatever the reason, remains fresh in Asian memory.[66] As noted in chapter 5, the Clinton administration's focus on liberalization in APEC and the pursuit of a Free Trade Area of the Americas (FTAA) reinforced the sense that APEC was a forum of not one region, Asia Pacific, but two, Asia and the Americas.

Furthermore, America's perceived indifference to—or lack of imagination for—how its behavior was viewed by Asian countries, not just in times of distractions by crises elsewhere, but also even when it was in fact focused on Asia, has hindered its immense power resources from fully translating into a lasting influence in the region. U.S. objections to East Asia–only frameworks in the 1990s made Asians wonder:

> What, at the end of the day, was the U.S. priority—whether peace and stability or its influence in the region? When Asia was supposedly a dangerous place full of mistrust about each other's strategic intentions, wasn't it to be welcomed that East Asian countries consider getting together to discuss the economic issues of mutual interest—avoiding difficult issues at first and starting from more comfortable ones so as to gradually build mutual trust and explore where they could cooperate? Didn't it have confidence in the robustness of the relations with its treaty allies that had strived to establish liberal democracy? Couldn't it contain its perceived impulse to divide and conquer and, instead, embrace and foster East Asian regionalism, as it did for Europeans?[67]

Even if the conclusions were the same (that the United States would object to particular frameworks), Asian countries would have viewed Washington very differently if it had made a sincere effort to provide cogent arguments for dealing with problems in alternative ways.

Despite the recent setbacks to its image, the United States has by far the most influence in the region. A Southeast Asian senior diplomat observed with friendly candor, "Among the three major powers in the region—the United States, Japan, and China, we still think that the United States is the most benign, with all its problems of unilateralist tendencies and arrogance." Compared with Japan, which seemed insensitive to its neighbors' concerns and "emotional wounds," or China, which displayed "its willingness to use military means to deal with territorial disputes and threaten Taiwan . . . the United States has good intentions and, by not belonging to this region, can be trusted to play a role of an honest broker and to check Japan or China."[68] Although China's image in the region is further improving, the U.S. position as the stabilizer of last resort has not changed and will not change for the foreseeable future.

America should not, however, take its influence in the region for granted if it is to continue to position itself as an Asia Pacific power. Economic and military supremacy alone are not enough to maintain this influence. It is essential to be sensitive to and, where possible, further the region's aspirations. When U.S. policy is perceived to accommodate East Asian common interests and to demonstrate a strong commitment to regional stability and prosperity, U.S. influence will grow stronger and the momentum among East Asian countries for defensive regionalism, for example, is likely to decrease.

Option for a U.S. Grand Strategy

More fundamental are the strategies for dealing with emerging East Asian regionalism. One might say that the U.S. response to East Asian regionalism hinges on how the United States wants to deal with Japan and China. Of the four alternative ways of dissuading others "from ganging up against the United States" that have been suggested, one is "the broker and balancer of last resort," which implies "a more equidistant posture vis-à-vis Japan and China and greater reliance on local forces to establish and maintain the regional equilibrium."[69] If America finds it easier to play a balancing role in Asia with "a stable regional equilibrium with the Japanese alliance than without it," however, this would not be a comfortable option.

The second option is to encourage "pan-Asian regionalism while seeking to anchor it to a stronger trans-Pacific relationship with the United States— much as Washington has accommodated the drive for European integration, while seeking to harness an emerging European Community to U.S. interests through strengthened trans-Atlantic institutions." Critics argue, however, that pan-Asian regionalism, if closed, could have an adverse effect on U.S. interests. If China and Japan developed closer ties, for example, they "could reinforce residual mercantilist reflexes, and limit the scope of American diplomacy in the region. At the same time, other Asian countries would find the prospect of a Sino-Japanese condominium worrisome." They conclude, "At a minimum the United States needs to ensure healthy trans-Pacific economic links as a counterpoint to the further evolution of pan-Asian regionalism. And U.S. strategic interests are best served by cultivating close ties with Beijing as well as Tokyo."

A third option would be to contain China. However, that might merely isolate the United States rather than China "and risk inciting nationalism and neutralism among America's Asian friends."

A fourth option is "a 'Bismarckian' policy of engagement with Japan, China, and all other consequential states of Asia" in order "to consolidate a generally favorable territorial and political status quo in the region." Under this option, the United States would enlist Beijing in multilateral arrangements designed to regulate security, trade, and other transnational problems. It "would retain alliances with Japan and Korea as well as forward deployments of other U.S. units in the Asian Pacific area as an earnest example of U.S. intent to preserve a stable regional balance of power." "Operationally, [this option] implies preserving closer ties with China and Japan than they maintain with each other."

The fourth option has indeed been the U.S. strategy toward Asia, although U.S. administrations have not necessarily been consistent and adept in their management of their relations with Japan and China.[70] This option, some note, "offers the greatest benefits and the fewest risks," but "can be diplomatically demanding and far from cheap."

The second option is the most conducive to East Asian regionalism. It is unlikely that Japan and China will turn East Asia into a closed bloc. Unless Japan becomes open, there will be no pan-East Asian regionalism. At a minimum, any preferential trade agreement that involves developed countries such as Japan will have to meet WTO criteria for covering "substantially all the trade." In addition, Asian developing countries have already been pressing Japan to liberalize its sensitive agricultural produce, labor-intensive manufacturing goods, and, more recently, services such as nurses and caretakers. If the United States is worried about Japan's residual mercantilist reflexes, it would be more in the U.S. interest to encourage Japan to take up the challenges of East Asian regionalism and transform its economy and society into a more open one.

Likewise, China has to give up its residual protections to promote East Asian regionalism. As a first step in that direction, China must faithfully implement its WTO commitments, or other countries in the region will be reluctant to place their confidence in additional international agreements with China. In response to those who worry that China and Japan might form a "condominium," the ASEAN countries and South Korea, in particular, are urging the two to overcome their historical animosities and promote East Asian regionalism. Once the drive toward regionalism takes a firm hold, it will be prudent for the United States to foster it as well so as to "harness it to U.S. interests," rather than run the risk of becoming irrelevant when Japan and China do achieve reconciliation.

Prospects

Although the U.S. approach to East Asian regionalism has changed from vehement opposition to benign neglect, the underlying view remains wary at best. The George W. Bush administration decided to pursue its own bilateral FTAs with East Asian countries (starting with individual ASEAN members) to wedge through their regionalism and showed a renewed interest in APEC. These responses, with their pragmatic focus, are generally constructive and can contribute to the development of multilayered frameworks in East Asia, yet are still eclipsed by Washington's traditional preference for bilateral relations with major powers in Asia and its current preoccupation with the war on terrorism. Meanwhile, East Asian regionalism, which has a lot of potential to promote U.S. interests, is gaining momentum on its own. As already mentioned, a piecemeal response, essentially to maintain the status quo, would not be in the U.S. interest as much as concerted support, which would give the United States more influence and opportunity to shape it.

China

As noted in chapter 7, the rise of China has changed the regional landscape. Now a link in the production network and an economy with growing domestic demand, China is contributing to the regionalization of the East Asian economy. At the same time, it has become an active promoter of regionalism. The first trend has firmly positioned China as an indispensable member of regional economic frameworks in East Asia and reinforced the second trend.

Evolution of China's Policy toward Regional Frameworks

China's role in East Asian regionalism was very limited until the late 1990s. Guided by a long-standing "victim mentality" and strong sense of vulnerability, China's leaders thought "the best way to protect China's sovereignty from being violated was to shun international institutions and regimes."[71] Since then, the government's policy toward regional multilateralism has passed through three stages as the Chinese economy became integrated into the global economy.

Throughout this process, China's leaders gradually became "aware of the necessity to play by the rules of the international game" and saw that "the best way to defend its interests in the international political, economic and security realms [was] to make its own voice heard in the rule-making process."[72] Nevertheless, they felt ill-equipped to manage complex multilateral relations, and therefore focused on bilateral ones.[73] From the 1980s to the mid-1990s, China's involvement in regional cooperation was basically passive and reactive. The primary motivation to participate in regional frameworks was not to help institutionalize them but to avoid being excluded from them. After participating in them, it tried to minimize their impact on the autonomy of its policy.[74]

Though still reactive, China's perception of the regional environment and regional multilateralism in particular underwent significant changes in the 1990s.[75] The government became more confident and comfortable with regional multilateral frameworks and then keen to capitalize on them. The isolation experienced after the Tiananmen Square incident in 1989 reminded China of the importance of securing a benign international environment that would enable it to focus on its domestic economic and social development. Thus it started giving more attention to its relations with neighboring countries. As China saw its economy rapidly grow, it became more confident and was increasingly viewed as indispensable to regional cooperation frameworks. Beijing became comfortable with the way regional multilateral frameworks such as APEC and ARF operated, with the strong influence of the "ASEAN way," which allowed China to prevent these forums from taking up agendas it was not ready to discuss and pushing it to change its policies against its will. While China's support of the ASEAN way may have been tactical rather than "out of a genuine commitment to its core principles," as suggested by its foreign policy practices toward Southeast Asia, Beijing's insistence on ASEAN norms such as equal participation, consensus, and seeking common ground while shelving differences and gradualism enhanced its legitimacy as a responsible major power.[76] Beijing also became eager to utilize regional cooperation frameworks to show that China was not the threat supposed because of the rapid growth of its economy and military budget.

It was not until the late 1990s that actual changes appeared in China's policy toward regional multilateral frameworks. The first turning point was the Asian financial crisis, which hit ASEAN hard both economically and politically. It prompted China to "accept interdependence as a fact of life" while opening up new opportunities for China to take a more active part in the regional affairs, which meant not only that China had "the opportunities to gain" but also that it had to "shoulder certain burdens and responsibilities."[77] As noted in chapter 7, the international praise China won by not devaluing the renminbi helped it boost confidence in its ability to positively shape the regional environment and gain "regional political influence."[78] In practice, however, "China has been highly selective in choosing the sorts of responsibilities it is willing to accept."[79] Nonetheless, the attack on the Chinese embassy in Belgrade during the 1999 war in Kosovo prompted Chinese analysts to conclude that, "in order to have a peaceful environment conducive to domestic development, China needed to be more *proactive* in shaping its regional environment."[80]

Because China's economy was not hit as hard as ASEAN's by the crisis and attracted an increasing share of FDI to East Asia, seemingly at the expense of ASEAN, diffusing the China threat theory became a high priority, "so that regional states will not coalesce to thwart China's economic growth."[81] It became imperative to reassure neighbors such as ASEAN countries that China had good intentions and provided economic opportunities for them. This was important not only for the economy (to enable it to react and catch up with the regional trend toward FTAs) but also for security policy.

Indeed, Beijing has recently been intensely focused on how its behavior is perceived, particularly by its neighbors, and how the neighbors can become more comfortable in dealing with China. It has emphasized its identity as a "responsible great power" and its foreign policy doctrine of China's "Peaceful Rise."[82] Beijing also changed its position on the U.S. security presence in Asia, now accepting that the United States has a role to play not only because of a desire to improve its relations with the United States but also its recognition that Asian countries want to avoid having to choose whether to be in the China or the U.S. "camp," and that the "U.S. security umbrella makes regional states more comfortable in dealing with China (thus China needs [the] U.S. to assure regional states)."[83] There is increasing appreciation in Chinese policy circles that "China's increased involvement in regional institutions demonstrates China's benign intention and its willingness to have its power constrained" and that regional multilateralism is "one of the keys for China and regional states to co-manage the rise of China and to shape the evolving regional order."[84] What frustrates Beijing is that despite these efforts, China's benign intention still remains in doubt, which "creates a new kind of 'victimhood syndrome'" and "undercuts support for China's current benign strategy toward the region."[85]

Nevertheless, China remains confident and realistic. In April 2004, in a speech at the Boao Forum for Asia, President Hu Jintao emphasized China's willingness to promote regional economic integration, explore "free trade arrangements of various forms," and "step up its coordination . . . on macro-economic and financial policies," "probe into the establishment of regional cooperation regime of investors, securities market, and financial institutions," and promote "institution building of all kinds . . . with a view to consolidating resources, prioritizing the key areas, and conducting performance-oriented cooperation."[86] He also signaled China's "overall embrace of multilateral cooperative security mechanisms," noting that China wants to facilitate security dialogue and military-to-military exchanges, but did not indicate China's readiness to move "from consultations and confidence-building measures (CBMs) to more codified and institutionalized security arrangements."[87]

> China will step up its cooperation and dialogue with other Asian countries in such security areas as regional counter-terrorism, combating transnational crimes, maritime security, and non-proliferation, giving full play to existing multilateral security mechanisms. China is ready to set up a military security dialogue mechanism with other Asian countries and actively promote confidence-building cooperation in the military field.[88]

Thus China's policy toward regional economic integration has acquired a more solid foundation from which to pursue security, economic, and political interests.

Enablers

Can China sustain a strategy of embedding itself in and being constrained by the regional framework while remaining realistic about the U.S. role in the region? As a rising power, China has many resources. First is its dynamic economy. With continued reform and opening, its long-suppressed entrepreneurial spirit has been spreading to the less dynamic parts of the economy, improved physical infrastructure has integrated the national economy, and its economic institutions have become more reliable and conducive to competition and innovation. With its huge pool of human resources and vast land mass, China will eventually become the largest power in Asia. Its increasing role in Asian regionalization, in providing both production sites and markets, has made it an important player in regional cooperation. The speed of its growth—the rate of change, as opposed to the absolute level—has had a significant psychological impact on China, its neighbors, and the world as a whole. The vision of China as a great power suddenly seems very realistic. There is a sense that the ups and downs of its economic performance may affect the speed but not the outcome. Thus China's neighbors are increasingly attentive to its interests and concerns.

Second is its strong political leadership, both in terms of personal quality and the decisionmaking process. The younger generation of leaders, detached from the past victim mentality, seems determined to sustain China's reform and opening in a pragmatic and balanced manner, and with more flexibility in foreign policies. Also, unlike their counterparts in democracies, they are, for now, free from messy democratic processes and can make bold moves once the political elites arrive at a consensus. The clear messages from its political leaders have earned significant diplomatic goodwill of ASEAN countries.

Constraints

China also has its own problems, most notably structural problems in the form of nonperforming loans, inefficient state-owned enterprises, high unemployment, widening income gaps between coastal and inland areas, serious environmental degradation, and energy shortages. In times of economic hardship, it will be difficult to continue further reform and opening. There is also a gap between the vision of political leaders and the actual implementation of it. China is still struggling to meet its WTO commitments in vast territories where local officials differ in their willingness and capacity to enforce rules and regulations. FTAs will put an additional burden on efforts to enforce international agreements. Also, some local authorities seem to have a different notion of international agreements. Remarking on the experience of businesspeople, Lee Kuan Yew, former president of Singapore and currently senior minister, noted that "Singaporeans take for granted the sanctity of contracts. When we sign an agreement, it is a full and final undertaking. Any disagreement as to the meaning of the written document is interpreted by the courts or an arbitrator. . . . For the Suzhou authorities, a signed agreement is an expression of serious and sincere intent, but one that is not necessarily comprehensive and can be altered or reinterpreted with changing circumstances."[89]

If China fails to faithfully implement its bold commitments, it will lose credibility with investors around the world. So far, Chinese leaders have seemingly been focusing on the political significance of FTA proposals and may not have paid enough attention to how to ensure their implementation on the ground. Structural problems can add to the tension between external policies and domestic capabilities and priorities.

In addition, weak institutional capabilities limit China's ability to propose new international rules. Although Chinese experts could propose effective rules that would find their way into regional and global agreements, there would be far more innovation if they had some experience encountering and solving problems under well-functioning market economy institutions on a daily basis.

Other constraints arise from China's autocratic political system. In the short term, its authorities might become even more autocratic to ensure that leaders' decisions are enforced. However, to be an attractive power in a region where an increasing number of people are enjoying democratic freedom, China has to be able to demonstrate that its own people can also enjoy an attractive living environment. Furthermore, the government's encouragement of anti-Japanese sentiment by allowing greater freedom of speech regarding anti-Japanese subjects and emphasizing Japan's wartime aggression and atrocity in schools, has ingrained a strong anti-Japanese sentiment in the younger generation.[90] In a survey of young people aged 24 or younger, 90 percent named Japan when asked if China has an enemy.[91] These situations, often widely reported in the Japanese media, have helped stir up anti-Chinese sentiment and reinforced the vicious cycle of mutual distrust.

Fifth is the persistent doubt among neighbors about China's benign intentions. Despite China's recent "charm offensive," there is lingering concern in the region about whether China will be a benign power once it has achieved economic development with corresponding military might.[92] Will China be tempted to use its power and influence to get its own way when it no longer feels the need to court its neighbors? This anxiety stems from the experience of having seen China's external policies abruptly shift according to its leaders' geopolitical calculations and visions, which have had decisive power in its autocratic political regime. Also, its harsh rhetoric in warning Taiwan's leader against calling for a referendum or other moves that Beijing interpreted as leading to independence was a reminder that economic development and the stable environment it requires might not always be China's paramount goal. Concern about the future intentions of a rising power can be alleviated, but not completely eliminated, by China's behavior today. The problem can only be solved by integrating China's economy with the regional and global economy and inducing economic and political changes in its domestic systems, beyond the point of no return.

Finally, as a result of the speed and impact of China's rise, combined with the recognition of the risks involved in its economic and political systems, countries in East Asia have a growing desire to avoid the concentration of economic activities in China and to create multiple growth centers in the region. They would move to dilute China's influence in regional forums and thereby assist in the reconfiguration of East Asian regionalism.

Options for China's Grand Strategy

Although China has a policy on regional economic integration, based on an integrated approach to pursuing security, economic, and political interests, its grand strategy is still evolving. It is seeking an optimal balance between a realistic orientation that would build up its own strengths and a coalition with other states that would balance the superpower and the liberal orientation so as to develop institutions for removing security dilemmas and nurturing stable international relations. The sixteenth National Congress of the Chinese Communist Party implied "a kind of 'two-headed' . . . grand strategy" consisting, on one hand, of "the moderate, prudently optimistic, and pragmatic principle of . . . [its] policy toward the United States, together with . . . the all-round 'good neighbor' policy and the positive involvement in economic globalization and various multilateral international regimes" and a firm determination, on the other hand, "to accelerate China's military modernization and to prevent or stop by almost any means if necessary the independence of Taiwan."[93] This strategy has been described as a combination of "'bandwagoning' and 'transcending', based [on] an un-excessive 'self-help.'"[94] Bandwagoning, as the term suggests, means constructing "a general relationship of accommodation with the United States and the Western community of nations under U.S. leadership" and "riding on the fundamental tide currents of the contemporary world," such as "globalization, domestic democratization, changes in international norms toward more justice, and multi-polarization."[95] Under this strategy, China would promote reform and opening up, conform to international norms, and learn advanced thinking from abroad. Transcending means developing "an international consensus or formal agreements on norms, rules and procedures" to solve problems. With respect to security problems, in particular, it means "trying to create, foster and develop regional and sub-regional security regimes."[96] Self-help means using one's own strengths, especially military and economic ones, and cooperating with other weak states facing similar threats so as to create or maintain an international balance of power that "buttresses the weak and restrains the strong."[97]

In fact, China has alternative grand strategies that balance the two-headed strategy in different ways. One such strategy places more emphasis on self-help because of a pessimistic assessment of the future Sino-U.S. power struggle. East Asian regionalism would serve as a means of multipolarization. The problem with this alternative is that other Asian countries would not be comfortable if they thought that by embracing East Asian regionalism they would be drawn into the Sino-U.S. power struggle.

A second alternative places more emphasis on bandwagoning and transcending, but only to complement self-help. With this option, the balance is perhaps closer to that of China's current strategy in practice and would have China strive to avoid confrontation with the United States and promote East Asian regionalism "to hedge against downturns in Sino-U.S. relations."[98] East Asian regionalism would be a secondary consideration, and China would remain opportunistic, moving on an ad hoc basis when it thinks it could wield diplomatic goodwill and influence in the region by doing so. However, it would try to avoid, as much as possible, systematic constraints on its diplomatic free hand.

A third alternative would focus on transcending—that is, on actively fostering and developing East Asian regionalism in a way that would make other East Asian countries feel comfortable. It would agree to have its power restrained by regional as well as global institutions and demonstrate this acceptance by fully implementing the rule of law and embracing democracy as the ultimate goal of its political reform. Under this strategy, China would develop into a genuinely responsible great power locked in by the institutional constraints of East Asian regionalism and global frameworks.

The last grand strategy, the most conducive to fostering East Asian regionalism, would require China to become much more confident in the strategic intentions of other major powers, particularly those of the United States. Furthermore, it would have to be politically stable, to deal with China's nationalism and anti-Japanese sentiment, in particular, which are so strong that accommodation with Japan and the United States would be highly unpopular. It must also be able to shape a favorable international environment. China will likely pursue the second grand strategy, and if it becomes more confident over time, will hopefully shift its course toward the third grand strategy.

Prospects

In the past several years, China has revolutionized its policy toward regional frameworks in Asia and now has concluded an FTA with ASEAN, actively promoted cooperation at regional forums such as ASEAN + 3, and advocated an East Asia summit. This change took place because of a shift in its grand strategy to political and security concerns. This seems to be a tactical change, in that China is hoping to become strong enough to eventually counterbalance the United States. As for regional institutions, both economic and political, China treats them as just a means to spotlight its image as a responsible great power and to enhance its political status and influence. Also, it is not yet ready to pave the way for reconciliation with Japan, as was evident during anti-Japanese demonstrations in April 2005. And as long as China lacks confidence in the strategic intentions of major powers, its domestic political stability, and its ability to shape the external environment positively, it will continue to take a tactical approach to regional institutions. Even so, China can enhance the effectiveness of its regional policies on economic integration to its advantage. Currently, the gap between the vision of political leaders and the actual implementation is a cause for concern. By focusing not on the geopolitical implications but on implementation, China would be able to earn its neighbors' confidence that China is genuinely intent on conforming to institutional constraints and ensuring that positive economic and social changes take place as a result of East Asian regionalism, as well as its accession to the WTO.

Conclusion

Japan, the United States, and China—all major powers with a strong influence on the shape of the regional economic order—need to address a number of policy issues if they are to have a positive effect on East Asian regionalism. Japan's problem is that it lacks a grand strategy from which to launch decisive reforms that would make its economy and society more open and attractive and win the trust of neighboring countries. For the United States, more high-level attention to regional policies toward Asia and encouragement of East Asian regionalism should replace its current piecemeal approach. The trouble with China's strategy is its tactical nature, which casts doubt on its credibility in the eyes of other countries in the region. An important step for China would be to implement its international commitments on the ground, while addressing neighbors' concerns about its rise as a military power with ambitions to dominate the region.

All the same, a real breakthrough in East Asian regionalism is now possible because these three powers have come into a historic alignment. Japan has finally started to visibly restructure its economy, driven by corporate restructuring and supported by changes in government policies, albeit not systematic ones. The U.S. attitude to East Asian economic regionalism has become much less negative, if not genuinely positive. The United States is pursuing bilateral FTAs with ASEAN countries, which provides a new impetus to East Asian regionalism. And China is putting considerable effort into domestic development and into securing a benign international environment conducive to such development. Its economy has become markedly more open and its foreign policy more sophisticated. Although Sino-Japanese relations remain thorny and China's growing influence and military buildup is making other countries nervous about how it is going to use that influence, each of the three powers is in fact contributing to what will be the building blocks for future regionwide frameworks. This is an unprecedented opportunity to promote East Asian regionalism as a unique layer of the international economic system. Positive alignment will also help strengthen important building blocks and, with improved Sino-Japanese relations, could take East Asian regionalism to the next stage of pan-regional integration.

How Economic Integration Changed East Asia

Regional economic integration has significantly changed the East Asian landscape in the past two decades. In the mid-1980s, East Asia did not have a regional identity. Its economies were not integrated in a de facto sense, much less an institutional one. Most Asian developing countries still protected domestic markets so they could pursue import substitution while promoting exports to U.S. and European markets from limited enclaves. Factories producing for the protected domestic markets operated below the minimum efficiency scale. Intraregional trade was driven mainly by bilateral trade with Japan. The region's countries exclusively followed the General Agreement on Tariffs and Trade (GATT) most favored nation (MFN) principle. Though the United States floated the idea of bilateral free trade agreements (FTAs) with the Association of Southeast Asian Nations (ASEAN) to create momentum for the GATT trade negotiations, ASEAN members were not ready for this, except Singapore, which had already become a free port. Forming a regional forum in East Asia was unthinkable, given the region's dependence on U.S. markets and the diverse economic systems, political regimes, and security policies found there.

Since then, the countries and economies of East Asia have experienced de facto economic integration and are in the early stages of institutionalizing it. At this point, East Asian regionalism is in a benign, significant, and promising state, though still fragile.

Stage 1: Competition among Proposals (1985–92)

East Asian regionalism took its first breath in 1985, when the September Plaza Accord brought about a sharp appreciation of the yen against the U.S. dollar. This triggered the regionalization of East Asian economies by forcing Japanese manufacturers to relocate their production bases abroad. Second, in his "fair trade speech" the day after the accord, President Ronald Reagan announced a multitrack strategy to explore regional and bilateral agreements with other nations with a view to opening their markets by threatening to close U.S. markets, if necessary. Thus East Asia came under protectionist and unilateralist pressure from the United States.

A surge in export-oriented foreign direct investment (FDI) from Japan and newly industrializing economies (NIEs) in the wake of the Plaza Accord and the resulting economic growth made local firms in ASEAN countries more open to partnership with foreign investors. Local governments, in competition with one another, also became more responsive to private sector requests. The subsequent rise of business costs in these countries shifted labor-intensive FDI to lower-cost countries such as China and Vietnam. The shift prompted local firms in more developed ASEAN countries to provide higher value-added products and to develop business networks with emerging economies. The need to develop backward linkages to enhance international competitiveness induced host governments to abandon import-substitution policies. This, in turn, provided the impetus for the integration of ASEAN markets. Though symbolic at first, the efforts for institutional economic integration within ASEAN eventually came to fruition in the ASEAN Free Trade Area.

In the latter half of the 1980s, U.S. trade policy posture stimulated Asian policymakers to consider institutionalized economic integration. First, the United States explored FTAs with Japan, South Korea, and other Asia Pacific economies but did not pursue them. It decided that an FTA with Japan or Korea would not produce significant market-opening results, when, in its view, most barriers were embedded in their domestic economic systems and cultures. FTAs would also be difficult to conclude with other Asia Pacific economies because the prospective partners differed greatly in their developmental levels, economic structures, legal systems, and cultures. Although Washington did not actually pursue the FTA idea, policymakers in the region feared that the U.S. "hub-and-spoke" approach to trade agreements might not only leave "spoke economies" at a disadvantage but also become a new vehicle for U.S. unilateralist pressure. In addition, the U.S.-Canada FTA signaled an alarming trend toward regionalism in the Americas.

In the late 1980s, both defensive regionalism (owing to the strong concern over U.S. unilateralism and protectionism) and intraregional interdependence (through the rapid growth of developing economies and interdependence within the region) prompted Japanese and Australian policymakers to consider the idea of an intergovernmental regional forum. Because of the dependence on U.S. markets, they decided to include the United States when the forum came into being in 1989, under the title Asia Pacific Economic Cooperation (APEC).

With the establishment of APEC, Washington grew interested in a multilateral regional economic framework in Asia, with the United States as a member, though it was strongly opposed to setting up such a framework without U.S. participation. This interest was fueled by Asia's rise in the world economy, the increasing intensity of intra-Asian economic relations, and concerns over Japan's possible dominance of the region. Also, the possibility of a regional forum in Asia without the United States (as in Australia's initial proposal of what later became APEC and in Malaysia's suggestion for an East Asian Economic Caucus, EAEC) persuaded Washington to try to participate in the new forum and preempt defensive regionalism in the Western Pacific. Washington's categorical objection to the EAEC proposal and its high-handed approach left a sense, even among the countries without compelling interests to promote it, that they should be able to choose for themselves whom to meet and talk to.

Regionalism at an East Asian or Asia Pacific level led the ASEAN countries to promote intra-ASEAN integration so as to avoid the marginalization of ASEAN. They agreed to establish the ASEAN Free Trade Area and from then on became more positive toward the institutionalization of the APEC and trade liberalization agenda in that forum.

In this period, regionalism put little emphasis on substance, despite the growing impulse to get together. In the absence of a regionwide framework, the tendency was to try to find a single formula that would accommodate all of the forces at play. Hence competing proposals were considered inconsistent, despite the emergence of multilayered thinking in the United States and Singapore. This explains the focus on membership in each framework, rather than on core objectives and specific measures that might be taken. As a result, no systematic effort was made to sort out the different motivations and assumptions of APEC members, so as to understand the difference between a holistic approach to secure stable growth in Asia and a focused approach to promote liberalization, between liberalization on an MFN basis and on a reciprocal basis, and between a consensus-oriented approach designed to nurture the members' willingness to liberalize and a structured approach designed to pressure the members to move forward. These differences became clearer when APEC shifted its attention from institution building to implementation in the next period.

Stage 2: Primacy of APEC (1993–98)

The trend toward a more open trade and investment environment through the interaction of foreign investors, local businesses, and host governments did not stop with the original ASEAN members. China's reform and opening accelerated in the early 1990s. ASEAN added four countries to its membership in the latter half of the 1990s and opened up new frontiers to be integrated into the globalized economy.[1] The boom in information technology (IT) and fierce competition under the short life cycle of technologies and falling prices prompted Western firms to use Asian production capacities extensively to achieve greater speed and lower cost. The drivers of intraregional trade became much more diverse than before, with U.S., European, and non-Japanese Asian firms playing increasingly important roles. The ASEAN countries, faced with competitive pressure from China and eager to capitalize on the opportunities that FDI brought about, developed a much more active interest in regional cooperation within and beyond ASEAN to improve their institutional capabilities and facilitate cross-border business activities.

Thanks to U.S. activism under the Clinton administration and ASEAN's greater confidence, APEC's trade liberalization agenda made significant progress after the first leaders' meeting in Seattle. That meeting, together with efforts of the Eminent Persons Group (EPG) directly reporting to it, helped APEC overcome bureaucratic resistance to its bold new visions. In November 1994, under the Indonesian chair, APEC leaders adopted the Bogor goal of liberalization in APEC by 2010 for developed economies and 2020 for developing economies. It was a surprising development, as Indonesia had been the member most cautious about liberalization, and added momentum to the GATT Uruguay Round negotiations. APEC was also instrumental in concluding the Information Technology Agreement in the World Trade Organization (WTO).

As bold as the visions were, members did not necessarily have the political commitment and institutional capabilities to follow through on them. Therefore as APEC moved from envisioning to implementing its ambitious goals, tension increased between those eager to promote regional trade and investment liberalization in APEC (the United States, Australia, New Zealand,

Canada, Singapore, and Hong Kong, but also Indonesia, after the adoption of the Bogor goal in 1994) and those with different priorities (Japan, South Korea, China, Taiwan, and ASEAN economies apart from Singapore), as well as between those insisting on liberalization on a reciprocal basis (the United States) and those opposed to preferential arrangements for APEC (other than the United States, though some countries such as Singapore and New Zealand were flexible). Although they managed to paper over this tension in successive leaders' meetings, matters came to a head when they were pursuing the Early Voluntary Sectoral Liberalization (EVSL) in 1998.

With the setback of EVSL, the limitations of a voluntary approach to trade liberalization became clear. The only way to liberalize highly sensitive items on an MFN basis was through WTO negotiations. An APEC FTA was not feasible given its diverse membership. Thus attention turned to the exploration of smaller (bilateral or subregional) FTAs as a realistic policy option.

Also, despite the considerable institutionalization and activism of APEC in the second period, it was not effective in checking the increasing momentum for regionalism in North America, not to speak of Europe. Asian policymakers began to recognize that regionalism was not a force they could stop but one they had to reckon with and manage to their benefit, where possible. Having been exposed to Washington's multitrack strategy and seeing that an APEC-wide FTA was not feasible, Asian policymakers concluded that APEC could not be expected to solve all the problems left by the WTO because it is part of a multilayered structure of international economic institutions. Hence they had to be creative in identifying the right agenda for the association and in exploring other possible layers. There was an increasing sense that it was more appropriate to conceive of APEC as a transregional than a regional body.

Throughout these explorations, APEC was incubating regional cooperation in Asia. It brought the region's governments and businesses together in many meetings and projects. It made them aware of their common problems, new measures for cooperation, and different priorities. In particular, the APEC discussions on trade and investment facilitation stimulated interest in taking more concrete measures through smaller groups or on a bilateral basis and enriched the elements of economic partnership agreements that combine liberalization and broader cooperation.

In response to the rapid development of APEC, ASEAN tried to remain viable by accelerating the schedule of the ASEAN Free Trade Area (AFTA) and taking the initiative in creating forums centering on it, such as the ASEAN Regional Forum, the Asia-Europe meeting, and various "ASEAN plus" meetings. Some ASEAN members worked hard to make an East Asia–only framework a viable part of the multilayered international institutions, through the establishment of an ASEAN + 3 (China, Japan, and South Korea) forum.

Stage 3: Experiments with New Assumptions (1998–2000)

Economic interdependence in the region deepened after the Asian financial crisis hit in the late 1990s. Despite a temporary reduction in domestic demand, production networks developed steadily, with the participation of investors in and outside the region. Lower corporation prices and deregulation of foreign capital in the wake of the crisis accelerated cross-border mergers and acquisitions. FDI from the United States and Europe increased their relative weight in such sectors as automobiles, electronics, distribution, and finance. At the same time, production processes became fragmented because of reductions in the cost of service links and the sophistication of the numerical control of manufacturing processes, which lowered the skill levels needed to perform certain manufacturing steps and made it much easier to locate those steps in developing countries. This led to ever-finer specialization among various countries, thus providing a unique opportunity for developing countries without indigenous capability to participate in production networks for technologically sophisticated products with promising growth prospects. Host governments competed to form a robust industrial cluster and sought complementary relations with other (potential) clusters in the neighborhoods, in a bid to become a regional center.

The Asian financial crisis also helped remove taboos on East Asia–only frameworks and FTAs. Releasing pent-up energy, East Asian countries began designing additional layers of multilayered international institutions that had been on their mind in the previous periods. The crisis encouraged the development of East Asia–only frameworks in several ways. First, the contagion reminded East Asian countries of their interdependence and common desire to survive the crisis, prevent future crises of this nature, and promote stable growth in the region in general. Second, the crisis crushed the confidence prevalent earlier in the region that made countries think they could count on the business activities and global institutions to remain dynamic without additional regional institutions or bilateral agreements. East Asian countries were now keen to explore whatever would work to overcome the crisis and revitalize their economies. Third, the crisis shifted economic gravity away from ASEAN to China and South Korea (after its sharp recovery) and prompted ASEAN to forge a closer linkage with Northeast Asia. Fourth, the crisis erased the fear of Japan's economic domination, making other East Asian countries more comfortable with institutionalized cooperation with Japan. Finally, because of the crisis, the United States seemed half-hearted about Asian economies in general, as indicated by the U.S. Trade Representative's narrow focus on EVSL in APEC in the middle of the crisis. Having seen Washington's categorical objection subside, Asian policymakers were less worried about U.S. reactions to East Asian regionalism.

The crisis also added momentum to bilateral FTAs. For one thing, the crisis helped East Asian countries overcome their traditional hesitation about preferential trade agreements. Economic stagnation and the need for better economic relations with Japan also encouraged South Korea to reach out to Japan in an effort to end the historical animosity and change the nature of the bilateral relations. Because economic gravity had shifted away from ASEAN to Northeast Asia, Singapore decided to go it alone and conclude bilateral FTAs with non-ASEAN countries, prompting other ASEAN members to follow suit. No longer feeling threatened by Japan's possible economic domination, other Asian countries proposed FTAs with Japan.

Although the financial crisis left East Asian countries resentful toward the United States and the International Monetary Fund (IMF) for the way they dealt with it, any resulting anti-American sentiment at this time was not instrumental in the development of East Asian regionalism. Rather, defensive regionalism arose from the limitations of the global system and the resulting need for regional financial cooperation, most notably in the form of the Asian Monetary Fund (AMF) proposal, which achieved its objective largely by inducing policy changes in the IMF. The Chiang Mai Initiative is a regional self-help mechanism to complement IMF efforts in future crises.

In the area of trade, the crisis urged hard-hit economies to become more attractive to investors, through domestic reform and liberalization of trade and investment. Their interest in East Asian regionalism was driven not by defensive regionalism but by the desire to promote intraregional economic interdependence and stimulate growth. The establishment of the WTO dispute settlement mechanism had also solved the problem of U.S. unilateral trade sanctions and reduced defensive motivations. The freedom of experimenting with various forums turned the attention of East Asian capitals to the substantive issues they were to deal with in each forum. Realistic views on APEC made them more proactive in creating frameworks for negotiating trade and investment liberalization that would better suit their situations. For practical reasons, then, they pursued bilateral FTAs rather than a pan–East Asian FTA. Although the growing regionalism elsewhere, particularly the

European Union's efforts to conclude FTAs with Mexico and other Latin American countries in response to the North American Free Trade Agreement (NAFTA) and the Free Trade Area of the Americas (FTAA) initiative, worried Asian economies, their response was to explore cross-regional FTAs such as FTAs with Mexico and Chile, and not necessarily in the form of regionalism within East Asia. Defensive regionalism therefore played more of a symbolic role in East Asian regionalism in that it helped legitimize East Asian–only frameworks.

In this period, the traditional obstacles to regionalism in East Asia were to some extent overcome. All having experienced the Asian financial crisis, the region's members had strong economic interests in common and a greater sense of cohesiveness. While they may not yet have developed a sense of community, they became much more willing to look for ways to cooperate better. Equally significant, U.S. reactions to East Asian initiatives for economic integration changed from categorical overall objection to opposition to the designs of particular proposals. East Asian capitals have become much more relaxed about U.S. reactions, feeling they can always discuss specific issues with the United States as they arise and rectify them as appropriate. In addition, East Asian countries are now much less wary of institutionalization and more comfortable with free trade agreements, albeit not with customs unions or currency integration.

Stage 4: FTA Race (2000 to the Present)

The most important factor in this period was the impact of the rise of China. China's accession to the WTO made it particularly attractive as an FDI destination, as investors expected improvements in its business environment. In becoming the world's factory and most dynamic market, China encouraged ASEAN countries to create industrial structures that were complementary to its own but that could also compete with each other. This, of course, added to the challenges of intra-ASEAN integration.

Since completing major negotiations for its accession to the WTO in 2000, China has become markedly more active in engaging in regional frameworks and has accelerated the FTA race among the major powers. When Japan moved to conclude FTAs with Singapore and South Korea, and the United States responded by starting negotiations with Singapore, China abruptly started to pursue a free trade agreement with ASEAN. Japan also began negotiating FTAs with individual ASEAN countries and then one with ASEAN as a whole. For its part, the United States had been preoccupied with the war on terrorism since the September 11 terrorist attacks, and then with the turmoil in postwar Iraq. It managed, however, to announce the Enterprise for ASEAN Initiative (EAI), which established a roadmap for bilateral FTAs between the United States and individual ASEAN members, based on the high standards set in the U.S.-Singapore FTA. In the second term of the George W. Bush administration, Washington became more concerned about the geopolitical impact of China's rise, but its Asia policy initiatives remained focused on the political and security areas.

This period also saw the development of the vision of East Asian regionalism under the "ASEAN + 3" framework. In 2001 the East Asia Vision Group proposed the formation of an East Asian community, with such elements as an East Asia Free Trade Area, an East Asia Investment Area, and an East Asia Summit. With their growing experience in bilateral and subregional FTAs, however, East Asian countries became realistic about what they could achieve at a pan–East Asian level and started to focus on immediately feasible functional cooperation under the ASEAN + 3 framework. Over the long term, they intend to let the bilateral and subregional FTAs take the lead outside the scope of the ASEAN + 3 forums and eventually integrate them into a pan-regional FTA. So far, the ASEAN + 3 framework has been a vehicle not for trade liberalization but for cooperation in various functional areas to facilitate trade and investment, close the developmental gaps among the members, and facilitate sustainable growth by addressing energy and environmental issues.

While overshadowed by the competitive dynamics evident in the proliferation of bilateral and subregional FTAs, intraregional economic interdependence has become the dominant underlying force. The further progress of regionalization, accelerated by China's rise, enhanced the East Asian countries' interest in facilitating intraregional business transactions. The proliferation of FTAs prompted the business sector to voice concerns over spaghetti-bowl effects and is expected to inform the ongoing bilateral FTA negotiations of Japan, for example, to make them building blocks of a pan-regional FTA.

At the same time, the rise of China has created new political dynamics. With the prospect of it eventually becoming the biggest power in the region, its neighbors have felt it essential to build a regional community and firmly integrate China in a rule-based system at both the regional and global levels. Such an approach would also enable them to manage this potentially volatile process.

More recently, the speed and impact of China's rise have been met with counteractions. Seeing economic activities increasingly concentrated in China and the risks imposed by its economic and political systems, other countries have grown eager to avoid further concentration by creating multiple growth centers in the region. Hence more economic arrangements are being considered within and beyond East Asia between countries other than China, with a potential for reconfiguring East Asian regionalism. Also at work is a desire to dilute China's political influence in the East Asian frameworks. The moves to invite India, Australia, and New Zealand to the East Asia summit in December 2005, so as to differentiate the premature summit from the ASEAN + 3 leaders' meeting, might turn out to be a precursor to the expansion of the membership of the East Asian community or the creation of a new layer, different from either ASEAN + 3 or APEC.

The challenge of managing the rise of China has also strengthened the desire of East Asian countries to get U.S. blessing and active support in this regional venture, as reflected in the efforts of some countries to enter into FTAs with the United States and Japan's attempt to invite the United States as an observer to the East Asia Summit of December 2005. In the meantime, the role of defensive regionalism has become markedly less conspicuous or important. Countries in the region are now more absorbed in designing and making the best possible use of new policy tools such as East Asian forums and free trade agreements.

The Impact of Regionalization and Regionalism on East Asia

Though an East Asian community has not been clearly defined, and this has caused controversies, the way East Asian economies have been integrated on a de facto basis reveals the benign nature of institutionalizing that integration. They have a strong incentive to remain open to other regions of the world. East Asia is a suitable unit for economic integration not because of mere economic interdependence but because of a specific attribute of that interdependence, namely, the development of production networks in which parts and materials go back and forth before being assembled into a final product. The economies in the region share a strong interest in further reducing the transaction costs involved in operating these production networks, so as to make them more competitive and investment in them more attractive. The overall aim is not to become a self-contained economic bloc.

This incentive informs their efforts to institutionalize regional integration. East Asian economic institutions, at least until the participating economies agree on common external tariffs of zero, will not resemble those of the European Community, which keeps a member state from eliminating its trade barriers ahead of other members. East Asian economic institutions will be more like those of NAFTA, in that a member will be free to conclude economic agreements with nonmembers, though arrangements will reflect the unique reality of the region.

The experience of the past two decades has made East Asian countries realistic about what they can achieve through regionalism. First, regional frameworks should be part of the multilayered structure of international economic institutions. They have found that neither APEC nor East Asian forums can solve all their problems. Second, institutionalization at a pan–East Asian level takes time. They are currently concentrating on immediately feasible functional cooperation under the ASEAN + 3 framework. Third, from the experience of FTA negotiations and the nature of FTAs less ambitious than previously envisioned, these countries have learned that to go further they need more domestic preparations (both political readiness and institutional capabilities).

As mentioned earlier, the East Asian countries have also been motivated to build a regional community in order to firmly integrate China in the rule-based system and manage this potentially volatile process. Naturally, they have a keen interest in making an East Asian community work.

Developments in the region over the past few decades have also affected the policies of the world's three major powers: Japan, China, and the United States. While often criticized for being slow and reactive, Japan has steadily overcome its political resistance to liberalizing sensitive sectors each time it has concluded a new FTA and has become more proactive. It, together with South Korea, has urged China to update the bilateral investment treaty and conclude a trilateral one with high-level disciplines. Nevertheless, Japan has yet to develop a comprehensive strategy for realizing economic integration in East Asia.

For China, the rise of regionalism in East Asia presented an opportunity to win the confidence of its neighbors and put up an institutional block to the moves to contain it. While the suspicion about its strategic intention will not disappear because of its size and historical self-image as the center of Asia, economic interests as well as political calculations (that engaging China will make it more benign) have promoted cooperation between China and its neighbors.

Washington has significantly moderated its attitude toward East Asian regionalism in the past decade. Rather than categorically opposing such a trend, the United States has started to proactively engage with the individual countries in the region to solidify its interests and influence.

The Promise of an East Asian Community

All three powers—Japan, China, and the United States—stand to benefit from making an East Asian community work. East Asia is going through historic geopolitical changes owing to the rise of China. The surge in political interest in the vision of an East Asian community suggests that the region is in search of a new order to accommodate China's growing power and influence and to maintain regional peace and stability. Economic integration will engage regional powers in stable regional interdependence, meaning that the prosperity of one will be in the interest of others and make them more predictable and reliable to each other. Moreover, the regular meetings of the leaders help stabilize relations among East Asian countries by providing venues for them to meet when bilateral relations are not cordial and thus keeping their dialogue open. Such interaction also allows their neighbors to urge them to improve their relations. For its part, China will be freed from the "China Threat theory" and be better able to secure a stable regional environment so that it can concentrate on its domestic development. In addition, the successful development of poorer countries in Asia through their integration with the dynamic regional economy will help promote political stability and reduce the possibility that these countries will become hotbeds of terrorism.

East Asian regionalism will induce Japan to make its economy and society much more open, and to face its neighbors' persistent mistrust without being shielded by the United States. This, in turn, will help revitalize and embed Japan in the region.

The United States will benefit from reduced regional tension and its security burden. A revitalized and trusted Japan will be a more valuable ally, and an economically dynamic Asia could help alleviate the structural imbalance in the global economy.[2] Needless to say, East Asian economies do not perceive their regionalism as being in conflict with the network of U.S. bilateral security alliances.

What the Three Powers Should Do

As seen in chapter 8, the three major powers are now aligned in an unprecedented way that makes a breakthrough in East Asian economic regionalism possible. Before this can happen, all three powers must move their policies in the right direction, as explained in the next subsections. Such developments will signal confidence in East Asian regionalism and focus the regional capitals' attention on the integration of bilateral FTAs into a seamless regional framework. Of course, the successful conclusion of the Doha development agenda of WTO negotiations is crucial to keeping regional frameworks, including those in East Asia, more open to the outside.

Japan

Japan has to solidify its more liberal trade policy (through the WTO and FTAs) and accompanying domestic reform with successful examples. It should conclude comprehensive and high-level FTAs with South Korea and ASEAN countries. These FTAs should have as many common elements as possible so they can converge into a regional multilateral FTA. Through these negotiations, Japan should demonstrate that it can liberalize sensitive sectors. Ideally, the liberalization should not be done on an ad hoc basis to reach individual agreements but through systematic programs of regulatory reform to make each sector more efficient and meet public policy goals more effectively. Japan's active contribution to WTO negotiations will provide it with an additional impetus for systematic reform at home. The successful conclusion of both FTA and WTO negotiations will add to the momentum for further reform and prepare Japan to play a more active role in promoting economic integration in the region.

Eventually, Japan's greater readiness should be supported by its neighbors' willingness to accept its role. Thus Japan should make a conscious effort to earn its neighbors' trust by articulating its national strategy and the role it is willing to play in the region. It also has to solve the history issues, fueled recently by the prime minister's visit to the Yasukuni Shrine, which has apparently damaged Japan's relations with China and aroused concern in other neighboring countries such as South Korea and Singapore.[3] The solution has to be a fundamental one, however, reached not under pressure from other countries but based on a national consensus on how to honor the war dead.

China

China should continue its efforts to open up and reform its economy, while faithfully implementing international agreements (its WTO commitment as well as its FTA with ASEAN) and showing its neighbors as well as foreign investors that it has the will and capacity to enforce international rules and improve the quality of its rule of law. At the same time, it should avoid commitments that cannot be realistically enforced. Also, to make the future integration of the existing separate FTAs smoother, China should participate in exploring the model elements of a regional FTA even when it is not ready for high-level elements. It would take a long time for China's local authorities in inland provinces to have sufficient capacity to implement international rules. Given the huge developmental gaps between coastal and inland areas, it would be unrealistic to apply the same time frame to the entire country. Therefore China could set up new "special economic zones" where high-level elements of FTAs are applied. This would allow more time for its less-developed regions to adjust and would pave the way for its more developed regions to participate early on in high-standard FTA negotiations among developed economies in East Asia.

For China to assume a greater role in promoting East Asian regionalism, it will have to help the younger generation overcome its narrow-minded nationalism and nurture a more balanced view of Japan. It should also allow Taiwan to participate in East Asian forums to reflect the reality of regionalization. Furthermore, if its military buildup continues, the neighboring countries as well as the United States will become more concerned about the lack of transparency in its military budget and the limited political freedom of its people. East Asia will not be able to build a true community as long as China's political system remains the same.

The United States

The United States should conclude high-standard FTAs with Asian economies, as it has already done with Singapore, and incorporate in them innovative rules that can in turn be adopted by other countries. It should actively (but not high-handedly) explore how the elements of its FTAs with ASEAN countries can be blended with those of FTAs among East Asian countries. It should also expand its capacity-building support for developing countries in East Asia. U.S. cooperation with other Asian countries to urge China to improve the implementation of its WTO commitments would enhance the quality of East Asian regionalism, given China's importance and influence in it. The active contribution by the United States to the WTO negotiations would help check East Asians' residual defensive motivations in promoting their regional cooperation.

Ideally, the United States should solidify the support for its current relaxed approach to East Asian regionalism by articulating, to both domestic and foreign audiences, how East Asian regionalism would be in the U.S. interest. These reasons could be turned into a more proactive policy to foster regionalism and make it as beneficial to the United States as possible. At the very least, Washington should determine what kind of East Asian regionalism it wants if the reality cannot be avoided and should work out how it can effectively influence specific features to its own benefit.

U.S.-Japan Cooperation

Even if both Japan and the United States take positive steps—that is, if Japan reforms its sensitive sectors and the United States becomes actively involved with East Asian economies—a Japan-U.S. FTA will not be feasible in the near future as long as Washington demands the complete liberalization of rice. Also, both countries need to substantially reduce, if not eliminate, the MFN tariffs on sensitive items to minimize the side effect of a bilateral deal, that is, trade diversion away from developing economies.

Tokyo and Washington could start cooperating without a bilateral FTA, however. They could jointly, possibly in cooperation with other advanced economies in APEC as well, develop common modules of rules, facilitate the interests of U.S. firms operating in the region to be reflected in Japan's FTAs with other Asian countries, and help less-developed economies in the region build the institutional capabilities needed to effectively implement FTAs and make their administrative procedures more efficient.

Key Uncertainties

Despite all its promising features, the prospects for an East Asian community remain under a cloud of uncertainty. Although this discussion has concentrated on the economic aspects of such a community, political uncertainties are bound to affect the momentum of economic cooperation as well, even if that cooperation has a positive impact on the political environment. After all, it would take a major transformation or metamorphosis of East Asian countries for them to build a regional community. Unless they change, the vision will not materialize.

Japan's Approach to History Issues

Without political leadership to address the lingering history problems and eliminate the sources of the neighboring countries' distrust, Japan will be thwarted in its efforts to build a regional community. Since the end of the cold war, the nature of the history problem has changed. Asian people now freely express their concerns about how Japan recognizes "history" issues and ask for compensation for their wartime sufferings. Government-to-government settlement of war-related claims does not guarantee public support for reconciliation, on which the ultimate solution to this problem depends. Many Asian policymakers have pointed out that if Japan hopes to gain the confidence of its neighbors, it needs to articulate its national strategy and the role it is willing to play in the region. This will require a long-overdue comprehensive review of Japan's national strategy. If Japan can overcome this historic challenge and earn the trust and due respect of the international community and its neighbors in particular, it would have a great impact on the confidence and vitality of its citizens and thus its quality and attractiveness as a society.

Sino-Japanese Relations

Violent anti-Japanese demonstrations on the streets of major Chinese cities in the spring of 2005 revealed a deep-rooted mistrust between the two countries. On the surface, the most important impediment to the improvement of the bilateral relations seems to be Prime Minister Junichiro Koizumi's visit to the Yasukuni Shrine. Some have suggested, however, that China would not even support Japan's bid for a permanent seat at the United Nations Security Council if the prime minister stopped visiting the shrine.[4] A more fundamental issue seems to be the geopolitical competition that has motivated China to block Japan's political rise.[5] In other words, while it is in Japan's interest to sort out how to deal with its history issues and do its best to earn its neighbors' trust, whether that would fundamentally change China's view of and policy toward Japan remains unclear.

China's Future: Its Political Reform and Strategic Ambitions

China's view of Japan relates to the question of what kind of power China is to become. Will it be a liberal democracy and benign power, once it has achieved economic development and corresponding military buildup? Will China be tempted to use its power and influence to have its own way when it no longer feels the need to court its neighbors? The anxiety looming in such questions stems from the experience of having seen China's external policies abruptly shift according to its leaders' geopolitical calculations and visions, which have had decisive power in its autocratic political regime. Also, the harsh rhetoric issued by the military in warning Taiwan against taking any action that Beijing might interpret as a move toward independence was a reminder that economic development and the stable environment conducive to it might not always be China's paramount goal. Concerns about the future intentions of a rising power can be alleviated by its behavior today but not completely eliminated. This problem can only be solved by integrating China's economy with the regional and global economy and inducing economic and political changes in its domestic systems, beyond the point of no return.

Insofar as China is not confident in the strategic intentions of the major powers or of its domestic political stability and ability to positively shape the external environment, its interest in regional institutions will remain tactical. China would try to promote East Asian regionalism on an ad hoc basis if it could wield diplomatic goodwill and influence in the region by doing so, but it would also try to avoid systematic constraints on its diplomatic free hand as much as possible.

U.S. Policy toward Asia

Will the United States engage with East Asia in a positive manner or continue its benign neglect? Asia is not a natural priority for the United States, whose status as a global superpower supersedes its position as "a Pacific power." Also, America is, above all, a Western Hemisphere power. Its neighboring areas necessarily weigh heavily in its strategic calculations because the problems there will have greater impact on it than the problems in other areas. As a consequence, U.S. policy toward Asia will remain subject to the distractions of responsibilities elsewhere in the world and the associated resource constraints. While the United States has recently strengthened its involvement in the region in response to China's rise—most notably in its tsunami search, rescue, and disaster relief operations—it is not clear how sustainable U.S. commitments in this region will be, especially in the event of crises elsewhere.

Of course, Washington is concerned about the geopolitical impact of the rise of China, particularly in view of its military buildup and lack of political reform.[6] Washington might revert to outright opposition to East Asian–only frameworks if it sees them as a potential vehicle of Chinese dominance.

The Question of Values

Will the countries in East Asia continue to ignore their differences in values regarding matters such as human rights and political freedom? For example, if East Asian frameworks turn out to be ineffective in inducing changes in authoritarian political systems and, on the contrary, are used by authoritarian states to impose greater influence or justify the status quo, democratic countries will be disillusioned. The United States might then revert to its explicit discouragement of East Asian regionalism and promote the idea of dividing the region into two competitive camps: maritime Asia, having strong relations with the United States and embracing a market economy and democracy on the one hand, and continental Asia, having China at its center, on the other. The division could turn out to be a blessing in disguise, however, if the cooperation of the maritime Asia, the United States, and other Pacific countries could create economic and other incentives that would induce positive transformation in continental Asia and eventually help make East Asian countries more cohesive.

Conclusion

Now that two decades have passed since the Plaza Accord, East Asia finds itself at another turning point. The region is faced with a geopolitical shift owing to the rise of China and the relative decline of Japan. The countries in the region are trying to cope with this process through community-building efforts aimed at economic cooperation, which in turn would institutionalize and facilitate the de facto economic integration.

Each of the three major powers has a decisive influence on the direction of this regional venture and has adopted a more positive approach to it. Japan, in an effort to regain international competitiveness, has started to reduce protection and subsidization of the politically sensitive sectors of its economy. China has substantially liberalized its economy through accession to the WTO and started promoting East Asian regionalism, though chiefly as a vehicle of its political and security policy. The United States has dropped its categorical objections to East Asian regionalism and begun engaging with the region through various channels, including bilateral FTAs. In a sense, the three powers have come into a historic alignment that makes it possible to take East Asian economic regionalism to a new level.

Therefore East Asia is at a critical juncture: it is poised to turn this venture into an effective subsystem of global institutions and a vehicle for alleviating mutual distrust and enhancing stability in the world's most dynamic region. Although formidable challenges lie ahead, East Asian regionalism holds great promise and is indeed worth pursuing.

Notes

Chapter One

1. East Asia refers to Northeast Asia and Southeast Asia.

2. ASEAN has ten member countries: Brunei, Cambodia, Indonesia, Laos, Malaysia, Myanmar, the Philippines, Singapore, Thailand, and Vietnam.

Chapter Two

1. Joint Announcement of the Japanese and Singapore Prime Ministers on the Initiation of Negotiations for Concluding a Bilateral Economic Partnership Agreement, October 22, 2000 (www.meti.go.jp/english/report/data/gJ-SFTA1-2e.html [March 2004]).

2. Preferential trade agreements are legally binding agreements for the reciprocal reduction or elimination of trade barriers between countries or customs territories that do not necessarily belong to the same geographical region. They generally do not guarantee free trade between countries and may be limited to certain products or may be one-way agreements. In the context of the World Trade Organization, PTAs correspond to regional trade agreements (RTAs). PTAs include free trade agreements (FTAs) and customs unions, as described in Article 24 of the General Agreement on Tariffs and Trade (GATT). An FTA is a type of PTA where each member applies its own independent schedule of tariffs to imports from nonmembers. A customs union is another type of PTA, which maintains a common external tariff on goods imported from nonmembers. The ASEAN Free Trade Area (AFTA), which was concluded in 1992, predated the Japan-Singapore agreement, but as a PTA exclusively among developing countries, it did not come under GATT Article 24.

3. Transcript of Prime Minister Goh Chok Tong's interview with Osamu Kobayashi, editor-in-chief of *Nikkei Business,* on December 19, 2000, at the Istana (www.gov.sg/singov/interviews/191200gct.htm [February 2004]).

4. For detailed accounts of the U.S.-Singapore FTA, see Tommy Koh and Chang Li Lin, eds., *The United States-Singapore Free Trade Agreement: Highlights and Insights* (Singapore: Institute of Policy Studies and World Scientific, 2004).

5. According to Lael Brainard, former deputy national economic adviser and deputy assistant to the president for international economics in the Clinton administration, the reason the administration was reluctant to move forward on the P5 FTA was not the lack of fast-track authority but its conscious decision: "The administration had a pretty strong group of cabinet secretaries and officials that argued against it. Those who opposed it felt that it would open the door to doing more of that kind of thing, which was not consistent with U.S. interests in promoting multilateral negotiations and broad regionalism and, in some respect, it did not include some of the most important trade partners in the region like Japan and South Korea." Lael Brainard, senior fellow, Brookings Institution, interview, January 30, 2004. Although the president's 1997 Trade Policy Agenda included negotiation of FTAs with individual Asia Pacific nations, with Australia, New Zealand, and Singapore mentioned as "a few of the possible partners in this respect," the Clinton administration did not follow through on this idea. See *1997 Trade Policy Agenda and 1996 Annual Report of the President of the United States on the Trade Agreements Program*, March 1997 (www.ustr.gov/html/1997tpa_forward.html [March 2004]).

6. Joint Statement by President Clinton, Prime Minister Goh Chok Tong of Singapore on U.S.-Singapore Free Trade Agreement, U.S. Newswire, November 16, 2000.

7. Carter Dougherty, "U.S.-Singapore Free-Trade Deal Seen as a 'Gateway' to Southeast Asia," *Washington Times*, November 17, 2000, p. B10.

8. "China to Bid for Free Trade Pact with ASEAN: Thai Official," *Malaysia General News*, November 17, 2000.

9. His Excellency Zhu Rongji, premier of China's State Council, speech at the Fourth ASEAN + China Summit (10 + 1) (translation), Singapore, November 25, 2000.

10. Chua Lee Hoong, "China 'Open to FTA' with ASEAN—In Time," *The Straits Times* (Singapore), November 26, 2000, p. 15.

11. Mary Kwang, "Beijing Urges Caution on Free-Trade Pacts," *The Straits Times* (Singapore), November 7, 2000, p. 17.

12. Transcript of remarks to the media by Prime Minister Goh on the discussion of the ASEAN + 3 Summit, Fourth ASEAN Informal Summit, November 24, 2000.

13. Edward J. Lincoln, *East Asian Economic Regionalism* (Brookings, 2004), p. 2. In fact, Lincoln asserts, not only Mahathir's EAEG but "much of the rhetoric concerning East Asian regionalism has sounded a strong anti-Western or anti-American theme." Malaysia first proposed the creation of an East Asian Economic Group—comprising ASEAN, China, Japan, and South Korea—in 1990. This initiative was strongly opposed by the United States and Australia, which feared that it would become a closed trade bloc. After consulting with ASEAN members, the Malaysian government then reformulated its proposal, calling instead for the creation of an East

Asian Economic Caucus, which would involve periodic consultations on economic issues of common concern.

14. Transcript of remarks to the media by Prime Minister Goh on the discussion of the ASEAN + 3 Summit.

15. In this book, "regionalism" refers to the creation of intergovernmental institutions designed to promote economic integration by liberalizing or facilitating trade or other forms of cross-border economic activities within a region. Various forms of regionalism require different levels of commitment from the participating governments. An FTA between countries in the same region is a solid form of regionalism. On the other hand, consultative bodies that do not involve legally binding agreements but aim at promoting economic integration among their members are a looser form of regionalism. The members of ASEAN tried various forms of economic cooperation, culminating in 1992 in the formation of the ASEAN Free Trade Area. However, there was no institutional framework for East Asia as a whole until the mid-1990s. The Asia Pacific Economic Cooperation (APEC), a consultative forum that covers East Asia, Oceania, and the Americas, is a loose form of regionalism in a region broader than East Asia. APEC focuses on deepening trans-Pacific ties, as opposed to ties within East Asia and as such is not a form of East Asian regionalism.

16. On the distinction between regionalization and regionalism, see Andrew Wyatt-Walter, "Regionalism and World Economic Order," in *Regionalism in World Politics*, edited by Louise Fawcett and Andrew Hurrell (Oxford University Press, 1995), pp. 77–121. According to Wyatt-Walter, economic regionalism is "a conscious policy of states or sub-state regions to co-ordinate activities and arrangements in a greater region and economic regionalization is the outcome of such policies or of 'natural' economic forces." For an analysis of the nature and effects of regionalization in East Asia, see, for example, Paolo Guerrieri, "Trade Pattern and Regimes in Asia and the Pacific," in *Asia-Pacific Crossroads: Regime Creation and the Future of APEC*, edited by Vinod K. Aggarwal and Charles E. Morrison (New York: St. Martin's Press, 1998), pp. 65–86; Jeffrey A. Frankel and Miles Kahler, "Introduction," in *Regionalism and Rivalry: Japan and the United States in Pacific Asia*, edited by Jeffrey A. Frankel and Miles Kahler (University of Chicago Press, 1993), pp. 1–18; Peter A. Petri, "The East Asian Trading Bloc: An Analytical History," in *Regionalism and Rivalry*, edited by Frankel and Kahler, pp. 21–48; Jeffrey A. Frankel, "Is Japan Creating a Yen Bloc in East Asia and the Pacific?" in *Regionalism and Rivalry*, edited by Frankel and Kahler, pp. 53–85; Robert Z. Lawrence, "Comment," in *Regionalism and Rivalry*, edited by Frankel and Kahler, pp. 85–87; Gary R. Saxonhouse, "Pricing Strategies and Trading Blocs in East Asia," in *Regionalism and Rivalry*, edited by Frankel and Kahler, pp. 89–119; Robert Gilpin, "Comment," in *Regionalism and Rivalry*, edited by Frankel and Kahler, pp. 119–22; and Lawrence B. Krause, "Comment," in *Regionalism and Rivalry*, edited by Frankel and Kahler, pp. 122–24. For a more recent perspective on East Asia's trade and investment links in and outside the region, see Lincoln, *East Asian Economic Regionalism*, pp. 42–113.

17. For various measures of diversity, see, for example, Lincoln, *East Asian Eco-*

nomic Regionalism, pp. 15–38; and John Ravenhill, *APEC and the Construction of Pacific Rim Regionalism* (Cambridge University Press, 2001), pp. 42–50.

18. Ravenhill, *APEC and the Construction of Pacific Rim Regionalism*, p. 48.

19. Peter J. Katzenstein, "Introduction: Asian Regionalism in Comparative Perspective," in *Network Power—Japan and Asia*, edited by Peter J. Katzenstein and Shiraishi Takashi (Cornell University Press, 1997), p. 23. See also Christopher Hemmer and Peter J. Katzenstein, "Why Is There No NATO in Asia? Collective Identity, Regionalism, and the Origins of Multilateralism," *International Organization* 56, no. 3 (2002): 575–607.

20. A State Department official noted that Washington's recent, much more relaxed attitude was based on perceptions of a diminished Asian threat, owing to the Asian financial crisis and Japan's stagnation, and on its recognition that ASEAN had become much more open (and therefore less vulnerable to the temptation of protection or to other outside influences). Personal interview, December 2003.

21. APEC is a regionwide consultative forum, organized in 1989, whose member economies are Australia; Brunei Darussalam; Canada; Chile; People's Republic of China; Hong Kong, China; Indonesia; Japan; Republic of Korea (South Korea); Malaysia; Mexico; New Zealand; Papua New Guinea; Peru; the Philippines; The Russian Federation; Singapore; Chinese Taipei; Thailand; United States; and Vietnam. Under the MFN principle, countries are required to treat all their trading partners equally. Exceptions can be made in certain circumstances, such as regional trade agreements.

22. Ryutaro Hashimoto, "Next Task for the WTO System and the APEC Process," *Journal of Northeast Asian Studies* 14 (Winter 1995): 30. The article is based on his speech, "Challenges for the World Economy in a Transitional Period and Development in the Asia-Pacific Region," delivered in Vancouver in May 1995.

23. "Towards an East Asian Community—Region of Peace, Prosperity and Progress," *East Asia Vision Group, Report 2001* (www.infojapan.org/region/asia-paci/report2001.pdf [February 2004]).

24. Howard H. Baker Jr., Ambassador Extraordinary and Plenipotentiary, United States, speech before "The Future of Asia 2004," June 3, 2004 (www.nni.nikkei.co.jp/FR/NIKKEI/inasia/future/2004/2004speech_baker.html).

25. Prime Minister Goh explained Singapore's strategy of bilateral FTAs as interim measures to achieve an East Asia Free Trade Area as follows: "One spoke from China to ASEAN, one spoke from Japan to ASEAN, through Singapore. But that is going to divide East Asia, when you have China and Japan contending for the love of ASEAN. . . . But at some part of time, we have got to link them together. . . . So, we take a building block approach or a bilateral approach to achieve the endgame of an East Asia Free Trade Area." See the transcript of questions and answers following the speech of Goh Chok Tong, Prime Minister, Republic of Singapore, "Challenges for Asia," March 28, 2003 (www.rieti.go.jp/en/events/03032801/qa.html [March 2004]).

26. Initially, Tokyo proposed that Australia, India, and New Zealand should join

the summit, whereas China tried to limit the membership to that of the ASEAN + 3 Summit. See, for example, Nojima Tsuyoshi, "Japan, China at Odds on Summit," *Asahi Shimbun (Asahi.com)*, April 1, 2005 (www.asahi.com/english/Herald-asahi/TKY200504010205.html [May 2005]). At the First East Asia Summit held on December 14, 2005, in Kuala Lumpur, Malaysia, the 16 leaders (13 from the ASEAN + 3 countries, Australia, India, and New Zealand) did not agree on whether to have Russia join, as China had reportedly advocated, and what roles the East Asia summit would play in community building in East Asia. The countries that supported the participation of the three countries (Australia, India, and New Zealand) in the summit were positive about the role of the East Asia summit in East Asian community building, whereas those against were reluctant to have the East Asia summit complicate community–building efforts through the ASEAN + 3 process. See, for example, Masakado Ishizawa, "Nichi Chu In, Shudoken Arasoi" (Japan, China, and India competed for the leadership), *Nihon Keizai Shimbun,* December 15, 2005, morning edition, p. 3.

27. A plurilateral agreement is between some but not all members of a larger multilateral trade agreement.

28. The most recent example is Lincoln, *East Asian Economic Regionalism,* pp. 255–56.

29. See, for example, U.S. Department of State, "Roundtable with Japanese Journalists, Secretary Colin L. Powell, Washington, D.C., August 12, 2004," where Secretary Powell urged Asian countries not to participate in Asia-only forums "in a way that undercuts the very, very fine and strong relations that the United States has with each and every one of our friends in Asia." Richard Armitage, former U.S. deputy secretary of state, criticized the proposed East Asia summit more explicitly, arguing that it would exclude the United States, which China was particularly enthusiastic about, and therefore could be seen as designed to weaken the U.S.-Japan alliance, the last thing the two countries would want in the face of a rising China whose strategic intention was uncertain. See Armitage, "Higashi Ajia Kyodotai eno Sanka wa Kokueki ni Narunoka" (Will participating in an East Asia community serve Japan's national interest?), *Wedge,* May 2005, pp. 5–6; and Yoichi Kato, "Higashi Ajia Kyodotai ni Hantai, A-mite-ji Zen Bei Kokumu Fukuchokan 'Bei Haijo, Ayamari'" (Objection to an East Asian community, Armitage, former U.S. Deputy Secretary of State, said, "Excluding the United States is a mistake"), *Asahi Shimbun,* May 1, 2005, morning edition, p. 1. In fact, Washington is not, at least officially, concerned about the rise of Chinese influence per se. On March 17, 2005, Secretary of State Condoleezza Rice espoused Washington's position on the rising Chinese influence: "We have no problem with a strong, confident, economically powerful China" as long as China's influence is positive and "the United States would welcome a confident China at peace with its neighbors and transforming its internal system at home." U.S. Department of State, "Rice's Trip to Asia-Pacific to Focus on Global Security Relations," March 18, 2005 (usinfo.state.gov/eap/Archive/2005/Mar/18-99197.html [May 2005]).

30. See, for example, Yasuhiko Ota, "Higashi Ajia Samitto, 'Kyodotai' e Ugoku"

(The East Asia summit started its way to a "community"), *Nihon Keizai Shimbun*, December 21, 2005, p. 2; and Tadanori Yoshida, "Chugoku, Kyocho wo Enshutsu" (China displays its cooperative attitude), *Nihon Keizai Shimbun*, December 16, 2005, morning edition, p. 8.

31. Kuala Lumpur Declaration on the East Asia Summit, Kuala Lumpur, December 14, 2005 (www.mofa.go.jp/region/asia-paci/eas/joint0512.html [January 2006]).

32. WTO, "Members and Observers," in "Understanding the WTO: The Organization" (www.wto.org/english/thewto_e/whatis_e/tif_e/org6_e.htm [May 2005]).

33. For the record of the negotiations on Multilateral Agreement on Investment (MAI), see Organization for Economic Cooperation and Development, "Multilateral Agreement on Investment: Documentations from the Negotiations" (www.oecd.org/daf/mai/index.htm [February 2004]).

34. See Arvind Panagariya, "The Regional Debate: An Overview," *World Economy*, June 1999, pp. 477–511: "Much of deep integration agenda can be pursued independently of a PTA. To justify PTA, one must identify extra gains resulting from a simultaneous pursuit of PTA and other deep integration agenda. Short of that, the two policies must be justified on their own merit." Combining these agreements would not produce extra economic gains but could improve the chances of their ratification and make each of them more comprehensive and thus more conducive to liberalization and reform than without the package deal. This does not justify PTAs so much as suggest how to improve their quality in specific situations.

35. Anne O. Krueger, "Free Trade Agreements versus Customs Unions," Working Paper 5084 (Cambridge, Mass.: National Bureau of Economic Research, April 1995).

36. Jeffrey A. Frankel, *Regional Trading Blocs in the World Economic System* (Washington: Institute for International Economics, 1997), p. 219.

37. On the bicycle theory, see I. M. Destler, *American Trade Politics*, 3rd ed. (Washington: Institute for International Economics, 1995), p. 17.

38. Robert B. Zoellick, U.S. Trade Representative, prepared statement before the Subcommittee on Trade, Committee on Ways and Means of the U.S. House of Representatives, May 8, 2001 (www.ustr.gov/speech-test/zoellick/zoellick_3.html [February 2004]). Also Zoellick, "Our Credo: Free Trade and Competition," *Wall Street Journal*, July 10, 2003, p. A10.

39. C. Fred Bergsten, "A Competitive Approach to Free Trade," *Financial Times*, December 5, 2002, p. 19. See also Anne O. Krueger, "Are Preferential Trading Arrangements Trade-Liberalizing or Protectionist?" *Journal of Economic Perspectives* 13 (Autumn 1999): 105–24, 120.

40. Jagdish Bhagwati, "Fast Track to Nowhere," *Economist*, October 18, 1997, pp. 21–23.

41. U.S. policymakers have occasionally mentioned this apparent similarity between U.S. trade policy and that of its trading partners. See, for example, Ralph Ives, "Advancing Competitive Liberalization: The Australia-U.S. Free Trade Agreement," IIBE&L International Visitor Lecture Series, Finders University, October 21, 2003 (www.iibel.adelaide.edu.au/docs/AdvancingCompetitiveLiberalisation~

RalphIves.pdf [February 2004]); and Franklin L. Lavin, "The U.S. and FTAs: Partnering for Mutual Benefits," The Indus Entrepreneurs (TiE), Singapore, October 29, 2003 (singapore.usembassy.gov/speeches/2003/Oct.29.shtml [February 2004]).

42. Ives, "Advancing Competitive Liberalization."

43. Bergsten called this "asymmetric liberalization" between "old rich" and "rapid growers." See C. Fred Bergsten, "Competitive Liberalization and Global Free Trade: A Vision for the Early 21st Century," Working Paper 96-15 (Washington: Institute for International Economics, 1996) (www.iie.com/publications/wp/1996/96-15.htm [February 2004]).

44. Officials and academics interviewed in 2002 and 2003 differed in their interpretation of Washington's benign neglect of East Asian regionalism. Preoccupied with the war on terrorism, Washington paid no high-level attention to East Asian regionalism.

45. I picked up this phrase from Simon Tay, National University of Singapore, during our conversation on Singapore's FTA strategy on November 3, 1999.

46. Hadi Soesastro, "Dynamics of Competitive Liberalization in RTA Negotiations: East Asian Perspective," PECC-LAEBA, "Regional Trade Agreements in Comparative Perspective," Washington, D.C., April 22, 2003 (www.iadb.org/intal/foros/LAsoesastro.pdf [February 2004]).

47. See Danielle Goldfarb, "The Road to a Canada-U.S. Customs Union," Paper 184 (C. D. Howe Institute, June 2003), pp. 7–11 (www.cdhowe.org/pdf/commentary_184.pdf [February 2004]); also, Bhagwati, "Fast Track to Nowhere," pp. 21–23.

48. Chairman's Statement of the Ninth ASEAN + 3 Summit, Kuala Lumpur, December 12, 2005 (www.aseansec.org/18042.htm [January 2006]).

49. Takashi Shiraishi, "The Rise of New Urban Middle Classes in Southeast Asia: What Is Its National and Regional Significance?" Discussion Paper Series 04-E-011 (Japan's Research Institute of Economy, Trade and Industry, February 2004).

50. Baker, speech before "The Future of Asia" (conference).

51. *East Asia Vision Group Report 2001*. Also, "The Future of Asia 2004," Tenth International Conference, sponsored by *Nihon Keizai Shimbun* (Nikkei), June 3, 2004. This conference put forth various new proposals to overcome political rivalry, historical animosity, and wide developmental gaps, and to drive East Asian cooperation forward. It reflects the growing enthusiasm and purpose among the regional political and business leaders in mid-2004. See, for example, "Dai 10 Kai Ajia no Mirai, Touron, 'Ajia no Shin Sedai ni Takusu Yume'" (10th conference, "The Future of Asia," Discussion, "The Dream for Asia's New Generation"), *Nihon Keizai Shimbun*, June 4, 2004, morning edition, p. 9, and Yasuhiko Ohta, "Kouen wo Kiite, Miete Kita Hatten Moderu" (Comments on the speeches, An emerging development model), *Nihon Keizai Shimbun*, June 4, 2004, morning edition, p. 9. English articles are available at www.nni.nikkei.co.jp/FR/NIKKEI/ inasia/future/2004/ [June 2004].

52. See, for example, Morton Abramowitz and Stephen Bosworth, "Adjusting to the New Asia," *Foreign Affairs* 82 (July/August 2003): 119–31.

53. I owe this expression to Mike M. Mochizuki, George Washington University, who shared it in our meeting on June 2, 2004.

54. For a simple model that demonstrates these effects, see Junichi Goto and Koichi Hamada, "Economic Integration and the Welfare of Those Who Are Left Behind: An Incentive-Theoretic Approach," *Journal of the Japanese and International Economies* 12 (March 1998): 25–48.

55. For example, Robert Scollay and John P. Gilbert, "New Regional Trading Arrangements in the Asia Pacific," *Policy Analyses in International Economics* 63 (Washington: Institute for International Economics, May 2001), pp. 68–69, 120. The authors estimate that an FTA among Japan, South Korea, and China would provide slight improvements in the economic welfare of Canada, Mexico, and Chile, showing that the net effects on outsiders may not always be negative even without taking dynamic effects into consideration.

56. The term "Washington consensus" was coined by John Williamson, senior fellow, Institute for International Economics. See Williamson, "What Washington Means by Policy Reform," originally published in April 1990 and updated in November 2002 (www.iie.com/publications/papers/williamson1102-2.htm [February 2004]). To Williamson's regret, the term was misinterpreted as "a set of neoliberal policies," when in fact he "never intended the term to imply polices like capital account liberalization (. . . [he] quite consciously excluded that), monetarism, supply-side economics, or a minimal state (getting the state out of welfare provision and income redistribution.)." See Williamson, "Did the Washington Consensus Fail?" Outline of remarks at the Center for Strategic and International Studies, November 6, 2002 (www.iie.com/publications/papers/williamson1102-2.htm [May 2004]).

57. Andrew Hurrell, "Regionalism in Theoretical Perspective," in *Regionalism in World Politics*, edited by Louise Fawcett and Andrew Hurrell (Oxford University Press, 1995), pp. 37–73, 73, argues that "a phased or 'stage-theory' approach to regionalism," that employs different theories to explain different stages of regionalism, while "theoretically somewhat unsatisfying," is "historically often very plausible."

58. Ravenhill, *APEC and the Construction of Pacific Rim Regionalism*, p. 15, considers this one of two impulses of "contagion" (the phenomenon that "regionalism in one part of the world fosters emulation by governments elsewhere"): "One is the desire to use mechanisms for promoting national objectives in a regional context that appear to have worked successfully elsewhere. The second is a defensive motive: the perceived need to emulate others in order to defend domestic interests that appear to be under challenge by a strengthening external entity." However, these two impulses "often operate together" and are hard to distinguish in actual situations. I call them both defensive regionalism.

59. Richard E. Baldwin, "The Causes of Regionalism," *World Economy*, 20, no.7 (1997): 865–88.

60. C. Fred Bergsten notes "the positive inspiration provided by European integration (especially the euro)" as one of "four basic reasons" for the resurgence of East Asian regionalism "at the outset of the 21st century" (the other three reasons are: "the

East Asian financial crisis; the failure of the WTO and of APEC to make headway on trade liberalization; and a broad disquiet with the behaviour of both the United States and the European Union"). See Bergsten, "East Asian Regionalism: Towards a Tripartite World," *Economist*, July 15, 2000, pp. 20–22.

61. Empirical evaluations of PTAs are reviewed by Richard E. Baldwin and A. Venables, "Regional Economic Integration," in *Handbook of International Economics,* edited by Gene M. Grossman and Kenneth S. Rogoff (New York: North-Holland, 1995), vol. 3, pp. 1597–1644.

62. Bergsten, "Competitive Liberalization and Global Free Trade."

63. Ibid.

64. See, for example, C. Fred Bergsten, "A Renaissance for U.S. Trade Policy?" *Foreign Affairs* 81 (November/December 2002): 86–98, and "A Competitive Approach to Free Trade." Also, Ives, "Advancing Copmpetitive Liberalization"; and Lavin, "The U.S. and FTAs."

65. World Bank, *Trade Blocs* (Oxford University Press, 2000), p. 2.

66. Gross national income (GNI) per capita is used here, in accordance with the Atlas method (current U.S. dollars) in the World Development Indicators Database (publications.worldbank.org/subscriptions/WDI/ [February 2004]). The Atlas method is the conversion factor the World Bank uses to calculate GNI (formerly referred to as GNP) and GNI per capita in U.S. dollars in order to reduce the impact of exchange rate fluctuations in the cross-country comparison of national incomes. The factor for any year is the average of a country's exchange rate for that year and its exchange rates for the two preceding years, adjusted for the difference between the rate of inflation in the country and international inflation. For details, see "World Bank Atlas Method" (www.worldbank.org/data/aboutdata/working-meth.html [May 2004]).

67. Miles Kahler, "Legalization as Strategy: The Asia-Pacific Case," *International Organization* 54 (Summer 2000): 549–71, 561.

68. For example, Shi Yinhong, "Sino-Japanese Rapprochement and 'Diplomatic Revolution,'" *Management and Strategy* (in Chinese) (April 2003), vol. 2.

69. The aspects of institutionalization concerning rules for the members are called "legalization," which Goldstein and others define by "three criteria: the degree to which rules are obligatory, the precision of those rules and the delegation of some functions of interpretation, monitoring, and implementation to a third party." Judith Goldstein, Miles Kahler, Robert O. Keohane, and Anne-Marie Slaughter, "Introduction: Legalization and World Politics," *International Organization* 54 (Summer 2000): 385–99. Measures such as holding regular summit meetings and setting up a secretariat for information sharing and logistical support show to some extent member governments' commitment to the forum and certainly some aspects of institutionalization but are not relevant to the degree of legalization. ASEAN countries in particular seemed wary of institutionalization in the early stage of APEC. This is most evident in the Kuching Consensus on the principles of ASEAN participation in APEC, agreed at the ASEAN Joint Ministerial Meeting (JMM) in Malaysia on

February 15, 1990. It states that APEC "should not lead to the adoption of mandatory directives" and "should proceed gradually and pragmatically, especially in its institutionalization." For the Kuching Consensus, see Ravenhill, *APEC and the Construction of Pacific Rim Regionalism,* pp. 104–05. The highly institutionalized European model was the last thing they wanted to see in APEC. See, for example, Eminent Persons Group Report, "Achieving the APEC Vision: Free and Open Trade in the Asia Pacific," August 1994: "We believe that we should avoid overinstitutionalization and over-bureaucratization; the approach followed by the European Community (EC) is one that is neither possible nor productive for the Asia Pacific; nothing in this Report should be read to imply any interest in emulating the European model" (www.apec.org/apec/publications/free_downloads/1997-1993.MedialibDownload.v1.html?url=/etc/medialib/apec_media_library/ downloads/misc/pubs/1994.Par.0001.File.v1.1).

70. Kahler, "Legalization as Strategy," p. 561.

71. Susumu Yamakage, *ASEAN Pawah: Ajia Taiheiyou no Chukaku e* (ASEAN power: toward the core of Asia Pacific) (Tokyo University Press, 1997), pp. 327–29.

72. Satoshi Kuwahara, "ASEAN no Keizai-Hatten Senryaku to Nichi ASEAN Kankei" (ASEAN's strategy for economic development and Japan-ASEAN Relations), manuscript in the author's possession.

73. Hashimoto, "Next Task for the WTO System."

Chapter Three

1. Walter Hatch and Kozo Yamamura, *Asia in Japan's Embrace: Building a Regional Production Alliance* (Cambridge University Press, 1996), pp. x–xi.

2. Data on Japanese outbound FDI are from the Ministry of Finance's statistics on a registered (not disbursed) basis and since 1989 are in Japanese yen. I have roughly converted them into U.S. dollars using the data provided by the Federal Reserve Bank of St. Louis (research.stlouisfed.org/fred2/series/EXJPUS/95 [April 2004]).

3. For the impact of the Plaza Accord and the subsequent trade frictions between NIEs and the United States, which in turn prompted the former to invest in ASEAN and China, see John Ravenhill, "Economic Cooperation in Southeast Asia: Changing Incentives," *Asian Survey* 35 (September 1995): 850–66.

4. For the impact of the FDI surge on the business orientation of local companies and, in turn, on ASEAN government policies, see Satoshi Kuwahara, "ASEAN no Keizai-Hatten Senryaku to Nichi ASEAN Kankei" (ASEAN's strategy for economic development and Japan-ASEAN relations), manuscript in the author's possession.

5. World Bank, *WDI-online* (publications.worldbank.org/subscriptions/WDI/ [April 2004]).

6. Ibid.

7. Kuwahara, "ASEAN's Strategy for Economic Development and Japan-ASEAN Relations."

8. Ministry of International Trade and Industry (MITI), "Prospects and Challenges for the Upgrading of Industries in the ASEAN Region," report presented by MITI Minister Hiroshi Kumagai at the second meeting of ASEAN economic ministers and MITI minister, Singapore, October 9, 1993.

9. The annual average growth rate was calculated using data on net inflows of FDI based on the balance of payments in current U.S. dollars, from World Bank, *WDI Online* (publications.worldbank.org/subscriptions/WDI/ [April 1, 2004]).

10. Kuwahara, "ASEAN's Strategy for Economic Development and Japan-ASEAN Relations."

11. Based on exports and imports of goods and services, from World Bank, *WDI Online*, retrieved on April 1, 2004.

12. Theodore H. Moran, "Parental Supervision: The New Paradigm for Foreign Direct Investment and Development," *Policy Analyses in International Economics* 64 (Washington: Institute of International Economics, August 2001), p. 16.

13. Ibid., p. 38.

14. WTO Secretariat, "Trade Policy Review: First Press Release, Secretariat and Government Summaries—Thailand: December 1995," PRESS/TPRB/21, December 1, 1995 (www.wto.org/english/tratop_e/tpr_e/tp21_e.htm [January 2006]).

15. The margin of preference for the AFTA-CEPT varies from country to country; for example, it allows reductions of up to half of the MFN rate in Indonesia, and more than half in Thailand. See WTO Secretariat, "Trade Policy Review—Indonesia—Report by the Secretariat," WT/TPR/S/117, May 28, 2003 (www.wto.org/english/tratop_e/tpr_e/s117-0_e.doc [January 2006]); and "Trade Policy Review—Thailand—Report by the Secretariat," WT/TPR/S/63, November 17, 1999 (searched from www.wto.org/english/ tratop_e/tpr_e/tpr_e.htm [March 2004]).

16. These respective figures are drawn from WTO Secretariat, "Trade Policy Reviews" for Thailand, PRESS/TPRB/21, December 1, 1995, PRESS/TPRB/122, December 10, 1999 (www.wto.org/english/tratop_e/tpr_e/tp122_e.htm [January 2006]), and WT/TPR/S/123, October 15, 2003 (searched from www.wto.org/english/tratop_e/tpr_e/tpr_e.htm); for Malaysia, PRESS/TPRB/67, December 1, 1997 (www.wto.org/english/tratop_e/tpr_e/ tp67_e.htm [January 2006]) and PRESS/TPRB/180, December 5, 2001 (www.wto.org/english/tratop_e/tpr_e/ tp180_e.htm [January 2006]); for Indonesia, PRESS/TPRB/94, December 1, 1998 (www.wto.org/english/tratop_e/tpr_e/ tp94_e.htm [January 2006]) and WT/TPR/S/117, May 28, 2003 (searched from www.wto.org/english/tratop_e/tpr_e/ tpr_e.htm [March 2004]); and for the Philippines, WT/TPR/S/59, August 27, 1999 (searched from www.wto.org/english/tratop_e/tpr_e/ tpr_e.htm [March 2004]).

17. Kuwahara, "ASEAN's Strategy for Economic Development and Japan-ASEAN Relations."

18. WTO Secretariat, "Trade Policy Review—Indonesia—Report by the Secretariat," WT/TPRB/94, December 1, 1998.

19. The history of ASEAN efforts for economic integration among its member-

ship goes back to a United Nations report commissioned by ASEAN foreign ministers in 1969 and submitted in 1972, which recommended three programs: "selective trade liberalization" (item-by-item preferential trade liberalization), "complementary agreements" (the division of components production and exchange of components produced in different member countries), and "package deal arrangements" (allocation of jointly owned industrial projects to ASEAN countries), which ASEAN foreign ministers decided to implement in 1975. See Joint Communiqué, Eighth ASEAN Ministerial Meeting, Kuala Lumpur, May 13–15, 1975, pars. 11, 12 (www.aseansec.org/1238.htm [April 2004]). For the origin of ASEAN economic cooperation, see Susumu Yamakage, *ASEAN: Sinboru kara Sisutemu e* (ASEAN: From symbol to system) (Tokyo University Press, 1991), pp. 193–200.

20. The ASEAN Chambers of Commerce and Industry, established in 1972, submitted recommendations on the measures to promote intra-ASEAN integration in preparation for the First ASEAN Summit in 1976 and have actively advocated ASEAN integration since then.

21. Japanese automakers were not the first to lobby for ASEAN integration. In 1976 the ASEAN Automotive Federation proposed a scheme for ASEAN Industrial Complementation (AIC), building on the Ford Motor Company's proposal of 1971. See Ravenhill, "Economic Cooperation in Southeast Asia," p. 852.

22. The idea was to divide the production of components for the "ASEAN car" among ASEAN members. See Joint Press Statement, Fifteenth ASEAN Economic Ministers Meeting, par. 7 (www.aseansec.org/6118.htm [April 2004]). The final package of automotive components was approved under the Basic Agreement on ASEAN Industrial Complementation, Manila, June 18, 1981 (www.aseansec.org/6377.htm [April 2004]). The package did not reflect the actual distribution of component production, but that desired by member governments. The private sector was by and large wary of using components with different specifications produced by other companies. ASEAN governments that adopted the program were not keen to see it implemented either. See Kuwahara, "ASEAN's Strategy for Economic Development and Japan-ASEAN Relations"; and "ASEAN ga Shin Jidousha Seisaku" (ASEAN's New Automobile Policy), *Nikkei Sangyo Simbun*, August 28, 1982, p. 7. AIJV was a program to promote joint industrial production under the Basic Agreement on ASEAN Industrial Joint Ventures (Jakarta, November 7, 1983) (www.aseansec.org/6378.htm [April 2004]). The private sector was deterred by long delays by state bureaucracies in approving proposals. See also Ravenhill, "Economic Cooperation in Southeast Asia"; and "MMC, Mitsubishi Corp. Consider Division of Auto Production in Asia," Jiji Press Ticker Service, May 30, 1984.

23. "Malaysian Govt Bent on Pushing 'National Car Project,'" Jiji Press Ticker Service, October 27, 1983; "Mitsubishi to Start Building Engine Plant in Indonesia," Japan Economic Newswire, November 28, 1983.

24. See Memorandum of Understanding Brand-to-Brand Complementation on the Automotive Industry under the Basic Agreement on ASEAN Industrial Complementation (BAAIC), Pattaya, Thailand, October 18, 1988 (www.aseansec.org/

806.htm [March 2004]); and Joint Press Statements, Twentieth ASEAN Economic Ministers Meeting, Thailand, October 17–19, 1988, par. 11 (www.aseansec.org/6123.htm [March 2004]).

25. "Toyota to Produce More Parts in ASEAN Countries," *New Straits Times* (Malaysia), April 19, 1995, p. 20.

26. Toyota spearheaded the use of BBC in setting up the production of steering gears in Malaysia and transmissions in the Philippines in 1992, in addition to the factories in Thailand and Indonesia. For the list of overseas production facilities with the timing of starting operations, see Toyota's Annual Report 2003, p. 115 (www.toyota.co.jp/jp/pdf/annual/03annualreport_j.pdf [March 2004]).

27. See Basic Agreement on the ASEAN Industrial Cooperation Scheme (www.aseansec.org/7945.htm [March 2004]); and Joint Press Statements, Twenty-Eighth ASEAN Economic Ministers Meeting, Jakarta, September 12, 1996, par. 15 (www.aseansec.org/7145.htm [March 2004]). For the list of 101 projects approved as AICO projects as of February 10, 2003, see the ASEAN Secretariat, "Approved AICO Applications" (www.aseansec.org/6398.htm [March 2004]).

28. See Kerry A. Chase, "From Protectionism to Regionalism: Multinational Firms and Trade-Related Investment Measures," draft manuscript (ase.tufts.edu/polsci/faculty/chase/protectionism.pdf [March 2004]), later published in *Business and Politics* 6 (August 2004): 1–36 (a pdf file available at ase.tufts.edu/polsci/faculty/chase/protectionism.pdf [January 2006]).

29. Vietnam joined ASEAN in July 1995, Laos and Myanmar in July 1997, and Cambodia in April 1999.

30. See Japan, Ministry of Economy, Trade and Industry (METI), *White Paper on International Trade 2001* (Tokyo, 2001), pp. 6–9.

31. Ibid., pp. 22–25.

32. Ibid.

33. On the assumption that most FDI from the British Virgin Islands and Cayman Islands to China came originally from Taiwan, see Japan External Trade Organization (JETRO), *Boueki Tousi Hakusho* (Trade and Investment White Paper), 2003, p.162.

34. For data on FDI (on a disbursed basis) to China, see JETRO, *China Data File 2002/3* (in Japanese), pp. 184–85, based on MOFTEC, *Almanac of China's Foreign Relations and Trade* (Beijing, various years) (data for 1986 to 2001); and JETRO, Trade and Investment White Paper, 2003, p.163 (data for 2002).

35. Calculation made using data from IMF, *Direction of Trade Statistics, Database and Browser* (Washington, 2004). East Asia here does not include Taiwan, which is not covered by the IMF trade statistics.

36. The trade intensity index measures the degree of trade integration between two countries (A and B) as A's export trade intensity with B ([A's export to B / A's export to the world] / [B's import from the world / total world import]) or as B's import trade intensity with A ([B's import from A / B's import from the world] / [A's export to the world / total world export]). An index higher (lower) than 1 is inter-

preted to indicate that a bilateral trade flow is larger (smaller) than expected given the partner country's importance in world trade.

37. Japan, METI, *White Paper on International Trade 2002* (Tokyo), pp. 15–16.

38. Francis Ng and Alexander Yeats, "Major Trade Trends in East Asia: What Are Their Implications for Regional Cooperation and Growth?" Policy Research Working Paper 3084 (Washington: World Bank, June 2003) (econ.worldbank.org/files/27878_wps3084.pdf [March 2004]).

39. Not all the sales to the host country were necessarily made by old import-substitution plants. A substantial part of the products sold locally were presumably for further reprocessing. Therefore, the data on sales destination underestimate the export-oriented nature of the business operation.

40. MITI, Dai 28 Kai Kaigai Jigyo Katsudo Doko Chosa (28th survey of overseas business activities), May 18, 1999; and METI, Dai 32 Kai Kaigai Jigyo Katsudo Doko Chosa (32nd survey of overseas business activities), rev. March 20, 2004 (www.meti.go.jp/statistics/index.html [March 2004]).

41. U.S. Department of Commerce (USDOC), "Revised 1990 Estimates," *U.S. Direct Investment Abroad: Operations of U.S. Parent Companies and Their Foreign Affiliates*, July 1993 (www.bea.doc.gov/bea/pi/idn0036.exe [March 2004]).

42. USDOC, "Revised 1995 Estimates," *U.S. Direct Investment Abroad: Operations of U.S. Parent Companies and Their Foreign Affiliates*, October 1998 (www.bea.doc.gov/bea/pi/idn0213.exe [March 2004]).

43. USDOC, "Revised 2000 Estimates," *U.S. Direct Investment Abroad: Operations of U.S. Parent Companies and Their Foreign Affiliates* (www.bea.doc.gov/bea/pi/USDIArevised2000.exe [March 2004]).

44. In 1989 and 1994 U.S. manufacturing affiliates in Asia and the Pacific (including Japan), on average, directed 66.8 percent and 66.6 percent of their sales, respectively, to other countries in Asia and the Pacific. In 1999 details on "other foreign countries" are available only for all industries (no separate data for manufacturing). The affiliates of all industries in countries for which data are available on average made 83.2 percent of the sales to other countries in Asia and the Pacific. See USDOC, "Revised 1989 Estimates," (www.bea.doc.gov/bea/pi/ idn0035.exe), "Revised 1994 Estimates" (www.bea.doc.gov/bea/pi/idn0189.exe), and "Revised 1999 Estimates" (www.bea.doc.gov/bea/pi/usdia99.exe), and *U.S. Investment Abroad: Operations of U.S. Parent Companies and Their Foreign Affiliates: Comprehensive Financial and Operating Data*" (www.bea.doc.gov/bea/ai/iidguide. htm#link12b [March 2004]).

45. According to Walter B. Lohman, executive director, U.S.-ASEAN Business Council, Inc., "U.S. firms have been in support of ASEAN integration since the mid-1990s." Personal interview, November 3, 2003. See also, for example, U.S. Department of State, "ASEAN Cooperation Plan," *Fact Sheet*, December 4, 2002 (www.state.gov/p/eap/regional/asean/fs/2002/16599.htm [March 2004]).

46. Sven W. Arndt and Henryk Kierzkowski, "Introduction," in *Fragmentation: New Production Pattern in the World Economy*, edited by Sven W. Arndt and Henryk Kierzkowski (Oxford University Press, 2001), p. 4.

47. Kyoji Fukao, Hikari Ishido, and Keiko Ito, "Vertical Intra-Industry Trade and Direct Investment in East Asia," Discussion Paper 03-E-001 (Tokyo: Research Institute of Economy, Trade and Industry [RIETI], January 2003) (www.rieti.go.jp/jp/publications/dp/03e001.pdf [February 2004]).

48. Carliss Y. Baldwin and Kim B. Clark, "Managing in an Age of Modularity," *Harvard Business Review* 75, no. 5 (September-October 1997), pp. 84–93.

49. RIETI, "Kyousouryoku no kenkyu (19)— Mojuruka" (Study on competitiveness (19)—modularity), *Nihon Keizai Shimbun*, January 29, 2002, morning edition, p. 29.

50. See Atsuo Kuroda, *Meido in Chaina* (Made in China) (Toyo Keizai Shimpo-sha, 2001), pp. 79–133; and Kwan Chi Hung, "China's Immiserizing Growth," *China in Transition*, August 16, 2002 (www.rieti.go.jp/en/china/02081601.html [February 2004]).

51. Masahisa Fujita, Paul Krugman, and Anthony J. Venables, *The Spatial Economy: Cities, Regions and International Trade* (Cambridge, Mass.: MIT Press, 2001), pp. 11, 346.

52. Satoshi Kuwahara, "Higashi Ajia oyobi Tonan-Ajia Chiiki ni okeru Sangyoshuseki Keisei" (Formation of industrial clusters in East and Southeast Asia), in *Gendai Ajia no Furontia* (The frontiers of Asia today), edited by Hideo Kobayashi (Tokyo: Shakaihyoronsha, 2004), pp. 83–108.

53. Ibid., p. 91.

54. Kuwahara, ASEAN's Strategy for Economic Development and Japan-ASEAN Relations.

55. METI, *White Paper on International Trade 2001*, pp. 10–11.

56. Ng and Yeats, "Major Trade Trends in East Asia."

57. Ibid.

58. The share of VIIT for individual sectors is based on data for the simplex diagrams in Fukao and others, "Vertical Intra-Industry Trade."

59. Ibid.

60. The trade in agricultural and mining products is dominated by one-way trade in both the European Union (60.4 percent and 67.7 percent, respectively, in 2000) and East Asia (92.7 percent and 86.0 percent, respectively, in 2000), but the shares of both vertical IIT and horizontal IIT in these products are much higher in Europe (21.5 percent [agriculture VIIT], 18.0 percent [agriculture HIIT], 13.1 percent [mining VIIT] and 19.2 percent [mining HIIT]) than in East Asia (2.4 percent [agriculture VIIT], 1.4 percent [agriculture HIIT], 2.8 percent [mining VIIT], and 11.2 percent [mining HIIT]).

61. See, for example, "Agriculture Getting Aggressive and Export-Oriented" (in Japanese), *Mainichi Shimbun*, morning edition, July 5, 2003, p. 11; "Vegetables and Fruits Taking a Chance in Asia" (in Japanese), *Tokyo Yomiuri Shimbun*, morning edition, July 7, 2003, p. 8; and other sources cited in chapter 5, n. 22.

62. USDOC, "Revised 1999 Estimates." Because many East Asian companies avoid disclosing data on their operations, the only regional aggregate available was for Asia and the Pacific.

63. These Monetary Authority figures are based on the detailed 1995 Asian input-output tables compiled by the Institute of Developing Economies (IDE), JETRO. See Economic Policy Department, Monetary Authority of Singapore, *Macroeconomic Review* 2 (January 2003): 64–65 (www.mas.gov.sg/resource/download/MRJan2003_upload.pdf [February 2004]).

64. Sun-Bae Kim, "Regional Commentary: Asia's Brave New Business Cycle Part II: Intra-Regional Trade," *Asia-Pacific Economics Analyst,* no. 2002/15, Goldman Sachs Asia Economic Research Group, September 2, 2002.

65. Dick Li, Jonathan Anderson, and Sun-Bae Kim, "What Is Driving Asia's Exports to China?" *Asia-Pacific Economics Analyst,* no. 2003/01, January 17, 2003.

66. Ibid.

67. Monetary Authority of Singapore, *Macroeconomic Review* 2, p. 65.

68. Walter Hatch, "Japanese Production Networks in Asia: Extending the Status Quo," in *Crisis and Innovation in Asian Technology,* edited by William W. Keller and Richard J. Samuels (Cambridge University Press, 2002), pp. 23–56.

69. See, for example, Hatch and Yamamura, *Asia in Japan's Embrace,* p. 198. They criticize the APEC goal of liberalization by 2010 for developed economies and 2020 for developing economies, arguing: "It shows again that Western policymakers do not understand the nature of Japan's developmentalism, which uses exclusionary relationships more often than explicit government policies to bar unwanted imports."

70. Hatch, "Japanese Production Networks in Asia."

71. Takahiro Fujimoto, "The Japanese Supplier System and Modularity" (in Japanese), in *Modularity—The Essence of New Industrial Architecture,* edited by Masahiko Aoki and Haruhiko Ando, RIETI Economic Policy Review (Toyokeizai Shimpo-Sha, March 2002), pp. 169–202.

72. For example, cross-shareholding declined sharply in the second half of 1990s. See Fumiaki Kuroki, "Cross-Shareholdings Decline for the 11th Straight Year (FY2001 Survey)," Financial Research Group, NIL Research Institute (www.nli-research.co.jp/eng/resea/econo/eco021001.pdf).

73. Fujimoto, "The Japanese Supplier System and Modularity," p. 175.

74. Kuroda, *Maido in Chaina,* pp. 106–08; and Mitsuhiro Seki, *Sekai no Kojo / Chugoku Kanan to Nihon Kigyo* (The factory of the world: Southern China and Japanese firms) (Sinhyoron, 2002), p. 165. It is also noted that Alibaba.com, an online business-to-business marketplace (www.alibaba.com) has reportedly decided to establish an office in Japan to serve Japanese companies increasing their procurement from Chinese companies. See "China's Alibaba Moves into Japan with Prospects for Japan's Increased Procurement from China," *Nihon Keizai Shimbun,* morning edition, July 15, 2003, p. 11.

75. See "The Most Popular Employers in Chinese Students' Eyes" (in Chinese) (www.chinahr.com/promotion/investigate/); and C. H. Kwan, "Why Japanese Firms Are Unpopular?" *China in Transition,* April 2, 2003 (www.rieti.go.jp/en/china/03040201.html). Also Kuroda, *Maido in Chaina,* pp. 255–57.

76. JETRO, *Zai Ajia nikkei seizogyo no keiei jittai—2002 nendo chosa* (Business condition of Japanese manufacturing in Asia—FY2002 report), March 2003.

77. Kyoji Fukao, "How Japanese Subsidiaries in Asia Responded to the Regional Crisis: An Empirical Analysis Based on the MITI Survey," in *Regional and Global Capital Flows: Macroeconomic Causes and Consequences,* edited by Takatoshi Ito and Anne O. Krueger, *East Asia Seminar on Economics,* vol. 10 (University of Chicago Press, 2001), pp. 267–310.

78. On the Japanese government's assistance, see chap. 6, n. 13.

Chapter Four

1. There was one accord: the Bangkok Agreement, ratified in the mid-1990s by five countries, including South Korea.

2. AFTA is based on the enabling clause.

3. Tommy Koh, "Introductory Remarks," in *U.S.-Singapore FTA: Implications and Prospects,* edited by Tommy Koh, Kristin Paulson, Jose Tongzon, and Vikram Khanna, *Trends in Southeast Asia* Series 5 (Singapore: Institute of Southeast Asian Studies, July 2003) (www.iseas.edu.sg/52003.pdf [April 2004]).

4. Geza Feketekuty, former Senior Assistant U.S. Trade Representative, e-mail message to author, January 14, 2004. For the impact of the 1982 meeting on the U.S. pursuit of bilateral FTAs that started with Israel and Canada, see also Jeffrey J. Schott, "More Free Trade Areas?" in *Free Trade Areas and U.S. Trade Policy* (Washington: Institute for International Economics, 1989), pp. 4–5.

5. Feketekuty, e-mail to author, January 14, 2004. See also Stuart Auerback, "U.S. Going Its Own Way on Trade," *Washington Post,* July 29, 1984, p. G1.

6. President Ronald Reagan, Remarks to Business Leaders and Members of the President's Export Council and the Advisory Committee for Trade Negotiations, September 23, 1985.

7. Feketekuty, e-mail to author, January 14, 2004. A U.S.-ASEAN FTA was considered but was deferred when President Reagan's planned visit to southern Asia was canceled following the assassination of Benigno Aquino in the Philippines (on August 21, 1983). See William A. Niskanen, "Stumbling toward a U.S.-Canada Free Trade Agreement," Cato Institute Policy Analysis 88, June 18, 1987 (www.cato.org/pubs/pas/pa088es.html [March 2004]). Given Feketekuty's account that the U.S. government preferred to have the other party announce first and ASEAN's rejection of the idea, however, it is unlikely that the proposal for a U.S.-ASEAN FTA would have become official even if President Reagan had made a trip to ASEAN as scheduled.

8. Koh, "Introductory Remarks."

9. Tommy Koh's account quoted in "The Negotiator," *channelnewsasia.com,* November 23, 2002 (www.channelnewsasia.com/stories/todaynews/view/225/1/.html [accessed November 23, 2002, but no longer available on the public domain of the website]).

10. Joint Communiqué, Seventh ASEAN-U.S. Dialogue, Singapore, May 8–9, 1986, par. 25 (www.aseansec.org/5940.htm).

11. It was first proposed by USTR Yeutter when he visited Singapore in October 1987. See "U.S., ASEAN Eye Free Trade Pact," Japan Economic Newswire, February 10, 1988. In February 1988, the coordinators for the ASEAN-U.S. Initiative (AUI) agreed to launch a joint study on ASEAN-U.S. economic relations. See Joint Communiqué, Eighth ASEAN-U.S. Dialogue, Washington D.C., February 10–11, 1988 (www.aseansec.org/5941.htm). A joint study on AUI commissioned in July 1988 and completed in March 1989 recommended that ASEAN and the United States enter into an "umbrella (or framework) agreement" that would include a set of basic guiding principles for the conduct of trade and other economic relations between the two and the creation of a Consultative Committee composed of trade ministers and advised by experts and private-sector representatives. An ASEAN-U.S. FTA "should be the ultimate goal of the framework agreement," though it "would be very complex and . . . likely to take a long time to negotiate." The report recommended commissioning a comprehensive study of such an agreement, noting that it "could serve as a forerunner to a wider accord in the Asia-Pacific region." See Seiji Naya, Kernial S. Sandhu, Michael Plummer, and Narongchai Akrasanee, *ASEAN-U.S. Initiative: Assessment and Recommendations for Improved Economic Relations*, Joint Final Report (Institute of Southeast Asian Studies and East-West Center, 1989), pp. 186–96. The Memorandum of Understanding concluded on December 21, 1990, between the United States and the Association of Southeast Asian Nations, a form of trade and investment framework agreement (TIFA), proposed "to establish a Trade and Investment Cooperation Committee to monitor and review trade and investment relations, to identify opportunities for expanding trade and investment and related technology transfer and human resources development and to hold consultations thereon."

12. TIFA refers to "a treaty aimed at promoting trade and investment between the partners through making the existing rules and regulations work more smoothly." Walter Goode, *Dictionary of Trade Policy Terms*, 4th ed. (Cambridge University Press, 2003), p. 351. The United States has often concluded a TIFA with another country as a preparatory step to a free trade agreement. Feketekuty, e-mail to author, January 14, 2004.

13. "Mansfield Counsels Japan-U.S. Free-Trade Pact," Jiji Press Ticker Service, May 22, 1987; "Ma Chunichi Taisi, Jiyuu Boueki Jouyaku Teiketsu o—Nichibei Masatu Kaisho de Teian" (Ambassodor Mansfield proposes free trade treaty—to solve Japan-U.S. trade frictions), *Nihon Keizai Shimbun*, evening edition, January 6, 1986, p.1.

14. "Chunichi Beikoku Taishi ga Koen, Nichibei de Nousanbutsu no Jiyuu Boueki Joyaku o" (U.S. ambassador to Japan proposed Japan-U.S. free trade treaty to liberalize agricultutral produce in a speech), *Nihon Keizai Shimbun*, evening edition, July 24, 1986, p. 3.

15. Nichibei Jiyuu Boueki Kousou Kenkyuukai (Study group on Japan-U.S. free trade initiatives), "Chuukan Torimatome: Aratana Nichibei Kyoryoku Kankei Kouchiku ni Mukete—'Nichibei Keizai Kensho' o Mezashita 'Daburu Torakku Apurochi'" (Interim report: toward building a new cooperative Japan-U.S. relationship—a 'double-track approach' aimed at 'Japan-U.S. economic charter'"), Tokyo, June 1989.

16. USITC, *Pros and Cons of Initiating Negotiations with Japan to Explore the Possibility of a U.S.-Japan Free Trade Area Agreement,* Publication 2120 (Washington: Government Printing Office, September 1988).

17. See Inbom Choi and Jeffery J. Schott, *Free Trade between Korea and the United States?* Policy Analyses in International Economics 62 (Washington: Institute of International Economics, April 2001), p. 2: "Initial flirtations with the idea of a Korea-U.S. FTA actually date back to the second half of the 1980s." In 1988 Treasury Secretary James A. Baker III and Robert Zoellick, counselor to Secretary Baker, "constructed a paper, based on an analysis of the U.S.-Canada FTA, in which they argued that regional [FTAs] could strengthen the global system." The idea was to expand the U.S.-Canada FTA to individual countries in the Asia Pacific. See Yoichi Funabashi, *Asia Pacific Fusion, Japan's Role in APEC* (Washington: Institute for International Economics, September 1995), pp. 59, 108. For Baker's thinking on the strategic employment of bilateral FTAs around this time, see James Baker, "The Geopolitical Implications of the U.S.-Canada Trade Pact," *International Economy,* January/February 1988, pp. 34–41: "We might be willing to explore a 'market liberalization club' approach, through minilateral arrangements or a series of bilateral agreements. In this fashion, North America can build steadily momentum for more open and efficient markets. Ambassador Yeutter has reported that there are voices in other nations—including Japan, South Korea, Taiwan, and some of the nations of the ASEAN—that have indicated that they do not wish to be left behind." Later that year, Baker proposed "a free trade policy . . . in relation to the Asia and Pacific regions," including a U.S.-Japan bilateral FTA. See "MITI Wary of Free Trade Pact with U.S.," Jiji Press Ticker Service, June 20, 1988.

18. USITC, *The Pros and Cons of Entering into Negotiations on Free Trade Area Agreements with Taiwan, the Republic of Korea, and ASEAN, or the Pacific Rim Region in General,* Publication 2166 (GPO, March 1989).

19. Ibid.; and USITC, *The Pros and Cons of . . . Negotiations . . . with Japan.* Also, Feketekuty, e-mail to author, January 14, 2004.

20. I. M. Destler, *American Trade Politics,* 3rd ed. (Washington: Institute for International Economics, April 1995), p.126.

21. Trade relations between the United States and Japan became more strained through the 1980s as the bilateral trade imbalance grew and culminated in April 1987 in the imposition of punitive tariffs by the United States on Japanese products for the first time since World War II, in retaliation against alleged Japanese violation of a bilateral semiconductor agreement. It marked a radical shift in U.S. policy from trying to work out compromises to resorting to punitive action.

22. On the reaction to the U.S. FTA proposal, see Funabashi, *Asia Pacific Fusion*, p. 108: "Washington severely underestimated the negative reaction . . . in the region. Far from embracing the proposal, most Asia Pacific nations saw the prospect of a bilateral free trade agreement with the world's largest economy as a clear threat, particularly given America's proclivity toward unilateral trade actions."

23. The U.S.-Canada FTA was potentially (though not imminently) a precursor to an FTA covering the North American continent as President Reagan, before being elected president, had already proposed "a North American accord" consisting of Canada, Mexico, and the United States. See Ronald Reagan, *Official Announcement for Presidential Candidacy*, November 13, 1979. The Single European Act, which stipulated that the "internal market" (defined as "an area without internal frontiers in which the free movement of goods, persons, services and capital is ensured") be completed by December 31, 1992, was signed in February 1986 and came into force on July 1, 1987.

24. Because the countries in the region hesitated to form intergovernmental institutions, the task of familiarizing scholars, business leaders, and government officials with each other, deepening policy-oriented discussions, and thus preparing for the establishment of APEC fell to nongovernmental groups such as the Pacific Basin Economic Council (PBEC), a discussion group of business leaders established in 1967; Pacific Trade and Development (PAFTAD), a network of economists in the Asia Pacific launched in 1968, with some government officials also participating in their private capacities; and the tripartite Pacific Economic Cooperation Committee (PECC), consisting of academic, business, and government participants, established in 1980. For the role of PAFTAD and PECC, see Hugh Patrick, "From PAFTAD to APEC: Economists Networks and Public Policymaking," APEC Study Center Discussion Paper Series 2 (Columbia University, January 1997). For precursors to APEC, see also John Ravenhill, *APEC and the Construction of Pacific Rim Regionalism* (Cambridge University Press, 2001), pp. 50–54); and Edward J. Lincoln, *East Asian Economic Regionalism* (Brookings, 2004), pp. 114–39.

25. MITI was not Japan's only source of ideas on regional cooperation. In March 1988, in a speech in San Francisco, former prime minister Yasuhiro Nakasone emphasized economic policy coordination among the United States, Japan, and Asian newly industrializing economies and proposed a Pacific cooperation forum on economic and cultural issues, modeled after the OECD. "Nakasone Zen Shusho Bei de Kouen, Taiheiyou-ban OECD o" (Former prime minister Nakasone, in a speech in the U.S., advocates a Pacific version of OECD), *Nihon Keizai Shimbun*, March 13, 1988, morning edition, p. 2.

26. "Ajia Taiheiyou Keizai Kyouryoku, Tamura Tsusan-sho ga Shinkousou" (Asia Pacific economic cooperation, MITI minister Tamura's new proposal), *Asahi Shimbun*, January 10, 1988, morning edition, p. 1. In January 1987, Tamura also proposed a pan-Pacific meeting of ministers of industry with Australia, Canada, New Zealand, the United States, and Japan as the initial members. This previous proposal, which did not fly, did not include Asian developing countries and thus could not help

diversify Japan's trade structure to alleviate its trade friction with the United States. Hirokazu Okumura, former MITI official, e-mail to author, May 5, 2004. While based in JETRO, Sydney, in the late 1980s, Okumura traveled through ASEAN countries and persuaded their capitals to join what was later to become APEC.

27. For APEC's prehistory, see Noboru Hatakeyama, *Tsuushou Koushou: Kokueki o Meguru Dorama* (Trade negotiations: the drama in pursuit of national interests) (Tokyo: Nihon Keizai Shimbun Sha, 1996), pp. 140–49. Hatakeyama, former MITI vice minister for international affairs, became director general for the International Trade Policy Bureau several months before the first APEC ministerial meeting.

28. E-mail to author, March 30, 2004. On the other hand, according to former MITI official Okumura, ASEAN countries in the late 1980s were particularly concerned about the creation of the "Fortress Europe." E-mail to author, May 5, 2004.

29. According to a MITI study group report, the way "to shift from the over dependence on the U.S. markets to the burden sharing among regional economies" was to develop domestic demand and intraregional trade. See MITI International Economic Affairs Department, International Trade Policy Bureau, "Aratanaru Ajia Taiheiyo Kyoryoku o Motomete" (In quest of new Asia Pacific cooperation), *Ajia Taiheiyo Boueki Kaihatsu Kenkyu-kai Chukan Torimatome* (Interim report of the study group for Asia Pacific trade and development), June 1988.

30. Satoshi Kuwahara, "ASEAN no Keizai-Hatten Senryaku to Nichi ASEAN Kankei" (ASEAN's strategy for economic development and Japan-ASEAN relations), manuscript in the author's possession.

31. MITI in those days referred to the Asia Pacific region as centering around Japan, the United States, Canada, Australia, New Zealand, Asian NIEs (South Korea, Taiwan, Hong Kong, and Singapore), and ASEAN countries (Indonesia, Malaysia, the Philippines, and Thailand). See MITI, *Aratanaru Ajia*.

32. Hatakeyama, *Tsuushou Koushou*, p. 142.

33. E-mail to author, March 30, 2004.

34. Funabashi quotes Shigeru Muraoka, then MITI vice minister for international affairs, as stating: "It would perhaps be more effective to combat and contain U.S. unilateral actions on trade issues if we could include the United States in the forum." Funabashi, *Asia Pacific Fusion*, p. 58.

35. "Hirakareta 'Kyoryoku ni yoru Hatten no Jidai' e" (Entering an era of development through cooperation that has opened), Ajia Taiheiyo Kyoryoku Suishin Kondan-kai (Roundtable on the promotion of Asia Pacific), June 15, 1989.

36. MITI, *Aratanaru Ajia*. The report advocated four guiding principles for prospective Asia Pacific cooperation: a gradual process based on consensus, mutual respect and equal partnership, complementarity to existing bilateral and regional forums, and the centrality of the private sector and market mechanism.

37. For Australia's motives in proposing a regional forum in Asia Pacific, see John Ravenhill, "Australia and APEC," in *Asia-Pacific Crossroads: Regime Creation and the Future of APEC*, edited by Vinod K. Aggarwal and Charles E. Morrison (New York: St. Martin's Press, 1998), pp.143–64.

38. Robert James Hawke, "Regional Co-operation: Challenges for Korea and Australia," speech by the Prime Minister, Luncheon of Korean Business Associations, Seoul, Korea, January 31, 1989.

39. Ravenhill, "Australia and APEC," pp. 154–55; Funabashi, *Asia Pacific Fusion,* pp. 61–64.

40. In his speech, Prime Minister Hawke envisioned an OECD-type organization with "a capacity for analysis and consultation on economic and social issues" "to help inform policy development." He proposed three areas for cooperation: to "improve the chances of success of the Uruguay Round"; to "investigate the scope for further dismantling of barriers to trade within the region, consistent with the GATT framework"; and to "identify the broad economic interests we [the countries in the region] have in common." Hawke, "Regional Cooperation." See also Ravenhill, "Australia and APEC," p. 155.

41. Funabashi, *Asia Pacific Fusion,* p. 66.

42. Richard W. Baker, "The United States and APEC Regime Building," in *Asia-Pacific Crossroads,* edited by Aggarwal and Morrison, pp. 165–89.

43. Christopher Hemmer and Peter J. Katzenstein, "Why Is There No NATO in Asia? Collective Identity, Regionalism, and the Origins of Multilateralism," *International Organization* 56 (Summer 2002): 575–607; Peter J. Katzenstein, "Introduction: Asian Regionalism in Comparative Perspective," in *Network Power: Japan and Asia,* edited by Peter J. Katzenstein and Takashi Shiraishi (Cornell University Press, 1997), pp. 23–25.

44. For the U.S. perspective of the relation between hub-and-spoke architecture of the U.S. security engagement ("a fan spread wide, with its base in North America and radiating west across the Pacific") and APEC ("connecting those spokes is the fabric of shared economic interests now given form by the Asia Pacific Economic Cooperation [APEC] process"), see James A. Baker III, "America in Asia: Emerging Architecture for a Pacific Community," *Foreign Affairs* 70 (Winter 1991/92): 1–18, 4.

45. Secretary of State George P. Shultz, Address before the Association of Indonesian Economists, Jakarta, July 11, 1988. Furthermore, in December 1988, Senator Bill Bradley proposed a Pacific Coalition to promote multilateral trade negotiations, Pacific economic integration and a closer partnership between developing and industrializing countries. See USITC, *The Pros and Cons of ... Negotiations ... with Taiwan, the Republic of Korea, and ASEAN.* Also, the following February Senator Alan Cranston recommended that President Bush set up a Pacific Basin forum that would include not only U.S. allies but also "the Soviets, as well as their allies North Korea and Vietnam," to discuss "free trade, economic development and environmental protection." See "Senator Proposes Pacific Summit," Jiji Press Ticker Service, February 14, 1989.

46. Shultz, Address before the Association of Indonesian Economists.

47. James A. Baker, III with Thomas M. DeFrank, *The Politics of Diplomacy: Revolution, War & Peace, 1989–1992* (New York: G. P. Putnam's Sons, 1995), p. 609; Walter S. Mossberg and Alan Murray, "Departure of Treasury Secretary Baker Would

Bring Halt to Initiative in Asia," *Wall Street Journal*, August 3, 1988, p. 22.

48. Robert Fauver, e-mail to author, December 17, 2003.

49. Ibid. On this point, W. Allen Wallis, undersecretary of state for economic affairs under Secretary Shultz, who raised the possibility of creating a Pacific Basin government organization similar to OECD, suggested that he was deliberately vague in describing the initiative so as not "to push more quickly than our Asian trading partners want to go." Wallis, "The U.S. and the Pacific Basin: Trade and Adjustment Issues," Address before the Asia Society in New York City, April 26, 1988, *Department of State Bulletin*, June 1988. See also Richard Katz, "Government-Level, Economic Forum Proposed for Pacific Rim; Aspects of Organization Would Resemble OECD," *Japan Economic Journal*, May 21, 1988, p. 15. The same consideration was presumably behind the Shultz speech.

50. Fauver, e-mail to author, December 17, 2003.

51. Mossberg and Murray, "Departure of Treasury Secretary Baker Would Bring Halt to Initiative in Asia."

52. Funabashi, *Asia Pacific Fusion*, p. 128.

53. See n. 17.

54. Former State Department official, interview, December 12, 2003.

55. Former State Department official, e-mail to author, December 17, 2003.

56. Baker and DeFrank, *The Politics of Diplomacy*, p. 609.

57. Ibid.

58. Funabashi, *Asia Pacific Fusion*, p. 62.

59. Secretary of State James A. Baker, III, "A New Pacific Partnership: Framework for the Future," Address to Asia Society, June 26, 1989.

60. Baker's thinking was that regional agreements "could help lay the institutional groundwork for ongoing economic cooperation. Issues come and go. But institutions abide." Baker and Defrank, "*The Politics of Diplomacy*, p. 605.

61. Ibid.

62. Indonesia agreed, on the condition that APEC would not create new institutions. Malaysia, while objecting to the formation of an economic bloc and institutionalization, did not object to its participation in the ministerial meeting. Kuwahara, "ASEAN's Economic Development Strategy."

63. Baker and DeFrank, *The Politics of Diplomacy*, p. 610.

64. Former State Department official, telephone interview, December 17, 2003.

65. "Chairman's Summary Statement," First APEC Ministerial Meeting, Canberra, Australia, November 6–7, 1989 (www.apecsec.org.sg/apec/ministerial_statements/annual_ministerial/1989_1st_apec_ministerial/chair_summary.html [April 2004]).

66. Joint Statement, First APEC Ministerial Meeting, Canberra, Australia, November 6–7, 1989 (www.apecsec.org.sg/apec/ministerial_statements/annual_ministerial/1989_1st_apec_ministerial.html [April 2004]) and "Chairman's Summary Statement."

67. Ravenhill, *APEC and the Construction of Pacific Rim Regionalism*, pp. 104–05.

68. "Kristoff Cool to Japan's Regional Cooperation Plan," Japan Economic Newswire, February 24, 1995. Sandra Kristoff, U.S. ambassador to APEC, was responding to Japan's 1995 MOFA proposal for Partnership for Progress. Evidently, she stated the same view as an important principle of APEC at the official-level meetings in the early 1990s.

69. Baker, "The United States and APEC Regime Building," p. 183; and Ravenhill, *APEC and the Construction of Pacific Rim Regionalism*, p. 96.

70. For U.S. positions on cooperation projects in APEC, see, for example, Ravenhill, *APEC and the Construction of Pacific Rim Regionalism*, p.102.

71. U.S. Department of State, "U.S.-Mexico Free Trade Agreement," *Dispatch* 1, no. 18 (December 31, 1990) (dosfan.lib.uic.edu/ERC/briefing/dispatch/1990/html/Dispatchv1no18.html [February 2006]).

72. President George Bush, "Remarks Announcing the Enterprise for the Americas Initiative," June 27, 1990.

73. World Trade Organization, "Understanding the WTO," September 2003, p. 20 (www.wto.org/english/thewto_e/whatis_e/tif_e/understanding_e.doc).

74. Azam Aris, "KL to Push for East Asia Pact," *Business Times*, December 11, 1990, p.1.

75. When Malaysian Primary Industries minister Lim Keng Yaik revealed this proposal for the first time on December 6, 1990, Malaysian Trade and Industry minister Rafidah Aziz, who was in Brussels for the GATT talks, reportedly laughed at the news and said, "I'm the Trade Minister. They can't decide this without me." Fagan D, "East Asian Trading Bloc Plan," Courier-Mail, December 7, 1990, and "Gatto Koushou Ketsuretus no Baai, Dokuji no Boueki Brokku o—Mareisia, Teian o Yotei" (Malaysia plans to propose their own trade bloc should GATT talks fail), *Nihon Keizai Shimbun*, December 7, 1990, morning edition, p. 9; Hatakeyama, *Tsuushou Koushou*, pp. 162–63.

76. Robert Goh, "PM Calls for Asia Pacific Trade Bloc," *New Straits Times (Malaysia)*, December 11, 1990.

77. Ibid. Also quoted in Ruth Youngblood, United Press International, January 2, 1991.

78. "Li Peng Is Supportive of East Asia Market Idea," Japan Economic Newswire, December 13, 1990; Trade Minister Rafidah's comment quoted in S. Sivam, "Lukewarm Response to Malaysia's Trade Bloc Proposal," Inter Press Service, December 17, 1990.

79. Richard Solomon, then Assistant Secretary of State for East Asian and Pacific Affairs, quoted in Shiro Yoneyama, "U.S. Cools to Japanese Military Presence in Gulf," Japan Economic Newswire, December 21, 1990.

80. Ruth Youngblood, no title, United Press International, February 24, 1991.

81. "U.S. Reaction to Proposal for East Asian Economic Group," Central News Agency, March 15, 1991.

82. Michael H. Armacost, then U.S. Ambassador to Japan, quoted in "Asian Trade: Bigger, Maybe Not Better," *Economist*, March 9, 1991, p. 36.

83. Funabashi, *Asia Pacific Fusion*, p. 68.

84. Sappani Kamatchy, "ASEAN Endorses East Asia Economic Group," Japan Economic Newswire, October 8, 1991.

85. Joint Press Statement, Twenty-Third ASEAN Economic Ministers Meeting, Malaysia, October 7–8, 1991, par. 13 (www.aseansec.org/6126.htm [April 2004]).

86. Kamatchy, "ASEAN Endorses East Asia Economic Group."

87. Secretary Baker, "The U.S. and Japan: Global Partners in a Pacific Community," Address before the Japan Institute for International Affairs, Tokyo, Japan, November 11, 1991, Department of State Dispatch, November 18, 1991.

88. Text of Joint Ministerial Press Conference, Third APEC Ministerial Meeting. as released by the U.S. Department of State, Office of the Assistant Secretary/ Spokesman, Shilla Hotel, Seoul, Korea, Federal News Service, November 14, 1991.

89. Stephen Ward, "Malaysian Leader Lashes U.S. for Opposing Economic Body," *South China Morning Post*, October 15, 1992, p. 2.

90. Hatakeyama, *Tsuushou Koushou*, p.164. See also Funabashi, *Asia Pacific Fusion*, pp. 68–69.

91. Comment by Singapore's deputy prime minister Lee Hsien Loong on the relations between U.S.-Singapore TIFA and other agreements and frameworks is characteristic of Singapore, a staunch "multitracker": "This [TIFA] in no way undermines the EAEC or ASEAN. These are all complementary arrangements just as the U.S. bilateral free trade agreement with Canada in no way undermines APEC." Calvin Tan, "U.S., Singapore to expand economic ties with bilateral pact," Agence France-Presse, October 10, 1991.

92. Hatakeyama, *Tsuushou Koushou*, p.170–71.

93. Some controversial remarks were also made in a behind-the-scenes U.S. campaign against Malaysia's proposal, such as Baker's "unusually blunt admonition" to South Korea's foreign minister Lee Sang Ock, "Malaysia didn't spill blood for this country—but we did." See Don Oberdorfer, "U.S. Lobbies against Malaysian Trade Plan; Baker Protests Exclusion from a Proposed Economic Group of East Asian Nations," *Washington Post*, November 14, 1991, p. A40. Recalling this exchange, Baker noted, "My message was simple: All the countries are *not* equal. The South Koreans got it, and did not press for an EAEG." See Baker and DeFrank, *The Politics of Diplomacy*, p. 611. In addition, Malaysia complained that U.S. officials avoided serious discussions explaining why they thought EAEC was harmful when it was not even a trade agreement and warned Malaysians, for example, about Japanese economic dominance via closed business systems and Indonesians about growing Chinese influence in an effort to persuade prospective members to oppose to EAEC (personal conversations with Malaysian officials in 1995). U.S. officials denied these allegations. Groundless or not, they indicated a distinct lack of trust and candor between the parties involved.

94. Mary Kwang, "U.S., EC Trying to Block East Asian Growth: Mahathir," *The Straits Times* (Singapore), October 15, 1992, p. 3. This article quoted Mahathir's comments at the Europe East Asia Economic Forum held in Hong Kong.

95. Personal interview, December 12, 2003.

96. Baker and Defrank, *The Politics of Diplomacy,* p. 610.

97. Kwang, "U.S., EC Trying to Block East Asian Growth."

98. James A. Baker, "The United States and the Other Great Asian Powers: Russia, Japan and China," speech delivered to a conference sponsored by Baker Institute-Asia Society on China, the United States, and Asia, Houston, Texas, February 9, 1996 (www.rice.edu/projects/reno/speeches/19960209_Baker-Asianconf.html [June 2004]).

99. "Mahathir Says Economic Grouping Designed for Free Trade," Japan Economic Newswire, April 27, 1991.

100. Ibid.

101. "Higashi Ajia Chiiki Keizai Ken Koso, Nihon ni Fusanka Yosei, Bei Kokumu Chokan, Gaimusho ni Shokan" (Japan requested not to participate in East Asia regional economic zone initiative, in a letter to MOFA from U.S. Secretary of State), *Nihon Keizai Shimbun,* November 6, 1991, morning edition, p. 1; "Malaysian Daily Calls Japan, U.S. Hypocrites over EAEC," Japan Economic Newswire, November 14, 1991.

102. Baker, "The U.S. and Japan: Global Partners in a Pacific Community"; Baker, "America in Asia: Emerging Architecture for a Pacific Community," p. 6.

103. Baker, "America in Asia: Emerging Architecture for a Pacific Community," pp. 7, 3.

104. Joint Press Statement, Twenty-Third ASEAN Economic Ministers Meeting, Malaysia, October 7–8, 1991, par. 9.

105. Agreement on the Common Effective Preferential Tariff (CEPT) Scheme for the ASEAN Free Trade Area, Singapore, January 28, 1992 (www.aseansec.org/ 1164.htm [April 2004]).

106. Statement of Robert B. Zoellick, Undersecretary and Counselor, U.S. Department of State, at ASEAN Post-Ministerial Conference, "Six + Seven" session, July 24, 1992.

107. Joint Statement, Fourth APEC Ministerial Meeting, Bangkok, Thailand, September 10–11, 1992, paras. 23, 24 (www.apec.org/apec/ministerial_statements/ annual_ministerial/1992_4th_apec_ministerial.html [April 2004]).

108. Joint Statement, Fourth APEC Ministerial Meeting, par. 14, 16.

109. George Bush, President of the United States, "Remarks and a Question-and-Answer Session with the Economic Club of Detroit in Michigan," September 10, 1992; Agenda for American Renewal, folder "Agenda for American Renewal, Bush Administration 1992," OA/ID 08856, Roger Porter Files, White House Office of Policy Development, Bush Presidential Records, George Bush Presidential Library. A month later, in following up the presidential proposal, a Commerce Department official offered an "unofficial thought" about concluding FTAs with Asia and Pacific economies committed to liberalize trade and investment and to safeguard intellectual property, presumably Australia, Hong Kong, New Zealand, Singapore, and Taiwan. See Remarks by Franklin L. Lavin, deputy assistant secretary for East Asia

and Pacific, U.S. Department of Commerce, "After NAFTA: Free Trade and Asia," Heritage Foundation, Washington, D.C., October 6, 1992.

110. "Australia and Japan's Pacific Partnership and Our Trade Policy Options," speech by the prime minister, the Hon. P. J. Keating to the Japanese Chamber of Commerce and Industry, September 22, 1992.

111. Former State Department official, e-mail to author, December 17, 2003.

112. See, for example, Baker, "America in Asia," p. 6.

113. According to Funabashi, *Asia Pacific Fusion*, pp. 129–30, a few months before the 1995 Osaka meeting, Zoellick warned that if APEC failed, countries might want to move ahead with liberalization among the willing, which would either mean sector by sector or through free trade agreements.

114. The emphasis on membership is clear, for example, from the U.S. government's view occasionally expressed in those days that the proper region for economic cooperation was not East Asia but the Asia Pacific Region.

Chapter Five

1. Winston Lord, "A New Pacific Community: Ten Goals for American Policy," Opening Statement at Confirmation Hearings for Ambassador Winston Lord, Assistant Secretary of State-Designate, Bureau of East Asian and Pacific Affairs, March 31, 1993; President William Jefferson Clinton, "Building a New Pacific Community," speech at Waseda University, Japan, July 7, 1993 (www.mofa.go.jp/region/n-america/us/archive/1993/remarks.html).

2. Clinton, "Building a New Pacific Community."

3. Ibid.

4. Claude E. Barfield, "Trade, Investment, and Emerging U.S. Policies for Asia," in *Expanding U.S.-Asian Trade and Investment: New Challenges and Policy Options*, edited by Claude E. Barfield (Washington: American Enterprise Institute for Public Policy Research, 1997), p. 33.

5. Ibid.

6. Ibid., p. 39.

7. APEC Eminent Persons Group (EPG), "A Vision for APEC: Towards an Asia Pacific Economic Community," November 1993, p. 18, emphasis added (www.apec.org/apec/publications/free_downloads/1997-1993.MedialibDownload. v1.html?url=/etc/medialib/apec_media_library/downloads/misc/pubs/1994.Par.000 2.File.v1.1 [February 2006]).

8. See *Economic Report of the President, 1995* (GPO, February 1995), p. 204.

9. Ibid.

10. Ibid.

11. APEC EPG, "A Vision for APEC."

12. "APEC Leaders'Economic Vision Statement," Blake Island, Seattle, November 20, 1993 (www.apec.org/apec/leaders__declarations/1993.html [April 2004]).

13. APEC EPG, "Achieving the APEC Vision: Free and Open Trade in the Asia

Pacific," August 1994 (www.apec.org/apec/publications/free_downloads/1997-1993.MedialibDownload.v1.html?url=/etc/medialib/apec_media_library/downloads/misc/pubs/1994.Par.0001.File.v1.1 [February 2006]).

14. Ibid.

15. APEC, "APEC Economic Leaders' Declaration of Common Resolve," Bogor, Indonesia, November 15, 1994, par. 6 (www.apecsec.org.sg/apec/leaders__declarations/1994.html [May 2005].

16. Yoichi Funabashi, *Asia Pacific Fusion, Japan's Role in APEC* (Washington: Institute for International Economics, September 1995), p. 92.

17. APEC EPG, "Achieving the APEC Vision," p. 48.

18. Ibid., p. 28.

19. Lael Brainard, personal interview, January 30, 2004.

20. APEC, "APEC Economic Leaders' Declaration of Common Resolve," par. 6.

21. Ibid., par. 11.

22. APEC EPG, Executive Summary, "Implementing the APEC Vision," *Selected APEC Documents 1995*, p.153 (www.apecsec.org.sg/apec/publications/free_downloads/1997-1993.MedialibDownload.v1.html?url=/etc/medialib/apec_media_library/downloads/sec/pubs/1995.Par.0002.File.v1.1 [May 2005]).

23. APEC, "The Osaka Action Agenda; Implementation of the Bogor Declaration," adopted in Osaka on November 19, 1995 (203.127.220.112/content/apec/leaders__declarations/1995.downloadlinks.0002.LinkURL.Download.ver5.1.9 [February 2006]).

24. APEC Economic Leaders' Declaration for Action, Osaka, Japan, November 19, 1995, par. 5 (www.apec.org/apec/leaders__declarations/1995.html [April 2004]). On the ambiguities of the OAA, see John Ravenhill, *APEC and the Construction of Pacific Rim Regionalism* (Cambridge University Press, 2001), pp. 155–63.

25. APEC, "Osaka Action Agenda," pt. 1, sec. A, par. 4.

26. Ibid., sec. C, par. 1.

27. For Washington's difficulty with tariff reductions after the approval of the UR implementing legislation, see "Japan Proposes Delay in APEC Action Plans until Next Year's Summit," *Inside U.S. Trade*, June 2, 1995.

28. APEC, "Osaka Action Agenda," sec. C, par. 1.

29. WTO, "Information Technology Agreement—Introduction" (www.wto.org/english/tratop_e/inftec_e/itaintro_e.htm#1 [April 2004]). The leaders instructed their ministers "to identify sectors where early voluntary liberalization would have a positive impact on trade, investment, and economic growth in the individual APEC economies as well as in the region, and submit to us recommendations on how this can be achieved." APEC, "Economic Leaders' Declaration: From Vision to Action," Subic, The Philippines, November 25, 1996, par. 8 (www.apec.org/apec/leaders_declarations/1996.html [April 2004]). EVSL aimed at liberalization before the agreed-upon deadline of 2010 for industrialized economies and 2020 for developing economies, in fifteen sectors. Priority was given to nine sectors: environmental goods and services, the energy sector, fish and fish products, toys, forest products,

gems and jewelry, medical equipment and instruments, chemicals, and telecommunications mutual recognition agreement (MRA). The remaining six were oilseeds and oilseeds products, food, natural and synthetic rubber, fertilizers, automotive, and civil aircraft. See APEC, "Early Voluntary Sectoral Liberalization (EVSL)," Joint Statement, Ninth Ministerial Meeting, Vancouver, Canada, November 21–22, 1997, annex (www.apec.org/apec/ministerial_statements/annual_ministerial/1997_9th_apec_mi nisterial/annex.html [April 2004]).

30. APEC, "Early Voluntary Sectoral Liberalization."

31. On the process of negotiations and the assumptions of major players, see Ellis S. Krauss, "The United States and Japan in APEC's EVSL Negotiations: Regional Multilateralism and Trade," in *Beyond Bilateralism: U.S.-Japan Relations in the New Asia-Pacific,* edited by Ellis S. Krauss and T. J. Pempel (Stanford University Press, 2004), pp. 272–95.

32. APEC, "Economic Leaders' Declaration: Connecting the APEC Community," Vancouver, Canada, November 25, 1997, par. 6 (www.apec.org/apec/leaders__dec larations/1997.html [April 2004]).

33. Krauss, "The United States and Japan in APEC's EVSL Negotiations," p. 282.

34. According to Peter Starr, "U.S.-Japan Trade Rivalry Overshadows APEC Process," Agence France-Presse, November 19, 1998: "Ushering reporters into a news conference in Kuching, U.S. officials expelled all members of the Japanese media before U.S. Trade Representative Barshefsky arrived to declare confidently that Japan was 'isolated' and that all other members saw eye-to-eye with the United States." According to a Japanese official directly involved in the EVSL process, however, Asian countries, or for that matter even the United States, did not make much concession in the selected sectors. In the case of Asian countries, developing countries were allowed considerable flexibility. In the case of the United States, the selected sectors did not pose difficult problems to it. E-mail communications, April 24, 2004.

35. "Statement of the Chair," APEC Meeting of Ministers Responsible for Trade, Kuching, Sarawak, June 22–23, 1998, paras. 5 and 6 (www.apec.org/content/ apec/ministerial_statements/sectoral_ministerial/trade/1998_trade.html [April 2004]).

36. According to Krauss, "The United States and Japan in APEC's EVSL Negotiations," p. 279, "the Americans . . . felt that Japan . . . had to . . . make *some concessions* in all nine . . . sectors" (emphasis added). However, the Japanese official involved in the EVSL process recalls that the United States insisted on *complete liberalization,* not some concessions in all nine sectors. This all-or-nothing attitude of the American delegation allegedly closed off the possibility of a deal. In fact, had the American delegation allowed Japan some flexibility in the choice of items within the two sensitive sectors, Japan would have had a harder time persuading the domestic constituencies to accept the elimination of some sensitive tariffs. E-mail communications, April 27, 2004.

37. Lee Kim Chew, "Summit Leaves Shadow over APEC," *The Straits Times* (Singapore), November 22, 1998, p. 39.

38. See, for example, Peter Starr, "APEC May Blow Critical Chance to Assert Itself in Asian Crisis," Agence France-Presse, November 15, 1998; David Saunders, "HK Confident despite APEC Failure on Tariff; Secretary for Trade and Industry Bullish on Securing Sector Agreement," *South China Morning Post,* November 16, 1998, Business Post, p. 1; and Chew, "Summit Leaves Shadow over APEC."

39. Former Australian foreign minister Gareth Evans's comments quoted in Peter Starr, "APEC May Blow Critical Chance."

40. See, for example, "Japan under Unfair Attack at APEC: Malaysia," Asia Pulse, November 13, 1998; "China Reiterates 'Voluntary' Nature of Free Trade Plan," Japan Economic Newswire, November 14, 1998; "U.S. Says Won't Cut Tariffs Unilaterally under Liberalization Plan," Agence France-Presse, November 15, 1998; "Asians Back Japan in APEC Trade; Australia, New Zealand Opposed," Kyodo News Service, November 13, 1998 (in *BBC Summary of World Broadcasts,* November 16, 1998); and "Prospect Outlines for APEC," China Daily, November 22, 1998.

41. "Free-Trade Initiatives Progressing within APEC," China Daily, November 17, 1998.

42. "U.S. in the Firing Line over APEC Disappointment," Agence France-Presse, November 19, 1998.

43. Summit of the Americas, "Declaration of Principles: Partnership for Development and Prosperity: Democracy, Free Trade and Sustainable Development in the Americas," Miami, December 1994 (www.ftaa-alca.org/ministerials/Miami_e.asp [April 2004]).

44. *Economic Report of the President, 1995;* also *Annual Report of the Council of Economic Advisers* (GPO, 1995) (a257.g.akamaitech.net/7/257/2422/17feb20051700/www.gpoaccess.gov/usbudget/fy96/pdf/econ_rpt.pdf [April 2004]).

45. See, for example, James A. Baker III, "America in Asia: Emerging Architecture for a Pacific Community," *Foreign Affairs* 70 (Winter 1991/92: 1–18); Statement of Robert B. Zoellick, Undersecretary and Counselor, U.S. Department of State at ASEAN Post-Ministerial Conference (PMC) "Six +Seven" Session, Manila, Philippines, July 24, 1992.

46. "Hearing of the Trade Subcommittee of the House Ways and Means Committee, Subject: Fast Track Authority" (103 Cong. 1 sess.), Federal News Service, April 21, 1993.

47. State Department official, personal interview, December 9, 2003.

48. Lael Brainard, Senior Fellow, Brookings Institution, personal interview, January 30, 2004.

49. Office of the U.S. Trade Representative (USTR), *1997 Trade Policy Agenda;* and *1996 Annual Report of the President of the United States on the Trade Agreements Program,* March 1997 (www.ustr.gov/html/1997tpa_part2.html [April 2004]).

50. Ibid.

51. "Hearing of the Trade Subcommittee of the House Ways and Means Committee," Federal News Service.

52. APEC, "Osaka Action Agenda," pt. 2, sec. A.

53. The APEC leaders' meeting in 2002 recognized this problem of "accountability" and "instructed Ministers to improve the focus of [APEC] economic and technical cooperation and capacity building objectives and ensure that [their] actions are duly monitored and assessed, fully support APEC's trade and investment liberalization and facilitation goals and address the challenges of globalization." APEC Economic Leaders' Declaration, Los Cabos, Mexico, October 27, 2002 (www.apecsec.org.sg/apec/leaders__declarations/2002.html [February 2006]).

54. Robert A. Manning and Paula Stern, "The Myth of the Pacific Community," *Foreign Affairs* 73 (November/December 1994): 79–83, 86.

55. For further information on these frictions, see ibid.; and "The Gall of Al Gore," *The Straits Times* (Singapore), November 18, 1998, p. 44, which commented on Vice President Gore's speech criticizing the state of political freedom in Malaysia as the "wrong place, wrong time, wrong tone." See also "New Zealand Premier Criticizes U.S. 'Megaphone Diplomacy,'" Radio New Zealand International, November 17, 1998, in *BBC Summary of World Broadcasts*, November 19, 1998; and "APEC Adrift," *Financial Times*, November 19, 1998, p. 29.

56. Ravenhill, *APEC and the Construction of Pacific Rim Regionalism*, p. 214.

57. Ibid. For a Canadian perspective on this issue, see, for example, Richard Gwyn, "East against West Once More at APEC," *Toronto Star*, November 18, 1998, p. 25.

58. Joint Press Statement, Twenty-Sixth ASEAN Economic Ministers Meeting (AEM), Chiang Mai, Thailand, September 22–23, 1994, par. 21 (www.aseansec.org/ 2115.htm [April 2004]).

59. MITI, *Prospects and Challenges for the Upgrading of Industries in the ASEAN Region* (Tokyo, 1993).

60. Tan Kim Song, "ASEAN-Japan Joint Group for Indochina Trade," *The Straits Times* (Singapore), September 25, 1994, p. 2.

61. Joint Statement, Meeting of Heads of State/Government of the Member States of ASEAN and the Prime Minister of Japan, Kuala Lumpur, Malaysia, December 16, 1997, par. 8 (www.aseansec.org/5224.htm [April 2004]).

62. The projects were implemented with the help of experts outside the Japanese government such as the Asian Development Bank, local offices of the International Monetary Fund, and the business sector. METI official who designed the CLM-WG and AMEICC processes, e-mail to author, May 12, 2004.

63. Joint Press Statement, Twenty-Fifth ASEAN Economic Ministers Meeting, Singapore, October 7–8, 1993, par. 27 (www.aseansec.org/6128.htm [April 2004]).

64. Malaysia preferred to have the EAEC meet during the annual AEM meeting and Indonesia preferred putting the EAEC within APEC. See "Malaysia, Indonesia Differ on EAEC Setup," Japan Economic Newswire, July 17, 1993.

65. U.S. secretary of state Warren Christopher had already said in July 1993 that having the EAEC within APEC had "eased considerably" the U.S. concern that it might become a protectionist trading bloc but that the United States was still "puzzled and concerned about the exclusivity or apparent exclusivity of the EAEC' and would continue to watch its development. "Malaysia Feels U.S., Japan, S. Korea Pos-

itive on EAEC," Japan Economic Newswire, July 27, 1993. See also "Mahathir Does-n't Regret His Boycott of APEC Summit," Japan Economic Newswire, November 20, 1993. At the APEC informal summit in Seattle, which Mahathir did not attend because Washington had not supported the EAEC, President Clinton said "he [was] not against the EAEC if it [favored] regional economic cooperation and [did] not shut off opportunities for other countries." See "Mahathir Urges Japan, S. Korea to Join EAEC," Japan Economic Newswire, November 23, 1993. When Clinton and Mahathir met on May 6, 1994, Clinton gave no signal of U.S. support but Mahathir said "as a result of this meeting the relationship between Malaysia and the U.S. would be much easier." See Antonio Kamiya, "Mahathir Says Meeting with Clinton Eases Strained Ties," Japan Economic Newswire, May 7, 1994.

66. "Special State Department Briefing, Briefers: Asst. Secretary of State for East Asian & Pacific Affairs Winston Lord and Permanent Secretary of Foreign Ministry of Brunei Lim Jock Seng," Federal News Service, May 10, 1994.

67. Irene Ngoo, "EAEC Not Confrontational, ASEAN Members Reassure U.S.," *The Straits Times* (Singapore), May 11, 1994, p.12.

68. Manning and Stern, "The Myth of the Pacific Community," p. 83.

69. Siti Rahil, "U.S. Tells Japan It Opposes EAEC," Japan Economic Newswire, June 15, 1994.

70. "EAEC Continues to Haunt ASEAN," *Nation,* December 4, 1995. The article vividly depicts ASEAN's dilemma: "The problem is, the ASEAN countries are not in the mood to push this idea nor are they ready to dump the much delayed plan."

71. See Joint Press Statement, Twenty-Sixth ASEAN Economic Ministers Meet-ing, par. 25; and Joint Press Statement, Twenty-Seventh ASEAN Economic Ministers Meeting, Bandar Seri Begawan, Brunei Darussalam, September 7–8, 1995, par. 16.

72. Yang Razali Kassim, "Prospective EAEC Members Hold Talks, Agree to Meet More Often," *Business Times,* July 26, 1994, p. 3.

73. ASEAN secretary general Ajit Singh, who briefed the press, quoted in Lee Siew Hua and Sinfah Tunsarawuth, "Ministers to Reassure West over Caucus," *The Straits Times* (Singapore), July 26, 1994, p. 14; Kassim, "Prospective EAEC Members Hold Talks."

74. Song, "ASEAN-Japan Joint Group for Indochina Trade."

75. "Japan for Inviting Australia, NZ to EAEC Meeting," Xinhua News Agency, March 16, 1995. Funabashi, *Asia Pacific Fusion,* p. 207, quotes Yoshihiro Sakamoto, then MITI vice minister for international affairs, as saying that "Japan's consistent policy has been to advocate inclusion of Australia and New Zealand in the EAEC, in some part to avoid their incorporation into NAFTA."

76. U.S. ambassador to Japan Walter Mondale's characterization made in a meet-ing with MITI minister Hashimoto. See Funabashi, *Asia Pacific Fusion,* p. 110. On the U.S. concern about EAEC around that time, see, for example, "Bei, EAEC Kensei no Ugoki, Keidanren, Zaikaijin ni Shinchou Taiou Motomeru" (U.S. moves to check EAEC, requesting Keidanren and the business community to take a cautious atti-tude), *Tokyo Yomiuri Shimbun,* April 9, 1995, morning edition, p. 5.

77. See, for example, "Malaysia Tells Japan Not to Dictate ASEAN Talks on EAEC," Japan Economic Newswire, March 14, 1995.

78. See "Tokyo to Skip Proto-EAEC Meet, Inviting S.E. Asia Anger," Japan Economic Newswire, April 10, 1995. Also, "Nichi Chuu Kan tono Keizai Kaigo, ASEAN ga Enki e" (ASEAN to postpone economic meeting with Japan, China, and South Korea), *Nihon Keizai Shimbun,* April 12, 1995, morning edition, p. 5; and "ASEAN Postpones Informal EAEC Meet," Xinhua News Agency, April 13, 1995.

79. See, for example, "Gou, NZ no Sanka Teian, Nihon, '9 ka Koku Kaigou' ni" (Japan proposes that Australia and NZ participate and hold a nine-country meeting), *Nihon Keizai Shimbun,* March 17, 1995, morning edition, p. 5.

80. See, for example, "Tsusan Jikan Kaiken, ASEAN Kakuryou Kaigou, Nihon wa Fusanka no Kousan" (MITI Vice Minister press briefing: Japan is unlikely to attend ASEAN ministerial meeting), *Nihon Keizai Shimbun,* April 7, 1995, morning edition, p. 5.

81. Sid Astbury, "Japan's ASEAN Intentions Unclear," *Australian Financial Review,* April 3, 1995, p. 12.

82. Joint Press Statement, Second ASEAN Economic Ministers Retreat, April 28–29, 1995, Phuket, Thailand, par. 7.

83. Greg Earl, "McMullan Welcomes Breakthrough Pact," *Australian Financial Review,* September 11, 1995, p. 10.

84. Information from an observer at a press background briefing on April 28, 1995.

85. "Keizai Kakuryo no EAEC Hi-koushiki Kaigou, Nichi Chuu Kan ni Sanka Yosei—ASEAN, Rai Getsu Matsu Keikaku" (Informal EAEC economic ministers meeting; Japan, China and South Korea asked to participate, ASEAN plans it end of next month), *Nihon Keizai Shimbun,* March 10, 1995, morning edition, p. 8.

86. "Malaysia Tells Japan Not to Dictate ASEAN Talks on EAEC."

87. Ryutaro Hashimoto, "Next Task for the WTO System and the APEC Process," *Journal of Northeast Asian Studies* 14 (Winter 1995): 30.

88. Noboru Hatakeyama, "Juusou-teki-na Kouryuu Mezasu" (Aiming at multi-layered relations), interview, *Tokyo Yomiuri Shimbun,* May 9, 1995, morning edition, p. 17 (author's translation).

89. Funabashi, *Asia Pacific Fusion,* p. 110.

90. Commission of the European Communities, "Towards a New Asia Strategy," Communication from the Commission to the Council, COM (94) 314 final, July 13, 1994 (europa.eu.int/comm/europeaid/projects/asia-itc/downloads/towards_a_new_asia_strategy.pdf [April 2004]).

91. Vikram Khanna, Catherine Ong, and Yang Razali Kassim, "Meeting of E. Asian and European Heads Urged to Boost Ties," *Business Times,* October 15, 1994, p. 2.

92. "Thailand Will Host Europe-Asia Summit: Chuan," *Business Times,* March 10, 1995, p. 3.

93. "Keynote Address by the Prime Minister of Singapore Mr. Goh Chok Tong at

the Opening Dinner Speech for the Europe/East Asia Economic Summit," October 12, 1994.

94. Ibid. See also Goh Chok Tong, speech delivered at the World Economic Forum, Davos, Switzerland, January 28, 1995.

95. Indeed, USTR Kantor told reporters after meeting with AEM on the sidelines of the APEC leaders' meeting in Osaka and agreeing to explore future linkages between AFTA and NAFTA, "The more meetings like this that occur, the more interaction between various regions of the world, the more we can address serious and important issues of the links between nations, and [the] better off we all are. So I welcome any meetings that are inclusive rather than exclusive." See Irene Ngoo, "ASEAN, U.S. to Explore Future AFTA-NAFTA Links," *The Straits Times* (Singapore), November 20, 1995, p. 3.

96. Greg Earl, "Canberra Fails to Win Asian Seat at Summit," *Australian Financial Review*, August 1, 1995, p. 6.

97. Siti Rahil Dollah, "Japan Agrees to Exclude Australia, NZ from Asia-EU Meet," Japan Economic Newswire, July 31, 1995.

98. Earl, "Canberra Fails to Win Asian Seat at Summit."

99. "Asia Sets Four Priorities for Summit with Europe Next Year," Agence France-Presse, November 19, 1995.

100. The remarks by the late Shunpei Tsukahara, then MITI minister, from the author's record of the Informal Meeting of the Asian Economic Ministers in Preparation for the ASEM, February 15, 1996.

101. Goh Chok Tong, Opening Statement, Fifth ASEAN Summit, December 14, 1995 (www.aseansec.org/5140.htm [April 2004]).

102. See Greg Earl, "Blocklines," *Australian Financial Review*, July 26, 1996, p. 22; and "Japan Said Not to Be Invited to ASEAN Summit This Year," Japan Economic Newswire, September 18, 1996.

103. "ASEAN, Japan to Hold Summit in Dec., Thai Minister Says," Japan Economic Newswire, April 29, 1997; Varunee Torsricharoen, "ASEAN to Hold Separate Talks with China, Japan, S. Korea," Japan Economic Newswire, May 31, 1997.

104. In October 1998, the Joint Press Statement of the Thirtieth ASEAN Economic Ministers Meeting (the first such meeting after Malaysia's prime minister Mahathir hosted the First ASEAN + 3 Summit) dropped the reference to the EAEC for the first time since its 1991 meeting (the first meeting after the proposal was made). See Joint Press Statement, Thirtieth ASEAN Economic Ministers Meeting, Makati City, Philippines, October 7–8, 1998 (www.aseansec.org/717.htm).

105. Former State Department official, phone interview, December 17, 2003.

Chapter Six

1. For Asian politicians' recognition of this point, see, for example, Edward Tang, "E. Asia Keen to Link Up with Group," *The Straits Times* (Singapore), December 16, 1998, p. 25.

2. See chapter 2, n. 56.

3. See Council on Foreign Exchange and Other Transactions, Subcommittee on Asian Financial and Capital Markets, "Lessons from the Asian Currency Crises—Risks Related to Short-Term Capital Movement and the '21st Century-Type' Currency Crisis," May 19, 1998 (www.mof.go.jp/english/tosin/e1a703.htm), which states that proposals for an AMF "took shape at the meeting of supporting countries for Thailand" hosted by the IMF in Tokyo on August 11, 1997, "where a heightened interest was expressed in examining the feasibility of a permanent institution created by Asian countries. This matter had been already discussed among ASEAN countries in the spring of 1997." Eisuke Sakakibara, "Nihon to Sekai ga Furueta Hi" (The day Japan and the world trembled) (Tokyo: Chuou Koron Shinsha, 2000), pp. 178–90, confirms that the vice minister of finance for international affairs and his staff started their action on this initiative immediately after the meeting of countries supporting Thailand on August 11, 1997. Sakakibara describes in detail the preparation for and setback of the AMF.

4. The Chiang Mai Initiative was put forward at the ASEAN + 3 meeting of finance ministers in May 2000. See Joint Ministerial Statement, ASEAN + 3 Finance Ministers Meeting, May 6, 2000, Chiang Mai, Thailand (www.mof.go.jp/english/if/if014.htm).

5. Chung Eui-Yong, Deputy Minister for Trade, Ministry of Foreign Affairs and Trade, "The Background of the Decision to Promote Free Trade Agreements, Progress Made and the Future Plan," speech delivered on December 17, 1998 (in Japanese).

6. Transcript of Prime Minister Goh Chok Tong's interview with Mr. Osamu Kobayashi, editor-in-chief of *Nikkei Business*, on December 19, 2000, at the Istana (www.gov.sg/sgip/intervws/0101-03.htm).

7. For reform measures related to trade and investment in particular, see, for example, Letter of Intent of the Government of Korea, December 3, 1997, par. 5; Memorandum on Economic Policies of the Royal Thai Government, May 26, 1998, par. 26; and Letter of Intent of the Government of Indonesia, October 31, 1997, pars. 38–40.

8. President Kim's determination is exhibited in the following press releases, for example: Kim Dae Jung, "Foreigners Will Invest When Reform Succeeds: President Kim," Inaugural Address, 1998-03011, February 25, 1998; "All-out Reforms, This Year's Administration Target," 1998-04-28; and "President Kim Urges Cabinet to Step Up Reform," Office of the President, Republic of Korea. Major economic reform measures were actually implemented. In 1998 the employment adjustment system was introduced to allow layoffs for managerial reasons, and mergers, acquisitions, and other forms of investment by foreign investors were liberalized and encouraged. See, for example, Korean Ministry of Foreign Affairs and Trade (MOFAT), "The Road to Recovery in 1999," May 27, 1999.

9. See, for example, Clyde Prestowitz, "Retooling Japan Is the Only Way to Rescue Asia Now," *Washington Post*, December 14, 1997, p. C1.

10. From the early stages of the crisis when speculators were looking for selling opportunities, there was an argument that the Japanese economy was the cause of the crisis. See, for example, "S. Korea Says Japanese Banks Are Cutting Credit," *Financial Times*, November 21, 1997, p. 1: Korea's finance minister reportedly said, "Japanese financial institutions are calling back loans instead of rolling them over," which had raised fears of a liquidity crisis since one-third of Korea's short-term debt of $68 billion had to be paid by the end of the year. Japan's Ministry of Finance immediately countered "that European banks had a higher proportion of lending in South Korea than Japanese groups," as reported in "Tokyo Washes Hands of Blame," *Financial Times*, November 22, 1997, p. 3. After the currency crisis developed into a full-blown economic crisis, a new version of arguments circulated blaming Japan's economy, such that stagnant domestic demand in Japan was responsible for Asia's deteriorating economy.

11. See, for example, "Where's Japan?" *Washington Post*, January 18, 1998, p. C8, which argues: "The time has come for Japan to stimulate its economy in a major way, in order to reduce its surplus with the world, provide an additional market for southeast Asia and do its part as a major world power." Also "Asia Will Not Forget," *The Straits Times* (Singapore), February 14, 1998, p. 40, which urged Japan to pump up demand, stabilize its banks and finance, and not abandon Southeast Asia as a production base.

12. See Secretary Robert E. Rubin, Testimony before the House Banking Committee, *Treasury News*, January 30, 1998, RR-2186 (www.treas.gov/press/releases/pr2186.htm); Deputy Secretary Lawrence H. Summers, Testimony before the Senate Finance Committee, *Treasury News*, February 4, 1998, RR-1295 (www.treas.gov/press/releases/pr2195.htm).

13. The Japanese government's assistance immediately after the crisis hit was mainly for stabilizing the currency in cooperation with the IMF. With the full-blown "economic" crisis, it took more comprehensive emergency measures, including economic packages such as Cabinet Decision, "Emergency Measures for the Economic Stabilization in Southeast Asia," February 20, 1998; Ministerial Meeting on Economic Measures, "Comprehensive Economic Measures," April 24, 1998 (www5.cao.go.jp/98/b/19980424b-taisaku-e.html); and Ministerial Meeting on Economic Measures, "Emergency Economic Package," November 16, 1998 (www5.cao.go.jp/98/b/19981116b-taisaku-e.html). Individual measures included a $30 billion financial package by the new Miyazawa Initiative in October 1998. Those packages and measures were used to implement specific programs, one example being a loan program to improve the financial condition of crisis-hit Japanese companies in Asia and help them maintain their overseas operations in the region.

14. In the Japan-ASEAN summit meeting held on December 16, 1998, some ASEAN country leaders stated that they were grateful for Japan's assistance provided in the middle of its own difficulties.

15. See, for example, Mohd Arshi Daud, "Goh Calls for Global Leadership to Tackle Financial Crisis," *Malaysian Economic News*, BERNAMA, November 16, 1998.

16. See, for example, "APEC Adrift," *Financial Times*, November 19, 1998, p. 29.

17. The origin of the P5 initiative apparently goes back to the U.S. Trade Representative's 1997 Trade Policy Agenda in March 1997. Though the Clinton administration as a whole was not enthusiastic, the report apparently sent a powerful signal to these countries. Shortly after it was released, New Zealand's international trade minister Lockwood Smith said he hoped to start negotiations for an FTA with the United States, "promoted by American interest in an agreement." See "Free Trade with U.S. on Agenda," *Dominion*, May 5, 1997, p. 3. U.S. ambassador Josiah Beeman reportedly dampened this hope by stating that a U.S.–New Zealand FTA would depend on fast-track authorities. See Simon Kilroy, "U.S. Raises Free-Trade Deal Idea," *Dominion*, May 10, 1997, p. 2. As noted before, however, it was not necessarily because of the lack of fast-track authorities but because the administration could not reach a consensus on the efficacy of small, bilateral FTAs. In 1998, Singapore's prime minister Goh reportedly suggested, at USTR's prodding, a five-country FTA during the talks with President Clinton. See Victoria Main, "Five Get Set for Rippingly Liberalized Free Trade Deal," *Dominion*, September 20, 1999, p. 2. In May 1999, New Zealand's prime minister, Jenny Shipley, revealed her intention to contact Australia and Singapore to investigate their possible involvement in a Chile–New Zealand FTA. See "Shipley Works on Four-Way Free Trade," *Dominion*, May 15, 1999, p. 2. In August, New Zealand and Australia agreed to explore the possibility of extending the CER to Chile, Singapore, and the United States. See Victoria Main, "New Partners Courted for CER," *Christchurch Press*, August 5, 1999, edition 2, p. 9. President Clinton promised Prime Minister Shipley that he would get back to her on a P5 FTA in 10 to 14 days and publicly commented that P5 was "a very interesting idea" after the meeting. Brian Fallow, "Hope for 5-Way Trade Depends on U.S. Priorities," *New Zealand Herald*, September 17, 1999.

18. "ASEAN, Japan, ROK, and China Hold 1st Summit," Jiji Press Ticker Service, December 15, 1997.

19. From the MOFA website (www.mofa.go.jp/mofaj/kaidan/kiroku/s_obuchi/arc_98/viet98/gaiyo.html [April 2004]).

20. Tim Johnson, "Malaysia, Singapore Call for East Asia Trading Bloc," Japan Economic Newswire, December 15, 1997.

21. "Kim Suggests Vision Group for E-Asian Economic Cooperation," *Korea Times*, December 16, 1998.

22. Joint Statement on East Asian Cooperation, Meeting of the Heads of State and Government of ASEAN, China, Japan, and the Republic of Korea, November 28, 1999 (www.mofa.go.jp/region/asia-paci/asean/pmv9911/joint.html [April 2004]).

23. The Chiang Mai Initiative was put forward at the ASEAN + 3 Finance Ministers Meeting in May 2000. See Joint Ministerial Statement, ASEAN+ 3 Finance Ministers Meeting, May 6, 2000, Chiang Mai, Thailand (www.mof.go.jp/english/if/if014.htm).

24. "EU/Mexico: Partnership Agreement Signed," European Report, December 10, 1997.

25. "EU-Mexico Accord Opens Way to Free Trade Talks," Agence France-Presse, December 8, 1997.

26. For the origin of the Mexico-Japan FTA, see Noboru Hatakeyama, "Short History of Japan's Movement to FTAs," *Journal of Japanese Trade and Industry*, November/December 2002, pp. 24–25.

27. The feasibility study on the Japan-Mexico FTA was launched by JETRO and SECOFI (Mexico's Ministry of Commerce and Industry) in February 1999.

28. "Nikkan, Kako no Mondai ni Shushifu, Kin Dai Chu Kankoku Daitouryou, Shunou Kaidan de Meigen" [Korean President Kim Dae Jung called in the summit meeting for an end to the problems of the past], *Tokyo Yomiuri Shimbun*, October 8, 1998, evening edition, p.1. In the joint press conference with Prime Minister Obuchi, President Kim stated: "The 20th century was the era of ethnocentric nation-states while the 21st century will be the era of globalism. The legacy of the 20th century has to be cleared off here." "Record of the Joint Press Conference of Prime Minister Keizo Obuchi and Korean President Kim Dae Jung," October 8, 1998 (in Japanese) (www.kantei.go.jp/jp/obutisouri/speech/1998/1008nikkan.html [April 2004]). In an address to the Japanese Diet, President Kim also stated that he was sure that a Japan–Republic of Korea Joint Declaration (www.mofa.go.jp/mofaj/kaidan/yojin/arc_98/k_sengen.html [April 2004]) that he and Prime Minister Obuchi had made public would put an end to the history problem between the two governments. See "President Kim Dae Jung's Address to the Japanese Diet," October 8, 1998 (in Japanese).

29. See, for example, "Kim Dae Jung Calls for Truly Friendly Ties with Japan," Japan Economic Newswire, April 29, 1998; Goro Hashimoto, "Kim Seeks New Era in Japan-ROK Ties," *Daily Yomiuri*, April 30, 1998, p. 1.

30. Multilateral Trade Cooperation Team, Ministry of Foreign Affairs and Trade, South Korea, "Government Holds Workshop for the Korea-Chile Free Trade Agreement," July 29, 1999; Multilateral Trade Policy Team, Ministry of Foreign Affairs and Trade, South Korea, "The 1st Meeting of the High-Level Working Group for the Korea-Chile Free Trade Agreement," April 12, 1999; "Frei Signs Free Trade Agreement with South Korea," *News Review*, September 16, 1999.

31. It took three ministerial meetings to launch a study on bilateral economic relations and to confirm that it would cover ("not exclude") the issue of a bilateral FTA. On November 13, 1998, Korea's minister of trade Han Duck-Soo met with Japanese MITI minister Kaoru Yosano in Kuala Lumpur on the fringes of an APEC ministerial meeting and proposed a joint examination of future Japan-Korea economic relations, which would also cover the possibility of establishing a bilateral FTA. On November 28, 1999, cabinet ministers of Japan and South Korea met in Kagoshima and confirmed that the two countries would launch the "Track Two" study. Finally on December 5, 1998, it was confirmed that the study would not exclude the possibility of an FTA at a joint government-private sector investment promotion conference held in Seoul during Minister Yosano's visit.

32. "Nikkan Keizai Ajenda 21" (in Japanese) (www.mofa.go.jp/mofaj/area/korea/agenda21.html [April 2004]).

33. Institute of Developing Economies, Japan External Trade Organization (JETRO), and Korea Institute for International Economic Policy (KIEP), "Towards Closer Japan-Korea Economic Relations: Proposal for Formulating a 21st Century Partnership (Joint Communiqué)," May 23, 2000 (www.ide.go.jp/English/Lecture/pressmenu/pressE00060601.PDF); Institute of Developing Economies (IDE), JETRO, "Toward Closer Japan-Korea Economic Relations in the 21st Century," March 2000 (www.ide.go.jp/English/Lecture/pressmenu/pressE00060602.PDF); and Korea Institute for International Economic Policy (KIEP), "Economic Effects of and Policy Directions for a Korea-Japan FTA," May 2000 (www.ide.go.jp/Japanese/Lecture/pressmenu/press00060604.PDF).

34. Joint Press Statement, Prime Minister of Singapore, His Excellency Goh Chok Tong, and Prime Minister of New Zealand, the Right Honourable Jenny Shipley, September 11, 1999.

35. Ibid.

36. Irene Ngoo, "Possible Free-Trade Pacts with Mexico and Chile," *The Straits Times* (Singapore), September 14, 1999, p.14; Lee Kim Chew, "S'pore to Help Speed Up Trade Liberalization," *The Straits Times* (Singapore), September 14, 1999, p. 14.

37. Jenny Shipley, post-APEC address to Auckland Chamber of Commerce, Carlton Hotel, Auckland, New Zealand, September 23, 1999. See also "Group to Be Set Up to Explore Singapore-Chile-New Zealand Free-Trade Pact," Xinhua General News Service, September 20, 1999.

38. See, for example, S. Durga Varma, "AFTA-CER Tree Trade Area Proposed," *Malaysia Economic News*, October 1, 1999.

39. See, for example, "Singapore Eying Free Trade Links with Europe," *Malaysia Economic News*, January 9, 2001.

40. See chapter 2, note 45.

41. For the perceived benefits of the prospective agreement from the two countries' perspective, see Joint Study Group Report, "Japanese-Singapore Economic Agreement for a New Age Partnership," September 2000 (www.meti.go.jp/policy/trade_policy/jsepa/study/data/092800_studyreport_e.pdf [April 2004]).

Chapter Seven

1. Chinese official with extensive experience in dealing with Asian countries, interview, October 24, 2003.

2. Tang Shiping and Zhang Yunling, "China's Regional Strategy," in *Power Shift: China and Asia's New Dynamics*, edited by David Shambaugh (University of California Press, 2005), pp. 48–68.

3. Ibid., p. 49. See also Mary Kwang, "Why China Speeded Up Plans for FTA with ASEAN," *The Straits Times* (Singapore), November 13, 2001, p. 16; "Lee Kuan Yew: Asia Grateful If RMB Remains Stable," Xinhua General News Service, March 11,

1998; "Malaysian FM Praises China's Efforts to Help Crisis-Hit Countries," Xinhua General News Service, May 27, 1998; and "Clinton Praises China for Resisting Pressure to Devalue Its Currency," Associated Press, June 27, 1998.

4. See for example, Gerald Segal, "Overrating China Is a Bad American Habit," *International Herald Tribune* (Neuilly-sur-Seine, France), June 22, 1988, p. 8; Gerard Baker, "Fed Official Confident over China Currency," *Financial Times*, June 24, 1998, p. 4; and "Yen's Fall Not to Force China to Devalue Yuan: Japan Official," Jiji Press Ticker Service, June 26, 1998.

5. Joint Statement, Meeting of Heads of State/Government of the Member States of ASEAN and the President of the People's Republic of China, Kuala Lumpur, Malaysia, December 16, 1997, par. 3 (www.aseansec.org/1817.htm [April 2004]).

6. "China Cautious on Proposed Asian Monetary Fund," Agence France-Presse, November 18, 1997, quotes Foreign Ministry spokesman Shen Guofang as saying, "The parties concerned have yet to conduct studies on this issue." By contrast, Ali Mamat, "Support for Asian Monetary Fund Vital, Says Mahathir," *Malaysia Economic News*, August 20, 1999, quotes Malaysia's prime minister Mahathir as saying that his Chinese counterpart, Zhu Rongji, had shown an encouraging response toward the AMF idea when it was raised during their bilateral discussion on August 18, 1999.

7. Leslie Fong, "China's Not in Competition with Japan," *The Straits Times* (Singapore), December 19, 2003, Commentary Section.

8. See, for example, C. H. Kwan, "The Rise of China and Asia's Flying Geese Pattern of Economic Development: An Empirical Analysis Based on U.S. Import Statistics," Discussion Paper Series 02-E-009 (Tokyo: Research Institute of Economy, Trade and Industry, July 2002) (www.rieti.go.jp/jp/publications/dp/02e009.pdf [April 26, 2004]). For example, there were widespread worries in the region that "with China out-competing them in the industrial sector, countries without the means to pull themselves up in the service sector may be pushed to de-industrialise, ending up as raw-material providers fuelling China's growth." Kao Chen, "Will the Dragon Hollow Out," *The Straits Times* (Singapore), September 15, 2001, p. H12-13. See also Ching Cheong, "China Gains Big in FTA Deal with ASEAN," *The Straits Times* (Singapore), November 30, 2001, p. 27.

9. See, for example, Jake Lloyd-Smith, "Beijing Moves to Reassure Neighbors of WTO Gains," *South China Morning Post*, December 1, 2001, p. 3.

10. Toshiya Tsugami, *Chugoku Taito* (The rise of China) (Tokyo: Nihon Keizai Shimbun-sha, 2003), pp. 210–13.

11. Fong, "China's Not in Competition with Japan."

12. The following discussion of the origin of the ASEAN-China FTA is based on Noboru Hatakeyama, "A Short History of Japan's Movement to FTAs," Part 3, *Journal of Japanese Trade and Industry*, March/April 2003, p. 42.

13. Ibid.

14. Differential and More Favorable Treatment Reciprocity and Fuller Participation of Developing Countries, Decision by GATT Contracting Parties, on November

28, 1979 (www.wto.org/english/docs_e/legal_e/enabling1979_e.htm) [April 2004]). The Framework Agreement, art. 3, par. 1, assumes that an ASEAN-China FTA will be in accordance with GATT, art. 24 (8) (b).

15. Chinese scholar involved in the China-ASEAN FTA study, interview, October 2002.

16. ASEAN-China Expert Group on Economic Cooperation, "Forging Closer ASEAN-China Economic Relations in the Twenty-First Century," Report, October 2001 (www.aseansec.org/newdata/asean_chi.pdf [April 2004]). Chairman of the Seventh ASEAN Summit and the Three ASEAN + 1 Summits, Press Statement, Brunei Darussalam, November 6, 2001, par. 3 (www.aseansec.org/534.htm [April 2004])

17. Ibid. For the Chinese perspective on its offer to ASEAN, see Mi Ligong and Lei Besong, "Premier Zhu Rongji Attends Sixth China-ASEAN Summit," Xinhua General News Service (reproduced in *World News Connection*), November 4, 2002.

18. Framework Agreement on Comprehensive Economic Cooperation between the Association of Southeast Asian Nations and the People's Republic of China, November 5, 2002 (www.aseansec.org/13196.htm [April 26, 2004]). Also Chairman of the Eighth ASEAN Summit, the Sixth ASEAN + 3 Summit, and the ASEAN-China Summit, Press Statement, Phnom Penh, Cambodia, November 4, 2002, par. 26 (www.aseansec.org/13188.htm [April 2004]); and Framework Agreement, art. 3, par. 4 (a) (i).

19. Framework Agreement, art. 9.

20. "China, Thailand Sign Tariff-Free Agreement on Agricultural Products," Xinhua General News Service, June 18, 2003.

21. Protocol to Amend the Framework Agreement on Comprehensive Economic Cooperation between the Association of Southeast Asian Nations and the People's Republic of China, October 6, 2003 (www.aseansec.org/15157.htm [April 27, 2004]); see esp. art. 12A ("Agreements outside This Agreement").

22. Framework Agreement, annex 3B. Thailand and China implemented early harvest measures on additional items such as frozen chicken, fresh fish, and fresh flowers on January 1, 2004. See "Free Trade Arrangements between Thailand and China and under the ASEAN-Chinese Framework," *Thai Press Reports*, January 14, 2004.

23. Agreement on Trade in Goods of the Framework Agreement on Comprehensive Economic Cooperation between the Association of Southeast Asian Nations and the People's Republic of China, Vientiane, November 29, 2004 (www.aseansec.org/4979.htm [May 2005]).

24. Hadi Soesastro, "Building an East Asian Community through Trade and Investment Integration," Working Paper Series 67 (Honolulu: Center for Strategic and International Studies, April 2003) (www.csis.or.id/working_paper_file/26/wpe067.pdf [May 2004]).

25. "China's Economic Shift: New Investment Strategy," *Nation*, March 16, 2004.

26. Ibid.

27. Ibid.

28. Takashi Yoshida, "Chuugoku tono FTA ga Motarasu Boueki Tenkan Kouka" (Trade diversion effect of the FTA with China), *JETRO Sensor*, June 2004, p. 57.

29. Hisatsugu Nagao, "Tai to Chugoku, Kudamono Boueki Sokusin de Aratana Hinshitsu Kijun" (Thailand and China to adopt new quality standards for fruits to facilitate trade), *Nihon Keizai Shimbun*, April 25, 2005, morning edition, p. 8.

30. Joint Announcement on the Japan-Singapore Economic Agreement for a New Age Partnership (JSEPA) by the Prime Ministers, October 20, 2001 (www.meti.go.jp/policy/trade_policy/jsepa/press/html/102001_press.html [April 2004]).

31. Joint Announcement of the Japan and Singapore Prime Ministers at the Signing of the Agreement between Japan and the Republic of Singapore for a New Age Economic Partnership (Toward Dynamism and Prosperity for the 21st Century), January 13, 2002 (www.meti.go.jp/policy/trade_policy/jsepa/html/seimei-e.html [April 26, 2004]). For the full statement, see www.mti.gov.sg/public/ PDF/CMT/ FTA_JSEPA_Jointannouncement.pdf. Also, Exchange of Diplomatic Notes for the Entry into Force of the Japan-Singapore Economic Partnership Agreement (www.mofa.go.jp/region/asia-paci/singapore/jsepa0210.html [April 2004]). The agreement was signed on September 17, 2004 (www.mofa.go.jp/region/latin/mexico/agreement/joint.html [June 2006]) and entered into force on April 1, 2005. The agreement is conveniently referred to as the Japan-Singapore Economic Partnership Agreement (JSEPA).

32. Joint Announcement of the Prime Minister of Japan and the President of the United Mexican States on the Initiation of Negotiations for Concluding a Bilateral Agreement to Strengthen Their Economic Partnership, Los Cabos, Mexico, October 27, 2002 (www.mofa.go.jp/policy/economy/apec/2002/joint_me.html [April 2004]). Before agreeing to launch FTA talks, Japan and Mexico set up the Joint Study Group (agreed in June 2001), which completed its report in July 2002.

33. Japan-Mexico Joint Statement on the State Visit to Japan of President Vicente Fox Quesada of the United Mexican States—Strategic Partnership across the Pacific between Japan and Mexico in the New Millennium, October 16, 2003, par. 6 (www.mofa.go.jp/region/latin/mexico/joint0310.html [April 2004]); and "The Agreement between Japan and the United Mexican States for the Strengthening of the Economic Partnership," Joint Press Statement, March 12, 2004 (www.mofa.go.jp/ region/latin/mexico/joint0403.html [April 2004]).

34. METI briefing material (in Japanese) (www.meti.go.jp/policy/trade_policy/l_america/mexico/j_mexico/html/list.html [April 2004]).

35. Prime Minister Junichiro Koizumi of Japan and President Kim Dae Jung of the Republic of Korea, Opening Statements at the Joint Press Conference, March 22, 2002 (www.mofa.go.jp/region/asia-paci/korea/pmv0203/state.html [April 27, 2004]).

36. Joint Study Group Report, "Japan-Korea Free Trade Agreement," October 2, 2003 (www.mofa.go.jp/region/asia-paci/korea/fta/index.html [April 2004]).

37. Joint Announcement on the Japan–Republic of Korea Summit Meeting, Bangkok, October 20, 2003 (www.mofa.go.jp/region/asia-paci/korea/joint0310.html [April 27, 2004]); METI briefing material (in Japanese) (www.meti.go.jp/policy/trade_policy/epa/html/j_korea1.html [April 2004]).

38. Junichiro Koizumi, Prime Minister of Japan, "Japan and ASEAN in East Asia—A Sincere and Open Partnership," speech, Singapore, January 14, 2002 (www.kantei.go.jp/foreign/koizumispeech/2002/01/14speech_e.html [April 2004]).

39. Framework for Comprehensive Economic Partnership between Japan and the Association of Southeast Asian Nations, October 8, 2003 (www.mofa.go.jp/region/asia-paci/asean/pmv0310/framework.html [April 2004]).

40. Joint Announcement of the Japanese and the Thai Prime Ministers on the Initiation of Negotiations for Establishing the Japan-Thailand Economic Partnership Agreement, December 11, 2003 (www.mofa.go.jp/region/asia-paci/asean/pmv0310/framework.html [April 2004]); Joint Announcement of the Japanese Prime Minister and the Philippine President, December 11, 2003 (www.mofa.go.jp/region/asia-paci/philippine/joint0312.html [April 2004]); and Joint Announcement of the Japanese and the Malaysian Prime Ministers on the Initiation of Negotiations for Establishing the Japan-Malaysia Economic Partnership Agreement, December 11, 2003 (www.mofa.go.jp/region/asia-paci/malaysia/joint0312.html [April 2004]).

41. Ministry of Foreign Affairs (MOFA), "A Japan-Philippines Economic Partnership Agreement," Joint Press Statement, November 29, 2004 (www.mofa.go.jp/region/asia-paci/philippine/joint0411.html [May 2005]).

42. MOFA, Joint Statement at the Signing of the Agreement between the Government of Malaysia and the Government of Japan for an Economic Partnership, Kuala Lumpur, December 13, 2005 (www.mofa.go.jp/region/asia-paci/malaysia/agreement/joint0512.html [April 2006]).

43. MOFA, Ministry of Finance, Ministry of Agriculture, Forestry and Fisheries, and Ministry of Economy, Trade and Industry, "Nichi ASEAN Houkatsuteki Keizai Renkei Kyotei Kosho Dai Ikkai Kaigou Gaiyou" (Negotiations on Japan-ASEAN comprehensive economic partnership agreement—outline of the first round), April 18, 2005 (www.mofa.go.jp/mofaj/gaiko/fta/j_asean/kosho05_g.html [May 2005]).

44. "Another Major Move in China's Diplomacy: Commentary," *People's Daily Online*, October 10, 2003, argues that China adopted "a flanking tactic" of letting ASEAN spur a reluctant Japan toward East Asian regional cooperation (english.peopledaily.com.cn/200310/10/eng20031010_125711.shtml [April 2004]).

45. Kwang, "Why China Speeded Up Plans"; "Nation's Diplomacy Growing Maturely," *China Daily*, November 28, 2002.

46. Personal communications by e-mail, November 16, 2001.

47. "ASEAN, Japan Work towards Win-Win Trade Partnership," *The Straits Times* (Singapore), September 14, 2002; also information from an observer at the joint press conference after the AEM-METI meeting, September 13, 2002.

48. Information from an observer at the joint press conference after the AEM +

3 meeting, September 14, 2002.

49. Prime Minister Goh Chok Tong, "ASEAN's Global Competitiveness Outlook—Towards a Single Market," Keynote Address at the ASEAN Business and Investment Summit, Bali, Indonesia, October 6, 2003.

50. Premier Zhu of China, remarks to Hatakeyama on May 28, 2002, quoted in Noburu Hatakeyama, "A Short History of Japan's Movement to FTAs," Part 2, *Journal of Japanese Trade and Industry*, January/February 2003, p. 41.

51. Kwang, "Why China Speeded Up Plans."

52. Fong, "China's Not in Competition with Japan."

53. Ibid.

54. The U.S.-ASEAN Business Council called on the Bush administration and Congress to focus on the five major objectives; to "consolidate and further strengthen U.S. engagement in ASEAN, take initial steps toward the creation of a U.S.-ASEAN Free Trade Area, respond to ASEAN + 3 and bilateral trade initiatives in the region, promote trade and investment facilitation and liberalization, and encourage economic, financial, and other reforms in ASEAN." US-ASEAN Business Council, "ASEAN and Its Importance to the United States of America: The Urgent Need to Look to the Future while Building on the Past," February 2002.

55. Office of the U.S. Trade Representative, Statement of Robert Zoellick, U.S. Trade Representative upon Senate Approval of Trade Promotion Authority, August 1, 2002 (www.ustr.gov/releases/2002/08/02-80.htm [April 2004]).

56. For the U.S. digital trade agenda in a U.S.-Singapore FTA, see Sacha Wunsch-Vincent, "The Digital Trade Agenda of the U.S.: Parallel Tracks of Bilateral, Regional and Multilateral Liberalization," *Swiss Review of International Economic Relations* (Aussenwirtschaft) 58 (March 2003): 7–46 (www.iie.com/publications/papers/wunsch0303.pdf [April 2004]).

57. "ASEAN-U.S. Free Trade Pact Still a Long Way Off," *The Straits Times* (Singapore), interactive, April 6, 2002.

58. Ibid.

59. Woranuj Maneerungsee, "Thailand, U.S. Mull Steps to Bilateral Arrangement: Zoellick Talks of 'Building Blocks,'" *Bangkok Post*, April 5, 2002; Office of the U.S. Trade Representative, "United States and Thailand Sign Bilateral Trade and Investment Framework Agreement," October 23, 2002.

60. White House, Office of the Press Secretary, "Fact Sheet: Enterprise for ASEAN Initiative (EAI)," October 26, 2002 (www.state.gov/p/eap/regional/asean/fs/2002/16605.htm [April 2004]).

61. White House, Office of the Press Secretary, "Statement on U.S.-Thailand FTA Negotiations," October 19, 2003 (www.whitehouse.gov/news/releases/2003/10/print/20031019-1.html [April 2004]). The first round of U.S.-Thailand FTA negotiations was held in July 2004. Embassy of the United States of America in Thailand, "United States and Thailand Conclude Third Round of FTA Talks," Press Releases 012/05 April 8, 2005 (bangkok.usembassy.gov/news/press/2005/nrot012.htm [May 2005]).

62. John McBeth, "ASEAN Summit: Taking the Helm," *Far Eastern Economic Review*, October 16, 2003 (www.feer.com/articles/2003/0310_16/p038china.html [April 2006]).

63. Ibid.

64. Secretary of State Colin L. Powell, "Briefing with Assistant Administrator for United States Agency for International Development Ed Fox," December 27, 2004 (www.state.gov/secretary/former/powell/remarks/40057.htm [May 2005]). See also Alan P. Larson, Under Secretary for Economic, Business and Agricultural Affairs, "Response of the U.S. Government and the International System to the Indian Ocean Earthquake and Tsunamis," Testimony before the Senate Foreign Relations Committee, February 10, 2005 (www.state.gov/e/rls/rm/2005/42173.htm [May 2005]).

65. U.S. Department of State, "U.S., Japan Urge North Korea to Return to Six-Party Talks; Rice, Rumsfeld Issue Joint Statement with Japanese Ministers," February 19, 2005 (usinfo.state.gov/is/Archive/2005/Feb/22-497285.html [May 2005]).

66. R. Nicholas Burns, Under Secretary of State for Political Affairs, "The National Security and Foreign Policy Implications for the United States of Arms Exports to the People's Republic of China by Member States of the European Union," Testimony before a joint hearing of the House International Relations Committee and the House Armed Services Committee, April 14, 2005 (wwwc.house.gov/international_relations/109/bur041405.pdf [May 2005]).

67. U.S. Secretary of State Condoleezza Rice, "Remarks with Australian Foreign Minister Alexander Downer after Their Meeting," May 4, 2005 (www.state.gov/secretary/rm/2005/45632.htm [May 2005]).

68. White House, Office of the Press Secretary, "Joint Vision Statement on the ASEAN-U.S. Enhanced Partnership," November 17, 2005 (www.whitehouse.gov/news/releases/2005/11/20051117-4.html [April 2006])

69. Office of the United States Trade Representative, "United States, South Korea Announce Intention to Negotiate Free Trade Agreement," February 2, 2006 (www.ustr.gov/Document_Library/Press_Releases/2006/February/United_States,_South_Korea_Announce_Intention_to_Negotiate_Free_Trade_Agreement.html [April 2006])

70. East Asia Vision Group, "Towards an East Asian Community—Region of Peace, Prosperity and Progress," 2001 (www.mofa.go.jp/region/asia-paci/report2001.pdf [April 2004]).

71. Ibid.

72. Chairman of the Seventh ASEAN Summit and the Fifth ASEAN + 3 Summit, Press Statement, Bandar Seri Begawan, Brunei Darussalam, November 5, 2001, par. 26 (www.aseansec.org/5317.htm [April 2004]).

73. "Final Report of the East Asia Study Group," ASEAN + 3 Summit, Phnom Penh, Cambodia, November 4, 2002 (www.aseansec.org/viewpdf.asp?file=/pdf/easg.pdf [April 2004]).

74. Chair's Statement, Eighth ASEAN Summit, Sixth ASEAN + 3 Summit, and

ASEAN-China Summit, Phnom Penh, Cambodia, November 4, 2002, par. 20 (www.aseansec.org/13188.htm [April 2004]).

75. Chair's Statement, Ninth ASEAN Summit and the Seventh ASEAN + 3 Summit, Bali, Indonesia, October 7, 2003, par. 35 (www.aseansec.org/15259.htm [April 2004]).

76. Joint Ministers' Statement, Third Meeting of ASEAN Economic Ministers Meeting and Ministers of People's Republic of China, Japan, and Republic of Korea, May 4, 2001, Siemreap, Cambodia (www.aseansec.org/539.htm [June 2004]).

77. Chair's Statement, Eighth ASEAN + 3 Summit, November 29, 2004, Vientiane, Laos, par. 10 (www.aseansec.org/16847.htm [May 2005]).

78. Chair's Statement, Fifth AMM + 3, July 1, 2004, Jakarta, par. 7 (www.aseansec.org/16212.htm [May 2005]).

79. Nobutaka Machimujra, "Japan's Global Strategy and the Japan-U.S. Global Partnership on the 60th Anniversary of the End of World War II," speech in New York, April 29, 2005 (www.mofa.go.jp/policy/un/fmv0504/speech.html [May 2005]); "Higashi Ajia Samitto Kaisai de Kihon Goui" (Basic agreement made on holding an East Asia Summit), *Nihon Keizai Shimbun,* May 9, 2005, morning edition, p. 9.

80. "ASEAN: Sign the Pact or Stay Away," *Australian,* April 12, 2005, local section, p. 2.

81. Department of Foreign Affairs, Republic of the Philippines, "Opening Remarks of the Honoroble Alberto G. Romulo, Secretary of Foreign Affairs at the Briefing for the Ambassadors and Representaitves of ASEAN and the ASEAN Dialogue Partners on the ASEAN Ministerial Retreat," April 15, 2005 (ww.dfa.gov.ph/archive/speech/romulo/afteraseanretreat.htm [April 2005]). The retreat was held on April 10–12, 2005.

82. "India Invited to E. Asia Summit, U.S. Left Out," Japan Economic Newswire, May 9, 2005. ASEAN + 3 foreign ministers met in Kyoto, at the margin of the ASEM foreign ministers meeting. "Higashi Ajia Samitto Kaisai de Kihon Goui" (see n. 79).

83. Chair's Statement, Sixth ASEAN + 3 Foreign Ministers Meeting, Vientiane, Laos, July 27, 2005, par. 10 (www.aseansec.org/17601.htm [April 2006]).

84. Kuala Lumpur Declaration on the ASEAN + 3 Summit, Kuala Lumpur, December 12, 2005 (www.aseansec.org/18036.htm [April 2006]).

85. Kuala Lumpur Declaration on the East Asia Summit, Kuala Lumpur, December 14, 2005 (www.aseansec.org/18098.htm [April 2006]).

86. MOFA, "Nichi Chuu Kan Tousi Torikime Kyoudou Kenkyuu" (The joint study on trilateral investment arrangements among China, Japan, and Republic of Korea) (www.mofa.go.jp/mofaj/gaiko/investment/jck_kaigo.html [June 2004]).

87. Ibid.

88. Report of the Joint Study on the Possible Modality of Trilateral Investment Arrangements among the People's Republic of China, Japan, and the Republic of Korea (www.mofa.go.jp/mofaj/gaiko/investment/pdfs/jck_kaigo_04e.pdf [May 2005]).

89. MOFA, "Nichi-Chu-Kan Gaishou Sansha Iinkai Gaoyou" (Summary of the

Three-Party Committee of the Foreign Ministers of the People's Republic of China, Japan, and the Republic of Korea), May 7, 2005 (www.mofa.go.jp/mofaj/kaidan/g_machimura/asem7_05/jc_gai.html [May 2005]).

90. Robert Scollay and John P. Gilbert, "New Regional Trading Arrangements in the Asia Pacific?" *Policy Analyses in International Economics* 63 (Washington: Institute of International Economics, May 2001), p. 150.

91. According to paragraph 3 of the Understanding on the Interpretation of Article XXIV of the General Agreement on Tariffs and Trade 1994, the "reasonable length of time" within which an FTA has to be completed should not exceed ten years except in exceptional cases.

92. Lee Hsien Loong, Singapore's prime minister, articulated this point as follows: "Second, we must strengthen co-operation amongst other Asian countries, so that even as China's economic weight grows, it does not become the only growth engine in East Asia. Cooperation amongst other Asian countries will produce a multi-focal, multi-connected pattern of growth, broader and more robust than a 'hub and spokes' configuration where every link either starts from or ends in China." See "The Future of East Asian Cooperation," speech delivered at the Eleventh International Conference on the Future of Asia, May 25, 2005, Tokyo, Japan (www.aseansec.org/17474.htm [June 2005]).

Chapter Eight

1. More recently, the territorial disputes over Takeshima (Tokdo, in Korean) Island and the sagging popularity of the Roh Moo-hyun administration have made it more difficult for South Korea to maintain this approach.

2. For discussions on Japan's national strategy, see Prime Minister's Commission on Japan's Goals in the 21st Century, "The Frontier Within: Individual Empowerment and Better Governance in the New Millennium," January 2000. The English version is available at www.kantei.go.jp/jp/21century/report/htmls/index.html (May 2004). Also, Task Force on Foreign Relations for the Prime Minister, "Basic Strategies for Japan's Foreign Policy in the 21st Century—New Era, New Vision, New Diplomacy," November 28, 2002 The summary in English available at www.kantei.go.jp/foreign/policy/2002/1128tf_e.html (May 2004). However, there has been no political initiative to comprehensively follow through on these recommendations, build a national consensus on Japan's purpose, and revise various policies, both domestic and external, to ensure that they consistently serve the national purpose.

3. Yoichi Funabashi, *Asia Pacific Fusion: Japan's Role in APEC* (Washington: Institute for International Economics, September 1995), p. 227. Other Asian countries resisted Japan's influence on the decision to locate the headquarters of the Asian Development Bank (ADB), so that it would be in Manila, not in Tokyo. Note, too, the anti-Japan riots at the time of Prime Minister Kakuei Tanaka's visit to the Southeast Asian countries in 1974 and cold reaction to Prime Minister Masayoshi Ohira's

pan-Pacific design in 1980. Ibid., pp. 227–30. Likewise, Japan avoided publicity on its APEC proposal and instead supported the Australian proposal.

4. Ibid., p. 224.

5. Ibid., p. 227.

6. Report of the Mission for Revitalization of Asian Economy, "Living in Harmony with Asia in the Twenty-first Century," November 17, 1999.

7. For the impact of the rise of China on Japan, see Naoko Munakata, "The Impact of the Rise of China and Regional Economic Integration in Asia—A Japanese Perspective," Testimony before the U.S.-China Economic and Security Review Commission, Hearing on China's Growth as a Regional Economic Power: Impacts and Implications (Washington, December 4, 2003) (www.uscc.gov/testimony/031204bios/naokmunakata.htm).

8. The report of the Task Force on Foreign Relations for the Prime Minister in November 2002 (cited in n. 2) states: "To revitalize Japan means that Japanese people and firms go into growing markets overseas, even more actively than before, and develop strategic networks that integrate domestic and overseas markets. Thus, Japan's prosperity will be achieved together with that of its partners. Japan should not turn inward-looking but base its strategy to expand its national wealth by the aggregate profits from both domestic and overseas markets. The highest priority for the Japanese economy is East Asia, which is the growth center for the world economy."

9. According to a report of the Ministry of Economy, Trade and Industry (METI), the FTA is one of the tools that integrated domestic and external economic policies can use to improve the business environment both domestically and abroad. Part of the rationale for pursuing the FTA (and other regional forums as well as the WTO) is to (1) promote expedient rule making, (2) maintain the momentum for multilateral liberalization, (3) gain experience with various types of international rule making, (4) avoid the disadvantages caused by lack of FTAs, and (5) undertake domestic structural reform. METI, *White Paper on International Trade 2001*, pp. 223–26.

10. This does not mean that all the firms in "competitive industries" are successful or that all the firms in "protected industries" are underperformers. The performance of individual firms varies depending on their corporate strategy. See Masahiko Aoki, "Tayouna Saino Ketsugo wo Chikara ni" (Combine diverse talents for a competitive edge), *Nikkei Sangyo Shimbun*, February 19, 2004, p. 1. In competitive industries, however, unsuccessful firms will eventually be forced out or have to turn around through market competition, whereas in protected sectors, unsuccessful firms tend to be allowed stay in business longer than warranted by market forces. T. J. Pempel argues that this system resulted from policy compromises within the Liberal Democratic Party, between an urban, big business-bureaucrat coalition, and a rural, small business-farmer coalition. See T. J. Pempel, "Decade of Political Torpor: When Political Logic Trumps Economic Rationality," in *Beyond Japanization: Region-Making in East Asia*, edited by Peter J. Katzenstein and Shiraishi Takashi (Cornell University Press, 2006), pp. 37–62.

11. "Kokusai Kyocho no Tame no Keizai Kouzou Chousei Kenkyu-kai Houkokusho" (Report of the study group on the adjustment of economic structure with a view to international cooperation), April 1986 (www.ioc.u-tokyo.ac.jp/~worldjpn/index.html [May 2004]).

12. Ministry of Foreign Affairs (MOFA), "U.S.-Japan Framework Talks" (www.mofa.go.jp/region/n-america/us/economy/date/17.html [May 2004]).

13. At first sight, regulatory reforms in the context of Japan-U.S. talks seem irrelevant to Japan's Asia strategy because the former involved deregulating such areas as financial services and telecommunications, which are usually not on the list of requests from Asian neighbors. However, demands from the United States and Asia were closely related in that Japan has to become much more open and competitive in the services sectors, so that it can substantially reduce the cost of service links between Japan and other Asian countries, broaden the base for economic growth, and become more confident in the "complementarity" with its neighbors, which are quickly catching up and becoming attractive markets for services as their income levels go up.

14. Walter B. Lohman, executive director, U.S.-ASEAN Business Council, personal interview, in which he revealed that U.S. firms had similar impressions of their Japanese counterparts: "Japanese firms concentrate on maximizing their performance in the existing environment and are good at overcoming the difficulties they face. American firms try to change the environment and approach their government. In this sense, the distance between business and government seems greater in Japan."

15. In a MOFA attitude survey on the WTO and FTAs conducted in February 2003, only 20 percent of the respondents were interested in FTA negotiations; 35 percent answered that exposing weak industries to fierce competition through an FTA is acceptable, 30 percent said it was unacceptable and they would rather not have an FTA in such a situation, 36 percent said they should accept an FTA that would allow foreign workers with professional skills to work in Japan, and 32 percent rejected such an FTA. See MOFA, "Keizai Gaiko (WTO, FTA) ni Kansuru Ishiki Chousa" (Attitude survey on economic diplomacy [WTO, FTA]), February 2003 (www.mofa.go.jp/mofaj/gaiko/wto/2003ec.html [May 2004]). On the other hand, when *Nikkei Sangyo Shimbun* conducted a survey of its e-mail magazine subscribers (mainly businesspeople), it found that 71 percent thought Japan should conclude FTAs with as many countries as possible, 23 percent said Japan should conclude FTAs with only certain countries (94 percent were positive about FTAs), and 53 percent answered that Japan should allow corporations to enter farming, enhance the competitiveness of agriculture, and turn it into an export industry. "Boueki Taisei to Nougyou Mondai" (Trade system and agriculture issue), *Nikkei Sangyo Shimbun,* February 27, 2004, p. 34.

16. A Ministry of Agriculture, Forestry, and Fisheries (MAFF) paper submitted to a discussion group organized by the prime minister's office emphasized, "It is necessary to fully study the benefits and costs of FTAs with specific countries," and

"care must be taken to avoid adverse effects on the structural reform of Japan's agriculture, forestry and fisheries." However, it no longer insisted that agriculture, forestry, and fisheries produce should be liberalized only through WTO negotiations, as it did before the conclusion of the Japan-Singapore Economic Partnership Agreement (JSEPA). MAFF, "Jiyuu Boueki Kyoutei to Nourin Suisan Gyou" (Free trade agreements and agriculture, forestry and fisheries); Dai 2 Kai Nichi-ASEAN Houkatsuteki Keizai Renkei Kousou wo Kangaeru Kondankai (The second meeting of the discussion group on the Initiative for Japan-ASEAN Comprehensive Economic Partnership), May 29, 2002 (www.kantei.go.jp/jp/singi/asean/dai2/2siryou4.pdf [May 2004]). See also "Nourin Suisan Sho Sougou Shokuryou Kyoku Kokusaibu Kokusai Chousei Kacho" (Director, International Trade Policy Coordination Division, International Affairs Department, General Food Policy Bureau, MAFF); Masaki Sakai, "Wagakuni no Shokuryo Anzenhosho to Nousanbutsu Boueki Seisaku—Jiyuu Boueki Kyoutei wo Megutte" (Japan's Food Security and Agriculture Trade Policy—on Free Trade Agreements), "Sangyo Kudoka" to Kanzei Seisaku ni Kansuru Kenkyuukai (Study Group on "Industry Hollowing-out" and Tariff Policy), April 25, 2002 (www.mof.go.jp/singikai/sangyokanze/siryou/a140517b.pdf [May 2004]).

17. Although it has been argued that Japan should have its version of a Trade Representative, such departments of government can only be effective when accompanied by close communications and trust among relevant agencies. For the proposal for creating a new organization to centralize the decisionmaking process, see Nippon Keidanren (Japan Business Federation), "Keizairenkei no Kyouka ni Muketa Kinkyu Teigen" (Urgent proposal for strengthening economic partnership), March 16, 2004 (www.keidanren.or.jp/japanese/policy/2004/020/honbun.html).

18. See, for example, "Ex-Snow Brand Milk Execs to Face Criminal Charges," Jiji Press Ticker Service, November 7, 2000; "Snow Brand Food Disguised Beef to Get Gov't Subsidies," Japan Economic Newswire, January 23, 2002; and "Police Building Beef Buyback Fraud Cases against 2 Co-ops," Japan Economic Newswire, April 19, 2004.

19. A former MAFF minister's comment, quoted in "'Hogo' Dakeja Dame, 'Shoku no Anzen' de Jimintou Nousui Zoku Henbou no Toki" (Time to change for the Liberal Democratic Party's agriculture tribe, food safety issues remind them that mere protection is no good), *Asahi Shimbun*, March 31, 2004, morning edition, p. 4.

20. Sourifu, Naikaku Souri Daijin Kanbou Kouhou Shitsu (Prime minister's office, prime minister's secretariat, public relations office), "Nousan Butsu Boueki ni Kansuru Yoron Chousa" (Public opinion poll on agricultural trade), October 10, 2000 (www8.cao.go.jp/survey/h12/nousan/index.html [May 2004]).

21. Ibid.

22. According to the Japan External Trade Association (JETRO), Japan's export of fresh apples to Taiwan in 2002 recorded a 488 percent increase over the previous year because Taiwan abolished its import quota following its accession to the WTO. As a result, Japan's overall export of fresh apples increased 370 percent in 2002. JETRO, "Nourinsuisan Butsu no Yushutu Jokyo" (The state of export of agricul-

ture, forestry, and fisheries), July 23, 2003 (www.jetro.go.jp/ag/j/export/committee/first/list/pdf/06.pdf [May 2004]). See also JETRO, "Higasi Ajia eno Nourinsuisann Butsu no Yushutsu Jirei" (Examples of agriculture, forestry, and fisheries exports to East Asia), September 12, 2003 (www.jetro.go.jp/ag/j/export/committee/first/2list/pdf/2_8_export.pdf [May 2004]).

23. "Nourinsuisan Shou no Yushutsu Sokushin Saku" (MAFF's export promotion measures), September 12, 2003 (www.jetro.go.jp/ag/j/export/committee/first/2list/pdf/2_2_maffshiensaku.pdf [May 2004]). See also "Nousan Butsu no Yushutu Sekkyokuka, Nousuisho ga Sokusin Shitsu Sechhi, Ajia Shojun" (MAFF turns aggressive in promoting agricultural produce, setting up the export promotion office, targeting Asia), *Sankei Shimbun*, March 2, 2004, morning edition, p. 9.

24. In 2000 Japan imported agriculture, forestry, and fisheries produce valued at 6,914 billion yen, whereas its export was valued at 315 billion yen. MAFF, "Free Trade Agreements and Agriculture, Forestry and Fisheries," cited in n.16. In 2005, its import and export values were 7,654 billion yen and 401 billion yen, respectively. Nourinsuisansho, Kokusaibu, Kokusai Seisaku Ka (MAFF, international department, international policy division), "Nourinsuisan Butsu Yushutunyuu Jouhou, Heisei 17 nen, 12 Gatsu Bun" (Export and import data of agriculture, forestry, of fisheries produce, December 2005), February 15, 2006 (www.maff.go.jp/toukei/sokuhou/data/yusyutu2005-12/yusyutu2005-12.pdf [May 2006]).

25. The comment was made to the press after the second meeting with President Vincente Fox of Mexico in October 2003 following Japan's failure to agree on an FTA with that country earlier that month. "FTA Koushou, Souki ni Saikai, Nihon, Mekishiko Shunou Icchi—Shushou, 'Nougyou Sakoku Dekinu'" (Japanese and Mexican leaders agree to soon reopen FTA talks, PM, "We cannot adopt an agricultural closed-door policy"), *Nihon Keizai Shimbun*, October 22, 2003, morning edition, p. 5.

26. MAFF, "Nousei Kaikaku no Suishin ni Tsuite" (On agricultural policy reforms), Shokuryou, Nougyou, Nousei Shingikai (Food, Agriculture and Agricultural Policy Council), December 9, 2003 (www.maff.go.jp/www/counsil/counsil_cont/kanbou/seisaku_singikai/6/siryo5.pdf [May 2004]).

27. Ibid.

28. Kazuhito Yamashita, "Nougyou, Chokusetsu Siharai de Kyousou Ryoku" (Enhance competitiveness of agriculture through direct payment), *Nihon Keizai Shimbun*, December 22, 2003, morning edition, p. 22 (www.rieti.go.jp/jp/papers/contribution/yamashita/02.html?mode=print [May 2004]). Yamashita is a MAFF official currently resident at the Research Institute of Economy, Trade and Industry (RIETI).

29. For the share of dedicated farmers, see MAFF, "Nougyou Kouzou Doutai Chousa Kekka Gaiyou" (Summary results of change in agricultural structure) (as of January 1, 2003), July 22, 2003 (www.maff.go.jp/toukei/sokuhou/data/kihon-kouzou2003/kihon-kouzou2003.htm [May 2004]).

30. For a summary of the Basic Plan, see Japan's Ministry of Agriculture, Forestry and Fisheries, "Summary of the New Basic Plan for Food, Agriculture and Rural

Areas," MAFF Update 585, May 20, 2005 (www.maff.go.jp/mud/585.html [June 5, 2005]); Kazuhito Yamashita, "Shokuryo, Nogyo, Noson Kihon Keikaku no Mondaiten (1)—'Midori' dewa nai 'Hinmoku Oudanteki Seisaku'" (The problems of the Basic Plan for Food, Agriculture and Rural Areas (1)—Non-product-specific measures that are not "green"), *Shukan Norin,* April 5, 2005, as reproduced at www.rieti.go.jp/jp/papers/contribution/yamashita/21.html (June 2005).

31. See, for example, Nippon Keidanren (Japan Business Federation), "Keizairenkei no Kyouka ni Muketa Kinkyu Teigen" (Urgent proposal for strengthening economic partnership), March 16, 2004 (www.keidanren.or.jp/japanese/policy /2004/020/honbun.html).

32. Junichiro Koizumi, Prime Minister of Japan, "Japan and ASEAN in East Asia—A Sincere and Open Partnership," speech, January 14, 2002, Singapore; Opening Statements at the Joint Press Conference with Prime Minister Helen Clark of New Zealand, May 2, 2002 (www.mofa.go.jp/region/asia-paci/pmv0204/ op_0502.html [May 2004]).

33. The emphasis on "functional cooperation" and the rejection of "putting an institution first" should be interpreted not as denying institutional frameworks such as ASEAN + 3 but as warning against making the institution an end in itself and a reminder of the importance of substantive cooperation to be conducted under institutional frameworks. Foreign Minister Yoriko Kawaguchi, "Shin Jidai ni okeru Ajia Chiiki Kyouryoku" (Asian regional cooperation in the new era). speech, May 21, 2002 (www.mofa.go.jp/mofaj/press/enzetsu/14/ekw_0521.html [May 2004]).

34. A high-standard FTA should be consistent with WTO rules (that is, FTAs among developing countries invoking the enabling clause do not meet this criterion) and should contain not only tariff elimination but also the liberalization of investment and services trade with the negative list approach, and rules on, at least, the protection of intellectual property rights (IPR), customs procedure, and transparency. How high a standard Japan can reach with other Asian countries remains to be seen. Compared with the Japan-Singapore FTA, the U.S.-Singapore FTA has much broader coverage of services and more extensive rules, such as detailed customs procedures, legal commitments on competition policy, protection for copyrighted works in a digital economy, and enforcement of IPR protection.

35. "Framework for Comprehensive Economic Partnership between Japan and the Association of Southeast Asian Nations," October 8, 2003, sec. 6 (www.kantei.go.jp/foreign/koizumispeech/2003/10/08wakugumi_e.html [May 2004]).

36. See, for example, Masaru Yoshitomi, *Ajia Keizai no Shinjitsu* (The truth of the Asian economy) (Tokyo: Toyo Keizai Shimpo Sha, 2003), p. 290.

37. MOFA, "Nihon no FTA Senryaku" (Japan's FTA strategy), 2002 (www.mofa.go.jp/mofaj/gaiko/fta/policy.pdf [May 2004]).

38. A survey of corporate managers of Japan, China, and South Korea jointly conducted by Nihon Keizai Shimbun Sha from Japan, International Business from China, and Maeil Business Newspaper from South Korea. "Nichi Chuu Kan FTA

'Hitsuyo' 7 Wari'" (70 percent consider Japan-China-ROK FTA 'necessary'), *Nihon Keizai Shimbun,* March 24, 2004, morning edition, p. 1.

39. "Kyoku-cho ni Kiku" (Interview with Deputy Secretary-General Lee, South Korea's National Security Council), *Nihon Keizai Shimbun,* February 15, 2004, morning edition, p. 2. Tokyo and Seoul had six rounds of FTA talks between December 2003 and November 2004 but have not reached agreement, with apparent differences on the approach to tariff reduction.

40. *Nikkei Sangyo Shimbun,* cited in n. 15.

41. "Nichi Chuu Kan FTA 'Hitsuyo' 7 Wari," cited in n. 38.

42. Japan's simple average tariffs are 2.9 percent for all products and 2.3 percent for nonagricultural products, whereas those of China are 10.0 percent for all products and 9.1 percent for nonagricultural products. MOFA, "Japan's FTA Strategy."

43. Yoriko Kawaguchi, Minister for Foreign Affairs, "Towards a Brighter Future: Advancing our Global Partnership," address at the Federation of Indian Chambers of Commerce and Industry, Delhi, India, January 8, 2003 (www.mofa.go.jp/region-/asia-paci/fmv0301/india.html [May 2004]).

44. As far as the East Asian security system is concerned, Japan is not considered a big power like the United States, China, and Russia, but a middle power like South Korea and ASEAN. Yoshihide Soeya, "Diplomacy Should Go beyond Alliance with U.S.," *International Herald Tribune / Asahi Shimbun,* July 3, 2003, as reproduced at www.rieti.go.jp/en/press/03070301.html (May 2004). See also Yoshihide Soeya, "Higashi Ajia Anzenhosho Sisutemu no Naka no Nihon" (Japan in the East Asian security system), in *Nihon no Higashi Ajia Koso* (Japan's East Asia initiatives), edited by Yoshihide Soeya and Masayuki Tadokoro (Keio University Press, 2004), pp.193–219. As far as the regional economic order is concerned, however, Japan still has significant power and influence as a big power, and it is in Japan's interest to use this power and influence, while still available, to build a stable regional order conducive to peace and prosperity in the region. To point out here that ASEAN countries hope for a stable Sino-Japanese relationship is not to deny that they might not want Japan and China to get so close that they would overshadow ASEAN, as noted at the beginning of this chapter.

45. Robert B. Zoellick, "Economics and Security in the Changing Asia-Pacific," *Survival* 39 (Winter 1997/1998): 40.

46. U.S. Department of Defense (DOD), Office of International Security Affairs, "United States Security Strategy for the East Asia-Pacific Region" (GPO, February 1995).

47. Richard W. Baker, "The United States and APEC Regime Building," in *Asia-Pacific Crossroads: Regime Creation and the Future of APEC,* edited by Vinod K. Aggarwal and Charles E. Morrison (New York: St. Martin's Press, 1998), p. 166.

48. Michael H. Armacost and Kenneth B. Pyle, "Japan and the Engagement of China: Challenges for U.S. Policy Coordination," NBR Analysis, vol. 12 (National Bureau of Asian Research, December 2001) (www.nbr.org/publications/analysis/pdf/vol12no5.pdf [June 2005]). Armacost and Pyle condense the funda-

mental principles into three: "1) to prevent the domination of the region by any other power; 2) to keep the region open to American trade and investment, the so-called 'open door'; and 3) to seek the spread of democratic government, the Wilsonian Principle of 'self-determination,' as the surest way to preserve peace and stability in the region."

49. DOD, "United States Security Strategy."

50. The exception to this observation, as noted in chapter 4, was the policy planning at the Treasury Department under the Reagan administration before APEC was launched, but the planning did not produce a concrete public proposal.

51. U.S. Trade Representative Robert Zoellick listed 13 factors to consider in selecting U.S. FTA partners, at a conference, "Free Trade Agreements and U.S. Trade Policy," at the Institute of International Economics, Washington, May 8, 2003: congressional guidance; U.S. business and agricultural interests, both current and future; impact on special products' sensitivities; seriousness of the partner about reaching high level agreements (FTA has to cover agriculture to be a "free trade" agreement); commitment of countries to the WTO; whether FTA can promote regional integration (for example, FTAA); impact of countries' economic reform, deregulation, and outward orientation; support of civil society (particularly on such issues as environment and labor); political security considerations, such as support for U.S. security policy; the need to counterbalance the inroads of others; regional balance (not just in the Western Hemisphere but also in Africa and Asia); the need to cover both developed and developing countries; and U.S. ability to manage administrative resources. This list does not suggest how to prioritize different potential FTA deals with different scores on each factor, but it does reveal the basic motivations of U.S. FTA policies, particularly when compared with the FTAs that Washington actually chose to negotiate.

52. Office of the U.S. Trade Representative (USTR), "USTR Reports on Free Trade Agreements in Southeast Asia," transcript of USTR Zoellick's press conference, Bangkok, Thailand, April 5 (Department of State Washington File, April 8, 2002) (usembassy-australia.state.gov/hyper/2002/0408/epf110.htm [May 2004]).

53. Office of the USTR, "Free Trade with Morocco: Helping to Solidify Economic Reforms," *Trade Facts*, January 21, 2003 (www.ustr.gov/regions/eu-med/middleeast/2003-01-21-morocco-factsheet.pdf); Office of the USTR, "Assessment of Morocco's Technical Assistance Needs in Negotiating and Implementing a Free Trade Agreements with the United States," January 21, 2003 (www.usaid.gov/regions/ane/documents/morocco-ta-trade03.pdf); Office of the USTR, "Free Trade with Central America: Summary of the U.S.-Central America Free Trade Agreement," *Trade Facts*, December 17, 2003 (www.ustr.gov/new/fta/Cafta/2003-12-17-factsheet.pdf).

54. USTR, "USTR Sees Increased Investment Potential for Thailand," transcript of USTR Zoellick's press conference, Bangkok, Thailand, April 4 (Department of State Washington File, April 4, 2002) (usembassy-australia.state.gov/hyper/2002/0404/epf413.htm [May 2004]).

55. USTR, "USTR Reports on Free Trade Agreements in Southeast Asia," transcript of USTR Zoellick's press conference, Bangkok, Thailand, April 5, 2002.

56. C. Fred Bergsten, "Foreign Economic Policy for the Next President," *Foreign Affairs* 83 (March/April 2004): 88–101, 89.

57. See, for example, Jeffery J. Schott, "Assessing US FTA Policy," in *Free Trade Agreements: US Strategies and Priorities*, edited by Jeffery J. Schott (Washington: Institute of International Economics, April 2004), pp. 359–81. In February 2006 the United States and South Korea announced their intention to negotiate a bilateral FTA. Remarks by U.S. Trade Representative Rob Portman and Republic of Korea Trade Minister Hyun-chong Kim, "Launch of U.S.-Korea Free Trade Agreement," Mansfield Room, U.S. Capitol, February 2, 2006, Washington (www.ustr.gov/assets/ Document_Library/Transcripts/2006/February/asset_upload_file804_8935.pdf [May 2006]).

58. Armacost and Pyle, "Japan and the Engagement of China," p. 39.

59. I. M. Destler, *American Trade Politics*, 3rd ed. (Washington: Institute for International Economics, 1995), pp. 41–63.

60. C. Fred Bergsten, "America's Two-Front Economic Conflict," *Foreign Affairs* 80 (March/April 2001): 16–27, 21.

61. C. Fred Bergsten, "A Renaissance for U.S. Trade Policy?" *Foreign Affairs* 81 (November/December 2002): 86–98, 88.

62. C. Fred Bergsten, "Foreign Economic Policy for the Next President," p. 89.

63. Ibid., p. 96.

64. James A. Baker, III, "A New Pacific Partnership: Framework for the Future," address to the Asia Society, June 26, 1989; Richard W. Baker, "The United States and APEC Regime Building," p. 166.

65. Baker, "The United States and APEC Regime Building," p. 166.

66. Brainard notes that "congressional restrictions on U.S. bilateral support for stabilization, enacted during the Mexican crisis, largely determined the initial U.S. decision not to aid Thailand in 1997." See Lael Brainard, "Capitalism Unhinged: The IMF and the Lessons of the Last Financial Crisis," *Foreign Affairs* 81 (January/February 2002): 192–98, 197. See also Paul Blustein, *The Chastening: Inside the Crisis That Rocked the Global Financial System and Humbled the IMF* (PublicAffairs, 2001), p. 79.

67. Han Sung-joo's comment quoted in Tim Shorrock, "East Asian Community Remains Elusive," *Asia Times Online*, February 2002 (www.atimes.com/china/ DB05Ad02.html [May 2004]).

68. Personal conversation, 2002. According to the diplomat, both Japan and China carry a historical burden: "The memory of wartime Japan remains heavy despite the decades of its postwar history as a peaceful nation, because we still have concerns about the quality of your political leaders, their lack of sensitivities to and the willingness to face and alleviate, if not heal, their neighbors' concerns and emotional wounds. We also remember China's support of communist insurgencies and, more recently, its willingness to use military means to deal with territorial disputes

and threaten Taiwan. Although it is quickly changing its approach to the region and making friendly gestures, we need more time to have confidence in China."

69. The quotations referring to the four options are from Armacost and Pyle, "Japan and the Engagement of China," pp. 39–42. Armacost and Pyle list U.S. approaches to triangular (that is, the relations among the United States, Japan and China) diplomacy to "dissuad[e] others from ganging up against the United States," which is also useful as the option for U.S. approaches to East Asian regionalism. Before discussing the four alternatives, they reject "a retreat to Fortress America" and "a reliance on collective security arrangements in Asia" as "academic."

70. Armacost and Pyle criticized the Clinton administration because "its approach [after 1995] was marked neither by consistency nor dexterity. Its management of U.S. ties with both Japan and China was erratic, and coordination with Japan of U.S. policies toward China was poor." Ibid., p. 42.

71. Wu Xinbo, "China: Security Practice of a Modernizing and Ascending Power," in *Asian Security Practice: Material and Ideational Influences*, edited by Muthiah Alagappa (Stanford University Press, 1998), p. 150.

72. Ibid., pp. 150–51.

73. Ibid., p. 149.

74. Seiichiro Takagi, "Chugoku to Ajia Taiheiyou Chiiki no Takokukan Kyoryoku" (China and multilateral cooperation in the Asia Pacific region), in *Kokusai Kankei— Ajia Taiheiyou no Chiiki Chitsujo* (International relations—the regional order in the Asia Pacific), edited by Kyoko Tanaka, vol. 8 of *Gendai Chugoku no Kouzou Hendou* (Structural changes of modern China) (Tokyo University Press, 2001), pp. 73–94.

75. For the changes in China's perception of its "periphery" in the early and late 1990s, see David Shambaugh, "Return to the Middle Kingdom? China and Asia in the Early Twenty-First Century," in *Power Shift: China and Asia's New Dynamics*, edited by David Shambaugh (University of California Press, 2005), pp. 23–47. See also Evan S. Medeiros and M. Taylor Fravel, "China's New Diplomacy," *Foreign Affairs* 82 (November/December 2003): 22–35.

76. Jurgen Haacke, *ASEAN's Diplomatic and Security Culture: Origins, Development and Prospects* (New York: RoutledgeCurzon, 2003), p. 113. For the nature of China's support of the "ASEAN way" in dealing with regional security issues, see pp. 112–38.

77. Tang Shiping and Peter Hay Gries, "China's Security Strategy: From Offensive to Defensive Realism and Beyond," Working Paper 97 (Enterprise for ASEAN Initiative, October 21, 2002), p. 6.

78. Tang Shiping and Zhang Yunling, "China's Regional Strategy," in *Power Shift*, edited by David Shambaugh, p. 52.

79. Ibid., p. 52.

80. Shambaugh, "Return to the Middle Kingdom?" p. 28.

81. Tang and Zhang, "China's Regional Strategy," p. 51.

82. See, for example, Xia Liping, "China: A Responsible Great Power," *Journal of*

Contemporary China 10, no. 26 (2001): 17–25 (www.stanleyfoundation.org/papers/xia.pdf [May 2004]). The Peaceful Rise theory was first put forward by Zheng Bijian, former vice principal of the Central Party School of the Chinese Communist Party in late 2003 during the Boao Forum for Asia. See Tang and Zhang, "China's Regional Strategy," pp. 49, 53. See also Robert W. Radtke, "China's 'Peaceful Rise' Overshadowing U.S. Influence in Asia?" *Christian Science Monitor,* December 8, 2003, p. 9.

83. Secretary Colin L. Powell, "Remarks Following Bilateral Meeting with Chinese Foreign Minister Tang," comments made in lobby, Hanoi, Vietnam, July 25, 2001 (www.state.gov/secretary/rm/2001/4277.htm [May 2004]); Roger Mitton, "Living with Elephants," *AsiaWeek.com,* August 31, 2001 (www.asiaweek.com/asiaweek/magazine/dateline/0,8782,172291,00.html [May 2004]); Tang and Zhang, "China's Regional Strategy," p. 53.

84. Tang and Zhang, "China's Regional Strategy," p. 53.

85. Ibid., p. 59.

86. Hu Jintao, "China's Development Is an Opportunity for Asia," speech at the annual conference of the Boao Forum for Asia, Boao, Hainan Province, China, April 24, 2004 (english.peopledaily.com.cn/200404/24/eng20040424_141419.shtml [May 2004]).

87. Tang and Zhang, "China's Regional Strategy," p. 50. See also, Shambaugh, "Return to the Middle Kingdom?" p. 40.

88. Hu, "China's Development Is an Opportunity for Asia."

89. Lee Kuan Yew, *From Third World to First: The Singapore Story: 1965–2000* (New York: HarperCollins, 2000), p. 653.

90. Yoshikazu Shimizu, *Chuugoku wa Naze Hannichi ni Nattaka* (Why China Became anti-Japanese) (Bungei Shunjiu, 2003).

91. Richard McGregor and David Pilling, "Old Sores Pain China and Japan: Economic Ties Are Growing but Antipathy Remains," *Financial Times,* August 26, 2003, p. 7.

92. See, for example, "East Asia's New Faultlines," *Economist,* March 14, 1998, p. 16; and Greg Sheridan, "Diplomatic Offensive Pays off with Beijing's Neighbors," *Australian,* September 6, 1999, p. 8.

93. Shi Yinhong, "National Direction of China in the Contemporary and Future World Politics: An Advocacy for 'Diplomatic Philosophy' and Grand Strategy," paper prepared for RIETI conference, "Asia in Search of a New Order," January 16–17, 2004 (www.rieti.go.jp/jp/events/04011601/pdf/shi.pdf [June 2004]).

94. Ibid.

95. Ibid.

96. Ibid.

97. Ibid.

98. Tang and Zhang, "China's Regional Strategy," p. 50.

Chapter Nine

1. Vietnam joined ASEAN in July 1995, Laos and Myanmar in July 1997, and Cambodia in April 1999.

2. While some estimates suggest that an FTA among ASEAN, Japan, South Korea, and China will have a slightly negative impact on the United States, it is smaller in magnitude than the negative impact of, say, a Free Trade Area of the Americas (FTAA) on many East Asian economies. Both of these negative impacts will be at least partly offset by dynamic effects not captured by static models and eventually rectified by the tariff reduction on an MFN basis through the WTO negotiations, for which major trading powers are striving to make regionalism a building block. For the impact of an ASEAN + 3 FTA and FTAA, see, for example, Robert Scollay and John P. Gilbert, "New Regional Trading Arrangements in the Asia Pacific," *Policy Analyses in International Economics* 63 (Washington: Institute for International Economics, May 2001), pp. 68–73. For the impact of an ASEAN + 3 FTA, see also Masaru Yoshitomi, *Ajia Keizai no Shinjitsu* (The truth of the Asian economy) (Tokyo: Toyo Keizai Shimpo Sha, 2003), pp. 286–87.

3. Kyodo News on the Web, "Singapore's Lee Blasts Koizumi's Hint of Visiting Yasukuni Shrine," May 18, 2005 (home.kyodo.co.jp/all/printer_friendly.jsp? an=20050518018 [June 2005]).

4. "Japanese Envoy Says China's Real Concern Is UN Bid, Not History," Agence France-Presse, May 18, 2005.

5. James R. Lilley, "All Not Quiet on the Eastern Front," *Wall Street Journal*, April 13, 2005, p. A18.

6. See, for example, U.S. Department of Defense, Office of the Assistant Secretary of Defense (Public Affairs), "Secretary Rumsfeld's Remarks to the International Institute for Strategic Studies," June 4, 2005 (www.defenselink.mil/transcripts/2005/tr20050604-secdef3002.html [June 2005]).

Index

Abdullah Ahmad Badawi, Datuk Seri, 121

AEM. *See* ASEAN economic ministers

AEM-METI Economic and Industrial Cooperation Committee (AMEICC), 94

AFTA. *See* ASEAN Free Trade Area

Agricultural trade: of Japan, 55, 108, 120, 143–44; liberalization by Japan, 4, 120, 142, 143–44, 158; liberalization by South Korea, 4; of Mexico, 120, 142

AIC. *See* ASEAN Industrial Complementation

AICO. *See* ASEAN Industrial Cooperation

AIJV. *See* ASEAN Industrial Joint Venture

AMF. *See* Asian Monetary Fund

Anti-Americanism and anti-Westernism, 10, 15, 175

ANZCERTA. *See* Australia–New Zealand Closer Economic Relations Trade Agreement

APEC. *See* Asia-Pacific Economic Cooperation

ARF. *See* ASEAN Regional Forum

ASEAN (Association of Southeast Asian Nations): closer economic relations (CER) countries, 93, 96, 111; consensus approach, 35; dialogue partners, 73, 127; economic cooperation within, 43–44, 94, 101, 122–23, 171; economic growth, 40; effects of financial crisis, 104; external relations, 96, 100–01, 122; foreign direct investment in member countries, 38–39; influence on regionalism, 93–94, 134–35; interests of members, 14; internal competition, 14; intra-industry trade, 44; meetings with other countries, 95–97, 173–74; membership, 46, 94, 100, 104, 172; participation in Asia-Europe meeting, 98; post-ministerial conferences, 106; potential free trade agreements, 117, 149; relationship with APEC, 69–70; relations with China, 112, 115, 116–19, 125, 160; relations with Japan, 29, 93–94, 96–97, 101, 120–21, 145–46; relations with NAFTA, 77, 93; relations with United States, 63, 77, 94–95, 124–25, 153–54, 177; summits, 44, 77; trade among members, 47, 48–49; trade liberalization, 43. *See*

also China-ASEAN free trade agreement
ASEAN + China summits, 9, 115, 116
ASEAN + 3 forums: as basis for regional community, 150, 177; Chiang Mai Initiative, 106, 107, 108, 116, 175; Chinese participation, 9, 115, 116; currency swaps, 103, 106; development, 105–06, 173–74; driving forces, 100, 101; economic ministers' meetings, 96–97; finance ministers' meetings, 106, 126; financial cooperation, 106–07, 126; foreign ministers' meetings, 95; functional cooperation, 126–27; goals, 128; health ministers' meetings, 127; potential free trade agreements, 117, 149; relationship to East Asia summits, 15, 21; relations with non-Asian countries, 9–10; scope, 4, 126–27, 150; summits, 9, 21, 99, 106, 126, 127, 128
ASEAN Business and Investment Summit, 122–23
ASEAN economic ministers (AEM) meetings, 93–94, 95, 111, 117
ASEAN Free Trade Area (AFTA): agreement, 44, 171; Common Effective Preferential Tariff, 43, 77; as defensive move, 79; driving forces, 29; impact on regionalism, 77, 79; implementation, 93, 173; launching, 83; potential expansion, 106, 111; proposal, 76–77
ASEAN Industrial Complementation (AIC), 44
ASEAN Industrial Cooperation (AICO), 44
ASEAN Industrial Joint Venture (AIJV), 44
ASEAN Regional Forum (ARF), 93, 95
ASEAN-U.S. Dialogue, 63
Asia-Europe meeting (ASEM), 93–94, 95–96, 98, 106
Asian Common Skill Standard Initiative for Information Technology Engineers, 127
Asian Development Bank, 107
Asian financial crisis (*1997–98*): APEC response, 105; changes in trade policies following, 18–19, 30; Chinese reaction, 161; effects, 11–12, 46, 102–05, 113–14, 174–75; IMF response, 35, 102–03, 107, 175; Japanese assistance, 104, 107; as motive for regionalism, 27, 30, 103; U.S. response, 102–03, 105, 156, 175
Asian Monetary Fund (AMF) proposal, 35, 103, 106, 107, 116, 175
Asia Pacific Economic Cooperation (APEC): achievements, 92–93, 173; ASEAN participation, 69–70; Bogor trade liberalization goals, 84, 85, 96, 172; consensus approach, 66; development, 78–79, 92; divisions within, 82–86, 91–92; Early Voluntary Sectoral Liberalization proposal, 82, 86–89, 100, 105, 108; early years, 70–71, 172–73; East Asia Economic Caucus proposal, 94–95; Eminent Persons Group, 78, 82–83, 84–85, 172; establishment, 65, 66, 171; free trade agreement proposals, 11, 83, 84, 85, 89; goals, 20, 70, 71, 92; human rights issues, 91; influence on regional cooperation, 92, 172–73; leaders' meetings, 8, 81–82, 83–84, 85–86, 87, 93, 125, 172; limitations, 20, 100; membership, 20, 66, 67, 69, 72, 78; ministerial meetings, 70, 78, 81; motivations of members, 79–80; Osaka Action Agenda, 85–86, 91; proposals, 65–67; response to financial crisis, 105; secretariat, 78; trade liberalization strategies, 82–86, 99–100, 172–73; as transregional forum, 92, 156, 173; unfulfilled expectations, 89–92. *See*

also United States, relations with APEC

Assembly factories. *See* Production networks

Association of Southeast Asian Nations. *See* ASEAN

Australia: APEC proposal, 65, 66–67, 69; closer economic relations with ASEAN, 93; economic policies, 66; exports, 67; inclusion in East Asia summits, 15, 16, 127, 128, 150; interest in East Asian regionalism, 66–67; participation in Asia-Europe meeting, 98; proposed free trade agreements, 105; role in East Asian forums, 132, 149–50

Australia–New Zealand Closer Economic Relations Trade Agreement (ANZCERTA), 78, 85

Authoritarian regimes, 33, 185

Autocratic regime, Chinese, 33, 164

Automobile manufacturing: in Indonesia, 44; Japanese firms, 44, 45–46, 58; in Malaysia, 44; production networks, 44, 45–46, 58

Baker, Howard, 12, 22

Baker, James A., 68–69, 73–74, 75, 76

Barshefsky, Charlene, 9

BBC. *See* Brand-to-Brand Complementation (BBC) scheme

Bergsten, C. Fred, 31

Bilateral free trade agreements. *See* Free trade agreements (FTAs), bilateral

Blanco, Herminio, 108

Boao Forum for Asia, 162

Bodharamik, Adisai, 124

Brand-to-Brand Complementation (BBC) scheme, 44

Brock, William, 62–63

Bush (George H. W.) administration: NAFTA negotiations, 71, 72, 74; relations with ASEAN, 77; trade policies, 71; views of Asian regional forums, 73–76, 81

Bush (George W.) administration: Asia policies, 123–25, 152–54, 159; Enterprise for ASEAN Initiative, 124, 152, 153, 177; free trade agreement negotiations, 125, 159; relations with China, 116; trade policies, 18, 155; trade promotion authority, 124, 155; war on terrorism, 23, 124, 125, 152, 176–77

Bush, George W., meetings with ASEAN leaders, 125

Business interests: American, 125; Japanese, 140–41, 142; U.S.-ASEAN Business Council, 51, 124, 125. *See also* Manufacturing; Production networks

Byrd, Robert, 64

Cambodia: trade flows, 49; Working Group on Economic Cooperation in Indochina, 94

Canada: APEC membership, 66. *See also* North American Free Trade Agreement

Canada-United States Free Trade Agreement (CUSFTA), 45, 63, 64, 170

CEPT. *See* Common Effective Preferential Tariff

Chiang Mai Initiative, 106, 107, 108, 116, 175

Chile, proposed free trade agreements, 105, 109, 111

China: attitudes toward contracts, 163; competition from neighbors, 165, 178; domestic demand, 57; economic reforms, 41; effects of financial crisis, 161; effects of rise of, 12, 177–78; exports, 118; fears of dominance, 2, 16, 177–78; foreign affiliates in, 51, 59; foreign direct investment from, 47; foreign direct investment in, 41, 46, 47, 161, 176; free trade agreement with Thailand, 118–19; goals, 23–24;

image in East Asia, 157, 161, 162, 164; implementation of free trade agreements, 163–64; implementation of WTO commitments, 26, 159, 163, 181–82; imports, 57; military buildup, 23, 25, 165, 182; nationalism, 182; nontariff barriers, 148; political leadership, 163; political system, 164, 182, 184; production network nodes in, 12, 30, 41, 53; relations with United States, 93, 116, 123–24, 157, 158, 161, 165, 166, 177; rise of, 23, 37, 132, 162–63; special economic zones, 41; Taiwan issues, 25, 164, 165, 182, 184; tariff rates, 148; trade with other East Asian countries, 47, 49–50; U.S. attack on Belgrade embassy, 116, 161; WTO accession, 30, 46, 115, 116, 117, 152, 176. *See also* Japan, relations with China

China, regional policies: APEC membership, 78, 116; bandwagoning strategy, 165, 166; benefits of regionalism, 180; constraints, 163–65; cooperation with Japan and South Korea, 128–29, 148; early harvest measures, 118–19; efforts to reassure neighbors, 161; evolution of, 115–17, 123, 160–62, 179; future of, 167, 184–85; influence on East Asian regionalism, 134, 148; interest in free trade agreements, 9, 117–18; interests, 13–14, 16; potential free trade agreements, 147–48, 167; recommendations, 26, 181–82; relations with ASEAN, 112, 115, 116–19, 125, 160; resources, 162–63; self-help strategy, 165–66; strategic options, 165–66; transcending strategy, 165, 166

China-ASEAN free trade agreement: framework agreement, 118; implementation, 4, 26; Japanese reaction, 121; negotiations, 12, 118; proposal, 9, 117–19

Chinese Taipei. *See* Taiwan

Clinton, Bill: announcement of trade negotiations with Singapore, 8; on NAFTA, 19

Clinton administration: Early Voluntary Sectoral Liberalization proposal, 86–89; Project 5 (P5) initiative, 105, 111; trade policies, 8, 81–82, 90, 152, 172; views of APEC, 81–82, 94, 152, 156

Common Effective Preferential Tariff (CEPT), 43, 77

Conformity Assessment Development Program in Industrial Standards, 127

Culture, Asian, 35

CUSFTA. *See* Canada-United States Free Trade Agreement

Customs unions, as alternative to bilateral free trade agreements, 147

Defensive regionalism. *See* Regionalism, defensive

Deng Xiaoping, 41

Developing countries: aid to, 70–71, 136, 137; benefits of locating manufacturing facilities in, 53; competition for foreign investment, 31; free trade agreements with developed countries, 32–33; participation in production networks, 20, 40–41, 52, 53, 174; tariffs, 17

Development cooperation, 19–20

EAEC. *See* East Asian Economic Caucus

EAI. *See* Enterprise for ASEAN Initiative

Early Voluntary Sectoral Liberalization (EVSL), 82, 86–89, 100, 105, 108

EASG. *See* East Asia Study Group

East Asia: anti-Americanism and anti-

Westernism, 10, 15, 175; regional identity, 22, 24, 91–92; values differences, 14, 33, 91–92, 185. *See also* East Asian economies

East Asian community: ASEAN + *3* as foundation, 150, 177; benefits of, 1; future of, 22, 183–85; importance as goal, 2–3; interest in, 3; Japanese vision, 149, 151; obstacles, 1; potential arrangements, 3–4; proposals, 126; short-term measures, 126; vision for, 12–13, 16, 126, 177. *See also* East Asian free trade area; Regionalism, East Asian

East Asian Economic Caucus (EAEC): agreement, 94–95; debates on, 75, 96; as defensive move, 79, 100; demise, 99; Japan's views of, 75–76, 96, 137; proposal, 9, 10, 72–73, 74, 79, 97; supporters, 97; U.S. objections, 73–76, 100, 171

East Asian Economic Group (EAEG), 10, 27, 35, 71–72

East Asian economies: competition among, 31–32; domestic demand, 41–42, 56–57; domestic reforms, 4, 36, 103; export markets, 56; extraregional dependence, 34–35; growth, 1, 40, 57; income differences, 33; interdependence, 29–30, 47, 131, 177. *See also* Asian financial crisis (*1997–98*); Foreign direct investment; Production networks

East Asian free trade area: interest in, 30, 106; obstacles, 129, 146; proposal, 9; stepwise approach, 129–31, 147; study of, 126. *See also* East Asian community

East Asia Study Group (EASG), 126

East Asia summits: benefit, 15; First (*2005*), 14, 127, 128, 150; participants, 127; participation of India, Australia, and New Zealand, 15, 16, 127, 128, 150; proposal, 9; relation-

ship to ASEAN + *3*, 15, 21; U.S. role, 127; U.S. view of, 15–16

East Asia Vision Group (EAVG), 12–13, 16, 22, 106, 126, 177

Economic integration. *See* Customs unions; East Asian community; Regionalism; Regionalization

Eminent Persons Group (EPG), 78, 82–83, 84–85, 172

Enterprise for ASEAN Initiative (EAI), 124, 152, 153, 177

Enterprise for the Americas Initiative, 71

Europe: affiliates of Japanese firms, 50; foreign direct investment from, 46; intra-industry trade, 52

European Union (EU): Asia-Europe meeting, 93–94, 95–96, 98, 106; association agreements, 32, 33; comparisons to East Asian regionalism, 3, 12–13; discrimination against nonmembers, 27; expansion, 32–33; free trade agreements with developing countries, 32, 33; free trade agreement with Mexico, 108; income differences of members, 32–33; relations with Asia, 97–98; trade interdependence, 47; trade with East Asia, 56

Europe–East Asia Economic Summit, 98

Evans, Gareth, 69, 98

EVSL. *See* Early Voluntary Sectoral Liberalization

Fauver, Robert, 68

FDI. *See* Foreign direct investment

Financial crisis. *See* Asian financial crisis (*1997–98*)

Foreign affiliates: in China, 51, 59; sales destinations, 50–51. *See also* Production networks

Foreign direct investment (FDI): attracting, 17, 39, 53–54, 103; in developing countries, 31, 38,

53–54; effects of Asian financial crisis, 46; effects on ASEAN policies, 39–43, 44; export oriented, 39, 40, 50; growth in *1980*s, 38–39; liberalization, 11; preferred policy environments, 45–46; sources, 46–47. *See also* Production networks

Fox Quesada, Vicente, 119

Free trade agreements (FTAs), bilateral: competition for, 12, 31, 104, 117, 121–23, 129, 131; cross-regional, 28; as first step toward regionalism, 21, 30, 177; goals, 19; increased interest in, 28, 30, 89, 103; increase in East Asia, 3, 8–9; international rules, 154; networks of, 78; overlapping, 13, 21, 146; political motivation, 31–32; as reinforcement for domestic reforms, 103; spaghetti bowl effect, 21, 130, 146, 147, 177; U.S. interest in, 90, 105, 124–25, 153, 154, 159, 170, 177; U.S. proposals, 62–65. *See also individual countries*

Free trade agreements (FTAs), regional. *See* Regional trade agreements; Regionalism

Free trade agreements (FTAs), subregional, 85, 129; Australia-New Zealand Closer Economic Relations Trade Agreement, 78, 85; overlapping, 13. *See also* ASEAN Free Trade Area; North American Free Trade Agreement

Free Trade Area of the Americas (FTAA), 33, 89, 156

FTAs. *See* Free trade agreements

General Agreement on Tariffs and Trade (GATT): as best forum for trade liberalization, 11; nondiscrimination principle, 11; Uruguay Round, 17, 71, 79, 84, 92, 172

Globalization: domestic adjustments,

155; East Asian regionalization as response to, 38–51

Goh Chok Tong, 8, 9–10, 98, 99, 106, 111, 122–23

Hashimoto, Ryutaro, 11, 95, 97, 99, 106

Hatakeyama, Noboru, 108

Hawke, Robert James, 67, 69

HIIT. *See* Horizontal intra-industry trade

Hiranuma, Takeo, 117

History problem, of Japan: efforts to overcome, 33; as issue in China, 34, 164, 181; Korean approach, 135; need for solutions, 181, 183–84; as obstacle to economic integration, 10, 24, 141; public opinion in other Asian countries, 24–25, 33, 141, 164

Hong Kong: affiliates of U.S. firms, 50–51; APEC membership, 78; exclusion from regional forums, 98, 150

Horizontal intra-industry trade (HIIT), 52, 55

Howard, John, 89

Hu Jintao, 162

Identity, regional, 22, 24, 91–92

IIT. *See* Intra-industry trade

IMF. *See* International Monetary Fund

Import-substitution policies, 40, 42–43, 45–46

India: inclusion in East Asia summits, 15, 16, 127, 128, 150; role in East Asian forums, 132, 150

Indochina, Working Group on Economic Cooperation in Indochina, 94

Indonesia: APEC meeting in Bogor, 84, 85, 172; automobile manufacturing, 44; economic performance, 40, 104; effects of financial crisis, 103, 107; export processing zones, 39; foreign direct investment in, 38, 39;

manufacturing growth, 40; support for ASEAN Free Trade Area, 77; tariff rates, 43; trade flows, 49, 50; trade-GDP ratio, 40; views of trade liberalization, 84

Information technology. *See* Technology

Information Technology Agreement (ITA), 86, 92, 172

Institutionalization: concerns about, 35–36; East Asian of East Asian regionalism, 178–79

International cooperation: global trend toward, 108; multilayered approaches, 2, 16, 20, 93, 95, 100, 151

International Monetary Fund (IMF): advocacy of economic liberalization, 38; Asian quotas, 35, 107; response to Asian financial crisis, 35, 102–03, 107, 175; Supplementary Reserve Facility, 107

Intra-industry trade (IIT): among ASEAN members, 44; benefits, 55; cross-regional, 56; in East Asia, 54–55; in Europe, 52; horizontal, 52, 55; intermediate goods, 54; vertical, 52, 54–55. *See also* Production networks

Investment: cooperation, 128–29; trade and investment framework agreements, 63, 74, 124, 125; trade-related investment measures, 45; treaties, 129. *See also* Foreign direct investment

Israel, free trade agreement with United States, 63, 64

ITA. *See* Information Technology Agreement

ITC. *See* U.S. International Trade Commission

Japan: affiliates of U.S. firms, 50; agricultural exports, 55, 143; agricultural imports, 108, 120, 143–44; automobile manufacturers, 44, 45–46, 58; business-government relations, 140–41; domestic markets, 24, 139, 140; dual structure of industrial sector, 139–40; economic performance, 10, 37, 104–05; economic restructuring, 24, 151–52; effects of Asian financial crisis, 104–05; fishery and forestry industries, 87, 88, 120; foreign direct investment from, 46, 47, 50, 136, 137, 170; foreign policy, 151; image in East Asia, 157; interests, 13; Ministry of Agriculture, Forestry and Fisheries, 143, 144; Ministry of Economy, Trade and Industry, 94, 117; Ministry of International Trade and Industry, 64, 65–66, 67, 93–94, 95, 96, 108; official development assistance, 71, 136, 137; political system, 140; possible UN Security Council seat, 34, 184; production networks of manufacturers, 38, 44, 45, 58–59, 136, 138–39, 170; regulatory reform, 139, 146; relations with South Korea, 33–34, 109, 110, 128–29, 135, 148, 175; relations with United States, 22, 63–64, 124, 125, 138, 151, 157, 183; trade, 47, 50, 51, 108, 136–37; yen appreciation, 38, 136. *See also* History problem

Japan, free trade agreements: with ASEAN, 145–46; with ASEAN members, 26, 121, 145, 146; benefits of, 141–42; bilateral, 4, 119–21; interest in, 30, 108, 110, 111; with Mexico, 119–20, 142; negotiations, 26, 119–21; potential, 64, 117, 147–48, 149; strategy, 145–48

Japan, regional policies: APEC proposal, 65–66, 67; Asian Monetary Fund proposal, 35; benefits of regionalism, 180; economic partnership agreements, 111–12, 120,

121, 122, 142, 146; effects of regionalization, 57–60; evolution of, 135–39, 179; free trade agreements, 26, 145–48; in future, 151–52; goals, 58; incrementalism, 119–21; influence on East Asian regionalism, 134; interests, 24; long-term vision, 144–45, 149–51; most favored nation liberalization, 11; participation in regional forums, 137, 138, 150–51; pragmatism, 97; recommendations, 26, 181; relations with ASEAN, 29, 93–94, 96–97, 101, 120–21, 145–46; response to financial crisis, 107; views of East Asian Economic Caucus, 75–76, 96, 137

Japan, relations with China: anti-Japanese sentiment in China, 23, 25, 164, 167, 182, 184; competition, 13–14, 25, 121–23; cooperation, 128–29, 148; history issue, 34, 164, 181; improving, 182; issues, 25, 34; as obstacle to regionalism, 4–5, 33; positive elements, 34; prospects for free trade agreement, 147–48; trade, 148

Japan, trade policies: agricultural liberalization, 4, 120, 142, 143–44, 158; gains from liberalization, 138; liberalization of sensitive industries, 87, 108, 111–12, 120, 122, 141–42, 158; multilateralism, 136; opposition to free trade agreements, 45; trade relations with United States, 65–66, 88, 136, 140

Japan-ASEAN Comprehensive Economic Partnership (CEP), 120, 121, 122, 146

Japan External Trade Organization (JETRO), 108, 143

Japan-Korea free trade agreement (JKFTA): Joint Study Group, 120; negotiations, 4, 26, 34, 120, 145; proposal, 109–10; as step toward

regional free trade agreement, 147, 149

Japan-Malaysia Economic Partnership Agreement (JMEPA), 121

Japan-Philippines Economic Partnership Agreement (JPEPA), 121

Japan-Republic of Korea Economic Agenda 21, 110

Japan-Singapore Economic Partnership Agreement (JSEPA): influence of business interests, 142; innovative measures, 142; negotiations, 8, 111–12, 119; proposal, 111–12; signing, 120

Japan-Thailand Economic Partnership Agreement (JTEPA), 121

JETRO. See Japan External Trade Organization

JKFTA. See Japan-Korea free trade agreement

JMEPA. See Japan-Malaysia Economic Partnership Agreement

Jordan, free trade agreement with United States, 8

JPEPA. See Japan-Philippines Economic Partnership Agreement

JSEPA. See Japan-Singapore Economic Partnership Agreement

JTEPA. See Japan-Thailand Economic Partnership Agreement

Kaifu, Toshiki, 75
Kantor, Michael, 90
Kawaguchi, Yoriko, 145
Keating, P. J., 78
Kim Dae Jung, 33–34, 103, 106, 109, 110, 128, 135
Koh, Tommy, 63
Koizumi, Junichiro, 119, 120, 121, 143, 145, 149, 181, 184
Korea. See North Korea; South Korea
Kuching Consensus, 70

Laos, Working Group on Economic Cooperation in Indochina, 94

Lee Jong-seok, 148
Lee Kuan Yew, 163
Li Peng, 71
Long Yongtu, 89

Macapagal-Arroyo, Gloria, 121
Maekawa Report, 140
MAFF. *See* Ministry of Agriculture,
    Forestry and Fisheries
Mahathir bin Mohamad, 10, 71–72,
    74–75, 94, 106
Major powers. *See* China; Japan;
    United States
Malaysia: affiliates of U.S. firms, 50, 51;
    automobile manufacturing, 44;
    East Asian Economic Caucus pro-
    posal, 9, 10, 72–73, 74; East Asian
    Economic Group proposal, 10, 27,
    35, 71–72; economic growth, 40;
    export processing zones, 39; First
    East Asia Summit, 14, 127, 128; for-
    eign direct investment in, 38, 39;
    Japan-Malaysia Economic Partner-
    ship Agreement (JMEPA), 121;
    manufacturing growth, 40; tariff
    rates, 43; trade flows, 49; trade-
    GDP ratio, 40
Mansfield, Mike, 63–64
Manufacturing: agglomeration, 53–54;
    Conformity Assessment Develop-
    ment Program in Industrial
    Standards, 127; electric and elec-
    tronics, 46, 52, 53, 55; growth in
    Southeast Asia, 40; Japanese indus-
    trial sector, 58, 139–40; machinery,
    54, 55; modularized products,
    52–53. *See also* Automobile manu-
    facturing; Production networks
METI. *See* Ministry of Economy, Trade
    and Industry
Mexico: APEC membership, 72; cur-
    rency crisis, 156; effects of NAFTA,
    28; free trade agreement with Euro-
    pean Union, 108; free trade
    agreement with Japan, 119–20, 142;

negotiation of NAFTA, 71; pro-
    posed free trade agreements, 111.
    See also North American Free Trade
    Agreement
Ministry of Agriculture, Forestry and
    Fisheries (MAFF), Japan, 143, 144
Ministry of Economy, Trade and
    Industry (METI), Japan, 117
Ministry of International Trade and
    Industry (MITI), Japan, 64, 65–66,
    67, 93–94, 95, 96, 108
Mitsubishi Motors Corporation
    (MMC), 44
Monetary Authority of Singapore, 56
Moran, Theodore H., 43
Mori, Yoshiro, 8
Most favored nation (MFN) trade lib-
    eralization, 11, 43, 84
Multilateral trade liberalization frame-
    works: advantages, 11, 147; role of
    regional agreements, 18, 31. *See
    also* General Agreement on Tariffs
    and Trade; World Trade Organiza-
    tion
Myanmar, Working Group on Eco-
    nomic Cooperation in Indochina,
    94

NAFTA. *See* North American Free
    Trade Agreement
Newly industrializing economies
    (NIEs), 39, 47, 65
New Zealand: Australia-New Zealand
    Closer Economic Relations Trade
    Agreement, 78, 85; closer economic
    relations with ASEAN, 93; free
    trade agreement negotiations with
    Singapore, 35, 110–11; inclusion in
    East Asia summits, 15, 16, 127, 128,
    150; participation in Asia-Europe
    meeting, 98; proposed free trade
    agreements, 105, 110–11; role in
    East Asian forums, 132, 150
NIEs. *See* Newly industrializing
    economies

North American Free Trade Agreement
(NAFTA): comparisons to East
Asian regionalism, 4; discrimination against nonmembers, 27;
effects on Asia, 90; goals, 19;
income differences of members, 32;
linkages with ASEAN, 77, 93; linkages with other free trade
agreements, 78; negotiations, 71,
72, 73, 79; trade interdependence,
47; trade with East Asia, 56
North Korea, 109, 148

OAA. *See* Osaka Action Agenda
Obuchi, Keizo, 109, 110, 111, 138
Official development assistance
(ODA), 71, 136, 137, 153
Ong Keng Yong, 125
Osaka Action Agenda (OAA), 85–86, 91

Panitchpakdi, Supachai, 95
People's Republic of China. *See* China
Philippines: affiliates of U.S. firms, 51;
economic growth, 40; export pro-
cessing zones, 39; foreign direct
investment in, 38, 39; Japan-
Philippines Economic Partnership
Agreement (JPEPA), 121; manufacturing growth, 40; tariff rates, 43;
trade flows, 49; trade-GDP ratio, 40
Plaza Accord, 38, 65
Plurilateral agreements, 2, 83, 90
Political systems: Chinese, 164, 182,
184; differences within East Asia,
33, 185
Preferential trade agreements (PTAs).
See Free trade agreements
Production networks: Chinese nodes,
12, 30, 41, 53; in developing countries, 20, 40–41, 52, 53, 174; efforts
to reduce transaction costs, 17, 20,
21, 29, 60–61, 131, 139, 149;
extraregional linkages, 56, 60; government policies promoting, 54;
growth of, 38, 52–53, 170, 174;

integration levels, 54–55; interest in
trade liberalization, 60–61; of
Japanese firms, 38, 44, 45–46,
58–59, 136, 138–39, 170; regionalization increased through, 52–54;
of Western manufacturers, 20, 46,
51, 56, 172, 174. *See also* Foreign
direct investment; Intra-industry
trade
Project 5 (P5) initiative, 105, 111
PTAs (preferential trade agreements).
See Free trade agreements

Rafidah Aziz, 74, 97
Ravenhill, John, 10
Reagan administration: proposed free
trade agreements, 62–65; relations
with Asia, 67–69; trade policies,
64–65, 170
Regional identity, 22, 24, 91–92
Regionalism: broad, 90; as complement
to globalism, 16–19, 30; European,
28, 33, 89; income differences and,
32–33; in North America, 28; open,
83, 84, 85, 89–90; welfare benefits,
28; Western hemisphere, 33, 71, 89,
156. *See also* European Union;
North American Free Trade Agreement
Regionalism, defensive: as driving
force, 27, 79, 114; East Asian Economic Caucus as example, 79, 100;
East Asian Economic Group proposal, 71–72; effects of financial
crisis, 103, 113–14, 175; meaning,
27; positive consequences, 100, 176;
reduction in, 114, 132, 178;
responses to U.S. policies, 65, 66,
171; U.S. efforts to preempt, 69, 76
Regionalism, East Asian: APEC influence on, 92, 172–73; ASEAN
influence on, 93–94, 134–35,
173–74; benefits of, 3, 131, 180;
closed, 4, 10, 37, 157–58; common
interests, 178; as complement to

globalism, 18–19; concerns about, 2, 10; driving forces, 26–32, 79, 114; effects, 169; expectations, 21, 179; free trade agreements as step toward, 21, 30, 177; future of, 3–4, 13, 14–15, 21–22, 132, 178–79, 180, 186; incremental approach, 30; inevitability, 90, 178; influences of major powers, 22–26, 134, 179; institutionalizing, 35–36, 178–79; multilayered approach, 2, 30, 79, 93, 149, 159; obstacles, 4, 10, 32–36, 79, 114, 176; phase one, 62, 79, 170–72; phase two, 81, 99, 172–74; phase three, 102, 174–76; phase four, 115, 176–78; political issues, 2, 34; social foundation, 22; U.S. concerns, 15–16, 67–69. *See also* East Asian community

Regionalization, East Asian: competition in, 61; effects on Japanese business networks, 57–60; evolution, 3, 10–11; extraregional linkages, 56–57; increase in, 46–51, 60; mechanisms, 51–54; as response to globalization, 38–51. *See also* Production networks

Regional trade agreements (RTAs), 62, 106, 129. *See also* East Asian free trade area; European Union

Relationalism, 58

Republic of Korea. *See* South Korea

Rice, Condoleezza, 125

RTAs. *See* Regional trade agreements

Salinas de Gortari, Carlos, 71

SARS. *See* Severe acute respiratory syndrome

Security issues, 125, 152, 154–55, 161

Severe acute respiratory syndrome (SARS), 127

Shultz, George P., 68

Singapore: affiliates of U.S. firms, 50–51; attitudes toward contracts, 163; foreign direct investment in

China, 47; Japan-Singapore Economic Partnership Agreement, 8, 111–12, 119, 120, 142; tariff rates, 147; trade and investment framework agreement with United States, 74; trade flows, 49

Singapore, free trade agreements: interest in, 104, 110–11, 175; negotiations with New Zealand, 35, 110–11; negotiations with South Korea, 145; proposed, 105, 111. *See also* U.S.-Singapore free trade agreement

Singh, Ajit, 94–95

Snow Brand Milk, 143

South Korea: affiliates of U.S. firms, 51; agricultural liberalization, 4; approach to Japanese history problem, 135; cooperation with Japan and China, 128–29, 148; financial crisis, 103, 107, 109; foreign direct investment in China, 47; influence on East Asian regionalism, 135; interests, 14; investment treaties, 129; relations with Japan, 33–34, 109, 110, 128–29, 135, 148, 175; structural reforms, 103; trade with other East Asian countries, 50

South Korea, free trade agreements: bilateral, 4; interest in, 30, 109–10; negotiations with Singapore, 145; negotiations with United States, 125; potential with China, 148; proposed, 111. *See also* Japan-Korea free trade agreement

Subregional free trade agreements. *See* Free trade agreements (FTAs), subregional

Suppliers. *See* Production networks

Taiwan: affiliates of U.S. firms, 50; APEC membership, 78; Chinese policies toward, 25, 164, 165, 182, 184; exclusion from regional forums, 98, 150, 182; foreign direct investment in China, 47

Takeshita, Noboru, 64, 65

Technology: Asian Common Skill Standard Initiative for Information Technology Engineers, 127; Information Technology Agreement, 86, 92, 172; manufacturing, 52

Thailand: economic growth, 40; export processing zones, 39; financial crisis, 107, 156; foreign direct investment in, 38, 39; free trade agreement negotiations with United States, 125; free trade agreement with China, 118–19; Japan-Thailand Economic Partnership Agreement (JTEPA), 121; manufacturing growth, 40; support for ASEAN Free Trade Area, 77; tariff rates, 43; trade and investment framework agreement with United States, 124; trade flows, 49; trade-GDP ratio, 40

Thaksin Shinawatra, 121

TIFAs. *See* Trade and investment framework agreements

Trade: Asian intraregional, 47–50; export markets, 56; intra-industry, 44, 52, 54–55, 56; sales destinations of foreign affiliates, 50–51. *See also* Production networks

Trade and investment framework agreements (TIFAs), 63; proposed ASEAN-United States, 125; U.S.-Singapore, 74; U.S.-Thailand, 124

Trade intensity (TI) index, 47–50

Trade liberalization: agricultural, 4, 120, 142, 143–44, 158; benefits of regionalism, 16–19, 31; competitive, 31; debates within APEC, 82–86; Early Voluntary Sectoral Liberalization proposal, 82, 86–89, 100, 105, 108; in East Asia, 31, 43; effects of foreign direct investment, 39–43; interest of foreign investors, 45–46, 60–61; most favored nation

(MFN) basis, 11, 43, 84; reciprocal, 82; unilateral, 31; U.S. policies, 18. *See also* Free trade agreements; Multilateral trade liberalization frameworks

Trade-related investment measures (TRIMs), 45

Tsunami aid, 125, 185

United Nations Security Council, 34, 184

United States: affiliates of Japanese firms, 50; economic effects of globalization, 155; economic performance, 37; foreign direct investment from, 46, 47, 50–51; hedge funds, 102; offshore outsourcing, 155

United States, free trade agreements: with ASEAN members, 159; bilateral, 26, 78, 153, 182; with Canada, 45, 63, 64, 170; with East Asian countries, 26, 78, 153, 159, 182; "hub-and-spoke" approach, 65, 78, 170; with Jordan, 8; potential, 64; quality, 154; with Singapore, 8–9, 63, 90, 112, 123, 124. *See also* North American Free Trade Agreement

United States, relations with APEC: under Bush (George W.) administration, 159; under Clinton administration, 8, 152, 156; East Asian Economic Caucus issue, 94–95, 171; expectations, 19, 171; as focus of East Asian relations, 76, 78–79, 81, 156; goals, 89–90, 91, 152; U.S. influence, 81–82; U.S. vision for, 69, 70–71, 74, 77

United States, relations with East Asia: American interests, 23, 152; anti-Americanism, 15, 175; APEC membership, 66, 67, 69; attack on Chinese embassy in Belgrade, 116, 161; benefits of regionalism, 180, 182; bilateral free trade agreements,

26, 78, 153, 159, 182; under Bush (George W.) administration, 123–25, 152–54, 159; business interests and, 125; under Clinton administration, 81–82, 94, 152, 156, 172; concerns about regionalism, 15–16, 67–69; constraints, 155–57; development assistance, 153; effects of financial crisis, 105; efforts to preempt defensive regionalism, 69, 76; foreign direct investment in, 46, 47, 50–51; foreign policy, 10; image of U.S. in Asia, 156–57; influence, 34–35, 134, 157; interest in free trade agreements, 90, 105, 124–25, 153, 154, 159, 170, 177; interests, 152; meetings with ASEAN, 63, 124; multilayered thinking, 79; objections to EAEC, 73–76, 100, 171; objections to EAEG, 72; policies on regionalism, 19–20, 26, 152–59, 179, 185; pragmatism, 154; recommendations, 182–83; relations with ASEAN, 63, 77, 94–95, 124–25, 153–54, 177; relations with China, 93, 116, 123–24, 157, 158, 161, 165, 166, 177; relations with Japan, 22, 63–64, 124, 125, 138, 151, 157, 183; response to financial crisis, 102–03, 105, 156, 175; role in East Asia summits, 127; security issues, 125, 152, 154–55, 161; trade, 3, 19, 51, 82, 154; trade and investment framework agreements, 63, 74, 124; trade issues, 65, 183; trade relations with Japan, 65–66, 88, 136, 140; tsunami aid, 125, 185; U.S. role in region, 23; view of East Asia summit, 15–16; views of Asian regional forums, 10–11, 67–69, 73–76, 78–79, 100, 105, 171
United States, trade policies: of Bush (George H. W.) administration, 71; of Bush (George W.) administration, 18, 155; of Clinton administration, 8, 81–82, 90, 152, 172; digital trade policy agenda, 124; multitrack strategy, 63, 64–65, 67, 69, 83, 90, 170; protectionism, 27, 65, 66, 155; trade and investment framework agreements, 63, 74, 124, 125; trade promotion authority, 124, 155; unilateralism, 65, 66, 175
U.S.-ASEAN Business Council, 51, 124, 125
U.S.-ASEAN Dialogue, 94–95
U.S.-ASEAN Free Trade Area, proposal, 124
U.S. International Trade Commission, 64
U.S.-Japan Security Consultative Committee, 125
U.S.-Singapore free trade agreement: implementation, 124; negotiations, 8–9, 90, 112, 124; signing, 124; Singapore's interest in, 63; U.S. interest in, 123
U.S. Trade Representative, 8–9, 62–63, 64, 90, 105, 124, 153–54
Uruguay Round, 17, 71, 79, 84, 92, 172

Values differences, 14, 33, 91–92, 185
Vertical intra-industry trade (VIIT), 52, 54–55
Vietnam: ASEAN membership, 94; economic reforms, 41; foreign direct investment in, 41; trade flows, 49; Working Group on Economic Cooperation in Indochina, 94
VIIT. *See* Vertical intra-industry trade

War on terrorism, 23, 124, 125, 152, 176–77
Washington consensus, 27, 102
Working Group on Economic Cooperation in Indochina, 94
World Bank, 32, 107
World Economic Forum, 98
World Trade Organization (WTO):

advocacy of economic liberalization, 38; APEC's role in, 92; as best forum for trade liberalization, 11; Chinese accession, 30, 46, 115, 116, 117, 152, 176; dispute settlement mechanism, 90, 114, 137–38, 175; Doha negotiations, 26, 180–81; establishment, 89; Information Technology Agreement, 86, 92, 172; lack of flexibility, 16–17, 30; membership, 16; regional agreements as complement to, 16–18; rules on

protectionism, 27
World War II: impact on Japan's relations with Asia, 135–36, 137, 141. *See also* History problem

Yasukuni Shrine, 181, 184
Yeo, George, 122
Yeutter, Clayton, 64

Zhu Rongji, 9, 115, 128
Zoellick, Robert, 68, 69, 77, 124, 153–54